A. C. Bradley and his influence in Twentieth-Century Shakespeare Criticism

A. C. Bradley and his influence in Twentieth-Century Shakespeare Criticism

KATHARINE COOKE

OXFORD
AT THE CLARENDON PRESS
1972

Oxford University Press, Ely House, London W. 1
GLASGOW NEW YORK TORONTO MELBOURNE WELLINGTON
CAPE TOWN IBADAN NAIROBI LUSAKA DAR ES SALAAM ADDIS ABABA
DELHI BOMBAY CALCUTTA MADRAS KARACHI LAHORE DACCA
KUALA LUMPUR SINGAPORE HONG KONG TOKYO

PRINTED IN GREAT BRITAIN
AT THE UNIVERSITY PRESS, OXFORD
BY VIVIAN RIDLER
PRINTER TO THE UNIVERSITY

FOR MY PARENTS

NORMAN AND BERTHA LEES

FOREWORD

THE basis of this book is a London University thesis accepted in 1967. Since then developments in Shakespearian studies have made some parts of that thesis seem a little old fashioned. The recognition of Bradley as a classic of which there were then signs is now much nearer to being an accomplished fact. As a reviewer in the *Guardian* wrote early this year, 'There is Bradley's *Shakespearean Tragedy*, of course', whereas the following pages will make it clear that there was, not so long ago, a time when a considerable amount of energy was spent in trying to demolish Bradley, whose criticism was thought to be a mirage to which schoolchildren and students were susceptible, but which the intelligent critic could see through.

Now that the struggle for recognition is largely over, the tone of the following pages sometimes seems unnecessarily defensive. This has not been altered because of a certain historical value. However, work on Bradley published since 1966 has been taken into account especially in two fields. The biographical chapter now incorporates additional material, as does the survey of works specifically about Bradley. Elsewhere footnotes and occasionally insertions make reference to more recent material, but these are not common.

1971 K. C.

CONTENTS

ACKNOWLEDGEMENTS

THE letters of A. C. Bradley to Gilbert Murray and his wife, Lady Mary, have been invaluable to me in coming to some understanding of the man Bradley was. To Mr. E. V. Quinn, the librarian of Balliol College, Oxford, who told me of them, and to the late Mrs. I. Henderson for permission to read the letters I wish to record my gratitude.

Thanks are due to Mr. Quinn also for help in finding what material there was at Balliol (including a lecture undiscovered elsewhere, 'The Teaching of English', and an undergraduate article by Bradley, 'Mr. Rossetti's Shelley') and for suggesting useful biographies of Bradley's contemporaries, and to Mr. D. F. Cook of the University Library, Liverpool, and Miss E. G. Jack of The Library, University of Glasgow, for their assistance.

For more extensive help I am immeasurably in the debt of Dr. P. M. Ball, my supervisor for the original thesis, of Royal Holloway College, University of London.

ABBREVIATIONS

A.M.	A. C. Bradley, *A Miscellany.*
A.C.S.	A. C. Bradley, 'Aristotle's Conception of the State'.
B.A.	*British Academy Annual Shakespeare Lecture.*
B.B.	A. C. Bradley, 'Bernard Bosanquet'.
C.E.	*College English.*
C.L.	*Comparative Literature.*
C.Q.	*Critical Quarterly.*
C.R.	*Contemporary Review.*
C.S.	*Critical Survey.*
D.N.B.	*Dictionary of National Biography.*
E. in C.	*Essays in Criticism.*
E.L.H.	*English Literary History*
H.L.Q.	*Huntington Library Quarterly.*
I.J.P.	*International Journal of Psychiatry.*
I.M.	A. C. Bradley, 'International Morality'.
I.R.	A. C. Bradley, *Ideals of Religion.*
J.A.A.C.	*Journal of Aesthetic and Art Criticism.*
J.H.I.	*Journal of the History of Ideas.*
J.R.L.B.	*John Rylands Library Bulletin.*
K.R.	*Kenyon Review.*
M.L.R.	*Modern Language Review.*
M.P.	*Modern Philology.*
N.R.	A. C. Bradley, 'Some Points in Natural Religion'.
O.L.P.	A. C. Bradley, *Oxford Lectures on Poetry.*
O.M.M.P.	A. C. Bradley, 'Old Mythology and Modern Poetry .
P.B.A.	*Proceedings of the British Academy.*
P.L.	A. C. Bradley, *Poetry and Life.*
P.Q.	*Philological Quarterly.*
S.A.B.	*Shakespeare Association Bulletin.*
S.P.	A. C. Bradley, *The Study of Poetry.*
S.Ph.	*Studies in Philology.*
S.Q.	*Shakespeare Quarterly.*
S.R.	*Sewanee Review.*

S.S.	*Shakespeare Survey.*
Sh.S.	*Shakespeare Studies.*
S.T.	A. C. Bradley, *Shakespearean Tragedy.*
T.E.L.	A. C. Bradley, *The Teaching of English Literature.*
T.I.M.	A. C. Bradley, *Tennyson's 'In Memoriam'.*
T.L.S.	*Times Literary Supplement.*
U.E.	*The Use of English.*
U.P.	A. C. Bradley, *The Uses of Poetry.*

Details of the works of A. C. Bradley are given in the Bibliography

I

INTRODUCTION

LITERARY fashion has been more than usually capricious in its handling of A. C. Bradley, so that any short summary of his position in twentieth-century criticism is certain to distort the facts. It is not sufficient to classify him with other literary and critical idols turned Aunt Sally, although there is enough evidence for this view; he was clearly not a critic maligned in his time and only appreciated generations later, although there is more evidence for this view than appears at first sight. His influence is not widespread enough for him to be truly seen as a major figure in twentieth-century literature although his name has become part of the jargon of criticism in a way which no other critical name of the century has paralleled. While it is possible to mention his name to students of English and receive in return a cold stare, it is difficult to find a work of Shakespearian criticism which omits all reference to his name.

In his essay on 'The Reaction against Tennyson' (first delivered in 1914 and later published in *A Miscellany*), Bradley himself remarked on the role which 'the wholesome work of reaction' had to play in establishing that which he considered most important in literature, a way to the poet's mind. He wrote:

The reaction against Tennyson is not, on the whole, a matter for regret. It was necessary, for one thing, in the interests of poetry itself. For the formal characteristics of his style were easily caught, and Tennysonian minor poetry, if less absurd than Byronic minor poetry, was quite as sickening . . .[1]

Remembering what J. I. M. Stewart called 'Bradley-and-water-critics'[2] this seems a strangely apposite commentary on

[1] *A.M.*, p. 3.

[2] J. I. M. Stewart, *Character and Motive in Shakespeare* (London, 1949), p. 80.

Bradley's position. What underlies it is almost a commonplace of critical histories. But as Quentin Bell wrote of the vicissitudes of fashion, in an article in the catalogue to the 1966 Roger Fry exhibition:

> in the case of a critic, the descending curve of popular favour is likely to be particularly abrupt. His real and permanent achievements become commonplace while his mistakes form a natural, and indeed a very proper target, for the younger men whose business it is to correct the errors of their predecessors.[3]

And Merritt Y. Hughes in an article, 'A Meditation on Literary Blasphemy', which went on to deal at length with the effect of F. R. Leavis on the value of Bradley's criticism, summed the matter up in two short sentences:

> Literary iconoclasm is the final remedy for literary superstition.

and

> Blasphemous impulses are part of the instinct for self preservation.[4]

What has been peculiar about the treatment of Bradley in this 'sifting process', as he himself called it, is the half-heartedness with which it has been carried on in published works and the fervour with which it has been taken up by the general reader. The best indication that the time for rehabilitation has come is not the amount of more recent criticism which acknowledges a debt to Bradley but the issue of his two most important works, *Oxford Lectures on Poetry* and *Shakespearean Tragedy*, as paperbacks, both in this country and in America.

In some ways the familiar pattern is further complicated by the fact that Bradley's work was received by converts. Reviewing *Shakespearean Tragedy*, *The Times Literary Supplement* wrote, 'Mr. Bradley had hardly begun his lectures before the echo of his voice made itself heard beyond the academic boundaries', and described the lectures as 'making a very unusual impression in Oxford and those who had not the chance of hearing them looked

[3] Quentin Bell, 'Roger Fry', article in *Vision and Design, The Life, Work and Influence of Roger Fry 1866–1934*, Catalogue to Arts Council Exhibition, 1966, p. 6.

[4] Merritt Y. Hughes, 'A Meditation on Literary Blasphemy' in *J.A.A.C.* xiv. 1 (Sept. 1955), p. 106.

forward with eagerness to their publication'.[5] It is perhaps small wonder that the work of reaction began immediately, most notably in A. B. Walkley's article, also in the *Times Literary Supplement*, less than two months after the original review, on 7 April 1905. The article, later reprinted in *Drama and Life*, is suitably respectful but iconoclasm had clearly set in:

> From what we have been saying it must not be thought that we undervalue the really important part of Mr. Bradley's book, his scrupulously careful examination of the text and his skill in bringing all 'into a concatenation accordingly' by means of the text. But to understand Shakespeare you have to supplement examination of the text by consideration of other matters, and it is here that we hold the Professor to be at fault. What is outside the text? He says (by implication) a set of real lives . . . we say, Shakespeare's dramatic needs of the moment, artistic peculiarities and available theatrical materials.[6]

Although this first salvo in the 'Stoll-Schücking' campaign is the most famous of the early blasphemies on Bradley, the attack had in fact begun earlier. On the 28 January 1905, the *Westminster Gazette* published a review of *Shakespearean Tragedy* by 'J. C. C.' (according to A. C. Bradley in a letter to Gilbert Murray, this was John Churton Collins). Here what can be called the 'How Many Children had Lady Macbeth?' campaign began with a vehemence besides which even F. R. Leavis's later skirmish seems half-hearted.

> The real points of interest and importance in the drama are not so much as touched on and the particularity with which what is touched on is dealt with is almost invariably in an inverse ratio to its interest and importance. Probably, for example, no intelligent reader of the play has ever had much difficulty in understanding Hamlet's relation to Ophelia—namely, that he was at first passionately in love with her, that then misunderstanding her reserve, and thinking that she was in league with his enemies, he suspected and mistrusted her, but that to the last something of his old love for her remained. This is discussed under nine headings . . . Every lecture teems with those irritating

[5] *T.L.S.*, 10 Feb. 1905.

[6] *T.L.S.*, 7 Apr. 1905. Reprinted with alterations in A. B. Walkley, *Drama and Life* (New York, 1907), p. 153.

superfluities, aggravated it may be added by the unnecessary diffuseness with which they are discussed. . . . Thus Professor Bradley treats us to special dissertations on such subjects as 'Did Lady Macbeth really faint?' 'Did Emilia suspect Iago?' 'Had Macbeth any children?'[7]

This attack provoked Gilbert Murray, Bradley's friend, to reply stating that he considered '*Shakespearean Tragedy* one of the most illuminating books I have ever read'.[8] Within a year, therefore, of the publication of these Oxford lectures, the shape of the controversy to come had been indicated. Sixty years later the same criticisms are being levelled against Bradley, their effect weakened by the passage of time, but that the process continues is a testimony to the fact that Bradley persists as a living influence in criticism.

For three decades after this Bradley's position in literary criticism was accepted without undue interest. There were those like J. Middleton Murry who declared discipleship, and, particularly later on, those who declared opposition, L. L. Schücking and J. M. Robertson among others. But in all this period Bradley was very much one amongst many critics. F. L. Lucas in 1927 wrote a book on tragedy without any reference to Bradley; in 1936 Harley Granville-Barker wrote a book on *Hamlet* also, and perhaps more surprisingly, without a reference to Bradley. It would be difficult to find two such works of a more recent period with similar omissions.

In these three decades the Shakespeare industry as a whole was in a relatively inactive state. 1930 marked the beginning of the great burst of scholarship and criticism which provided such an impetus that the industry is still proliferating at a remarkable rate. This renaissance provided such ardent supporters for Bradley as G. Wilson Knight and H. B. Charlton, as well as ferocious opponents like F. R. Leavis, L. C. Knights, and L. B. Campbell. The position was crystallizing; it was gradually becoming necessary for a critic to state whether he was for or against Bradley, though as yet this fact was unnoticed.

Not until a year after the event did Bradley's death give rise to the usual critical reappraisal. Then an article in the *Times Literary*

[7] *Westminster Gazette*, 28 Jan. 1905, p. 13. [8] Ibid. 30 Jan. 1905, p. 2.

Supplement in May 1936 lavished such praise on the dead critic as might have been thought to kill off any spark of interest in his work.

The article opens:

> It is we surmise, a not uncommon experience with those who have long practised the art of literary criticism to find themselves, when they return to the work of A. C. Bradley, satisfied with their own past performance precisely to the degree in which their judgments and conclusions have accorded with his. . . . The critic recognises, with a mixture of rueful and happy surprise, that in so far as he agrees with Bradley he is mature; and where he disagrees he has still a long road to travel. But he makes no doubt that the road will lead him back to Bradley again, and bring him under that sign to the thrill of critical certitude and the bliss of critical peace.[9]

In fact, a footnote in D. G. James's *Scepticism and Poetry*, published in 1937, is a sign that some critics were drawn to look at Bradley on account of this article.

> Some time after the above was written a reference in an article on A. C. Bradley in the *Times Literary Supplement* (May 23 1936) led me to read (what to my shame, perhaps, I had not formerly read) Bradley's lecture on Wordsworth in *Oxford Lectures*. The reader who feels that in the above section I have overemphasised one aspect of Wordsworth's imaginative life may be advised to read Bradley's remarkable lecture.[10]

Readers of this chapter on Wordsworth may well have followed James's advice and gone on to reconsider their opinion of Bradley's work as a whole.

But in 1937 Bradley received such publicity from a different quarter that the effect of the article's praise becomes insignificant. *Scrutiny*[11] had from the outset named Bradley as one of its enemies and F. R. Leavis's article on *Othello*, 'The Diabolic Intellect and the Noble Hero', is the loudest salvo in the attack. Leavis writes as though Bradley were no longer a significant figure and he was

[9] *T.L.S.*, 23 May 1936: 'A. C. Bradley: The Surrender to Poetry'.

[10] D. G. James, *Scepticism and Poetry: An Essay on the Poetic Imagination* (London, 1937), p. 164 n.

[11] Cf. F. R. Leavis, 'The Literary Mind', *Scrutiny*, i. 1, pp. 20–32 (1932), at p. 25.

merely calling up the ghost to prove just how dead the critic was. He begins by stating that:

not only Bradley but, in its turn, disrespect for Bradley (one gathers) has gone out of fashion (as a matter of fact he is still a very potent and mischievous influence).[12]

—but proceeds to hammer Bradley with such unremitting sarcasm that this article more than any other probably revived interest in Bradley's works. It would be a very unfeeling reader who, having read such sallies as: 'we must not suppose that Bradley sees what is in front of him'; 'with such resolute fidelity does Bradley wear . . . blinkers'; 'Bradley . . . in his comically innocent way . . .', did not turn with some curiosity to a Bradley long forgotten or maybe never read.[13] J. F. C. Gutteling in an article on 'Hamlet Criticism' succinctly described the effect of reading Bradley:

The student who reads Bradley's masterly essay is enthralled by an exposition so penetrating and so human, that he believes the ultimate truth about *Hamlet* has been said. It is only later, much later perhaps, that after re-reading Shakespeare's text he feels doubts rise within him whether Bradley's *Hamlet* and Shakespeare's correspond, whether the drama Bradley interprets is not a tragedy more consistent than the one which Shakespeare wrote.[14]

This process, provoked, as surely Dr. Leavis must have suspected, by his polemic, revitalized the criticism of Bradley for a new generation.

It was some time after this minor renaissance of Bradleyism that the attack of Miss L. B. Campbell was made in two separate articles in 1947 and 1949. She wrote then:

As a result of his letting Elizabethan ideas go by the board, he frequently concerned himself with problems that were irrelevant or

[12] F. R. Leavis, 'Diabolic Intellect and the Noble Hero: or the Sentimentalist's Othello', *Scrutiny* vi (Dec. 1937), pp. 259–83, reprinted in *The Common Pursuit* (London, 1952).

[13] J. M. Newton ('*Scrutiny*'s Failure with Shakespeare', *C.Q.* i. 2 (Spring 1966), pp. 144–68, has a different view: '*Scrutiny* has had the effect of discouraging many people from ever reading [Bradley's criticism]', p. 150.

[14] J. F. C. Gutteling, 'Modern Hamlet Criticism', *Neophilologus* xxv (1940), pp. 276–86, at pp. 277–8.

ignored the significance of evidence important to the tracing of the moral pattern in the plays, to which tasks he had set himself.[15]

To compare this with the remarks by J. C. C. in the *Westminster Gazette* of 1905 illustrates how much more serious critical attention was being accorded Bradley at this stage.

In the forty years which had elapsed since Bradley had been forced on the Shakespearian scholars of the century, various other approaches to Shakespeare had been mooted and either accepted or rejected, notably the Wilson Knight interpretation, the E. E. Stoll sceptical analysis, the historical criticism of Miss Campbell, and the *Scrutiny* approach to theme. This survey in its brevity does violent injustice to the history of twentieth-century Shakespeare criticism but it indicates at least that other alternatives were available by the time Miss Campbell turned her attention to Bradley. In the light of these alternatives it was possible to examine more precisely what Bradley proposed to do and how far he succeeded in doing it. In the earlier years the attitude of critics seemed to be that he sought to speak for Shakespeare as a prophet illuminating a divinity; either the prophecy was accepted by eager proselytes or rejected by the rational 'this side idolatry' Shakespeare students. As might be expected this latter view was usually productive of the more helpful criticism.

As criticism moved on from Bradley it was possible to define Bradleyism; most of the assumed definitions in use do grave injustice to his approach but at least the attempt was being made to understand Bradley's criteria and his work in relation to them. The time was then ripe both for the attacks of Leavis and the praise of the *Times Literary Supplement*. The 'sifting process' was becoming more critical. Miss Campbell's two articles examined in detail important aspects of Bradley's work; it was no longer sufficient to breathe his name in awe or jibe at it in passing. H. B. Charlton's fervent admiration no less than Miss Campbell's

[15] L. B. Campbell, 'Bradley Revisited: Forty Years After', *S. Ph.* xliv (1947), pp. 174–94; 'Concerning Bradley's *Shakespearean Tragedy*', *H.L.Q.* xlii (Nov. 1949), pp. 1–18. Both reprinted as appendix to 1961 edition of *Shakespeare's Tragic Heroes: Slaves of Passion*, first published 1930.

attack is controlled by an understanding that Bradley was working from one method out of many. Charlton wrote:

> Bradley's method was not new, and indeed, particularly in phrase, or at times even in diagnosis, it may not be approved by the particular psychological doctrine of to-day. But it is essentially the method of our greatest Shakespearian critics, and is none the worse for having been traditional for over two centuries.[16]

Since 1950 references to Bradley in works of Shakespeare criticism have become noticeably more critical, and shown considerably more desire to 'see the object as in itself it really is'. Thus Barbara Everett in an article 'The New King Lear' in the *Critical Quarterly* for 1960 wrote:

> Bradley's profound study of the play is remarkable, both for the way in which he feels a Romantic sympathy for, or participation in, the central character, to an extreme degree, and also for the way in which he soberly refuses to take it any further. If he directs the reader to a more 'transcendental' interpretation of the play, he does so hesitantly, hedging his observations round with careful reservations.[17]

—which shows a willingness to heed all that Bradley said, rarely found in earlier criticism.

In the last twenty years also there is evidence of scrutiny of the attitude to Bradley. Christopher Gillie wrote in *Essays in Criticism* after Leo Kirschbaum had published an article in that magazine criticizing Bradley for 'writing as though Banquo were an historical figure and not part of a drama'[18] in order to say 'My contention is that Bradley was right, and that the dramatic function of Banquo is subtler than Mr. Kirschbaum realises.'[19] Herbert Weisinger wrote an article called 'The Study of Shakespearian Tragedy since Bradley' which examined Miss Spurgeon, L. C. Knights, and Miss Campbell in turn, defended Bradley in relation to each, and concluded: 'Despite the trends which I

[16] H. B. Charlton, *Shakespearian Tragedy*, Clark Lectures 1946–7 (Cambridge, 1948), p. 4.

[17] B. Everett, 'The New King Lear', *C.Q.* ii. 4 (1960), pp. 324–39, at p. 328.

[18] L. Kirschbaum, 'Banquo and Edgar: Character or Function', *E. in C.*, vii. (1957), pp. 1–21, at p. 6.

[19] C. Gillie, Letter to, *E. in C.* vii. 3 (1957), pp. 322–4, at p. 322.

have briefly characterized here, the kind of approach which Bradley represents still seems to me the most fruitful for the understanding of tragedy.'[20]

More significantly still the Cambridge and *Scrutiny* school has been willing to accord him a place in the tradition of criticism. L. C. Knights, the author of a major attack in the thirties, wrote in 1959 of his debt to Shakespeare critics of the century 'from Bradley, through G. Wilson Knight, to more recent writers'.[21] Empson, a writer whose technique seemingly differed totally from Bradley's, wrote in his essay on the 'Fool in Lear':

> Going back to Bradley after I had drafted my piece, I was struck by how much I had unconsciously borrowed from him, how much broader and more adequate to the play his whole treatment seemed than mine, and what an enormous amount he gets said in his apparently brief and leisurely talks.[22]

If Empson was not ashamed to have been bettered by Bradley, Irving Ribner later was not afraid to admit: 'Although I have written in opposition to A. C. Bradley's principal tenets in his influential *Shakespearean Tragedy*, my great indebtedness to him will be everywhere apparent.'[23] Criticism is disentangling itself from the competitive as opposed to the critical attitude to Bradley. It is now no longer necessary for a writer to make his stand on Bradley; the heroics implied in the *Times Literary Supplement* remark in 1951, 'It seemed an act of tremendous courage in Professor H. B. Charlton a few years ago to descend upon Cambridge with the Clark lectures proclaiming "I am a devout Bradleyite" ',[24] are now comically out of date. It was possible in 1960, for John Bayley to undermine without flourish or fanfare the last bastion of anti-Bradleyism by writing: 'One can be sure that somewhere in that mind [of Shakespeare's]

[20] H. Weisinger, 'The Study of Shakespearian Tragedy since Bradley', *S.Q.* (1955), pp. 387–96, at p. 396.

[21] L. C. Knights, *Some Shakespearian Themes* (London, 1959), p. 11 (1964 edition).

[22] W. Empson, *The Structure of Complex Words* (London, 1951), p. 125.

[23] I. Ribner, *Patterns in Shakespearian Tragedy* (1960), p. 11.

[24] *T.L.S.*, 30 Mar. 1951: 'A. C. Bradley.'

the problem of Lady Macbeth's children would find its appropriate resolution.'[25]

All of these things are signs of a critical acceptance of Bradley—an acceptance which pays him the finest compliment of questioning by every means available his methods and assumptions. It hardly, therefore, seems surprising that Morris Weitz should devote so much attention to Bradley in his book *Hamlet and the Philosophy of Literary Criticism*. It seems that now when the 'sifting process' has done its work we can see Bradley as he rightly forecast we would see Tennyson: 'When the process is complete nobody troubles to dwell on the poet's defects, nobody is blinded by them to his merits, and it is possible to form a comparative estimate of his worth.'[26]

What makes Bradley's position so peculiar is that this natural development of critical independence and acceptance has been masked by a veneer of anti-Bradleyism which probably helps prevent his works being as widely read as they would otherwise be. The name of Bradley is probably better known among university students as a tag to represent the outdated than are any of the ideas contained in his work. It was thus possible for Sir Ifor Evans in a speech of thanks to Helen Gardner after a lecture on *King Lear*[27] to say quite *en passant*, 'I suspect that Bradley never went to the theatre', and meet with the hearty intellectual laughter of superiority which he was clearly counting on. Similarly and perhaps more seriously T. J. B. Spencer giving the British Academy Shakespeare lecture wrote: 'As for the Victorian critics (including Bradley), at a time when the dominant literary form had become the serious moralising novel, it is obvious that they are assuming the plays to be (as objects of criticism) something like *Middlemarch*.'[28]

What makes this type of criticism so damaging is that it bears no relation to the facts. Ifor Evans could not be expected to know whether A. C. Bradley went to the theatre. If he had been

[25] J. Bayley, *The Characters of Love: A Study in the Literature of Personality* (London, 1960), p. 41.

[26] *A.M.*, p. 4.

[27] H. Gardner, *King Lear*. John Coffin Memorial Lecture, University of London, 2 Mar. 1966.

[28] T. J. B. Spencer, 'The Tyranny of Shakespeare', *B.A.* (1959), pp. 153–71, at p. 163.

making a serious critical comment instead of an academic joke he would have taken the trouble to find out. Gilbert Murray, a close friend of Bradley's, was both writing for the theatre and translating plays. The letters from Bradley to Murray indicate that Bradley not only went to the theatre but was interested in contemporary drama. For example, in December 1904, at the time when *Shakespearean Tragedy* appeared, Bradley wrote to Murray that he went to see *Candida*: 'I should like to have seen *Candida* ten times over and find myself constantly thinking of it and am ready to forgive Shaw a good deal for it. And I thought G. Barker quite perfect.'[29]

All of this would be irrelevant to an understanding of Bradley if it were not that so much criticism has relied for so long on a Bradley who never really existed. For Spencer to say that Bradley treats the drama as something comparable to *Middlemarch* ignores so much of Bradley's work—the debt to Aristotle and Hegel—both writing before the 'dominant literary form had become the serious moralising novel', the chapters on the substance and structure of Shakespearian tragedy—and yet appears superficially so knowledgeable that many readers of the critic will look no further. This is why such remarks are harmful. Good criticism provokes further criticism and encourages a critical attitude to the works in question. Poor criticism is barren and unproductive, and Bradley has been subjected to a large quantity of this poor criticism; the criticism which has failed to examine the facts for itself and wishes to deter others from doing so. The reasons for this are complex and related to the movements of fashion in wider spheres than the study of Bradley.

It is hoped in this book to come to some understanding of the value of Bradley's work which will be free from the prejudices which acritical commentary has built up. Since Bradley is for so many present-day readers not the Bradley of *Shakespearean Tragedy* (1904) and *Oxford Lectures on Poetry* (1909), but the Bradley of *How Many Children had Lady Macbeth?* (1933) and Shakespearian critics' social jokes, it seemed best to work inward starting from the Bradleyan façade and aiming towards the essential

[29] Letter to G. Murray, Dec. 1904.

Bradley, evaluating what he said in terms of the reactions it has aroused and the influence it has had; for in reaction and influence the value of the critic must finally rest. If Bradley has succeeded in making the twentieth century alive to important aspects of Shakespeare's work, then his criticism will stand despite the fluctuations of fashion.

Because Bradley's relationship to modern Shakespeare criticism is a complex of the truly critical and the merely fashionable, it is not possible to deal with that relationship in what would perhaps be the most obvious way, that is chronologically. Under close scrutiny trends disappear amid detail; remarks which should be peculiarly modern are found among the critics of the past, prognostications of where criticism is going appear years before and again years after criticism in fact takes that path. Dates become almost meaningless; some writers are more 'modern' or more 'old-fashioned' it would seem, irrespective of their period. To preserve historical sequence it would be necessary to ignore so much or include so many exceptions that the exercise would become valueless. Moreover a historical approach tends to give the impression that criticism is marching on to perfection, with each critic seen as a stage on that journey and not as a critic in his own right.

History has not been forgotten, Chapter 8 sets the discussion in its proper time sequence, but it has been thought best to concentrate in the main part of the work on critical developments in ideas rather than historical progression.

2

LIFE AND MINOR WRITINGS

BEFORE losing sight of the Bradley who actually was in the ramifications of the Bradley which the twentieth century has built according to its own image, it will be useful to set down some of the basic facts of Bradley's life and work. The sources[1] for this material are few and scattered; even the short biographical obituaries published after his death offer only a bare outline, omitting long periods of Bradley's life altogether and dealing with the mere facts of much of the rest. Bradley's own letters to Gilbert Murray, which cover the last thirty-five years of his life, furnish the only details that survive; for the rest, biographies of other more prominent men offer some hints on Bradley's life and show us something of the society in which he lived.

Bradley's father was a man renowned in his own right; almost the typical 'Victorian' and apparently the typical 'Victorian father'. Mure in his article on F. H. Bradley describes him:

> A not uncommon 19th-century English type; an evangelical clergyman, noted for his polished but forcible sermons highly prolific, and a domestic tyrant. He had twenty-two children by two wives and he bullied them all. Herbert . . . is said to have been the only one of his offspring who ever stood up to this formidable *paterfamilias*.[2]

The Reverend Charles Bradley was born in Essex in 1789 of

[1] Cf. Bibliography: Sources of Biography.

[2] G. R. Mure, 'Men and Ideas. F. H. Bradley, Towards a Portrait', *Encounter* xvi (Jan. 1961), p. 28. According to R. Wollheim there were twenty children and one of his children, George Granville, could be no more precise than to say that there were thirteen children by the first wife (twelve of whom survived their father) and 'a large family' by the second. Twenty-two is probably only a notional number. Charles Bradley's granddaughter Margaret L. Woods in an unpublished volume of memoirs (Bodleian MS. Don. d. 129, fol. 154) has some interesting details on the parson's life, perhaps the most interesting of which is her 'suspicion that the Reverend Charles was a pious flirt'.

parents of Yorkshire origin. He took orders without obtaining a degree, although he lived for a while at St. Edmund Hall, Oxford. He held a number of livings in the south of England and, while still comparatively young, earned some repute as a preacher. A volume of sermons published in 1818 had reached an eleventh edition by 1854. At the same time a volume first published in 1825 reached a ninth edition. He married his first wife, Catherine Shepherd, in 1811 and had twelve children by her, the eldest son, Charles, earning himself a reputation in educational circles and the fourth son George Granville becoming Dean of Westminster.

In 1829 Charles Bradley became incumbent of St. James's Chapel, Clapham. This was then the centre of the evangelical Clapham Sect and Bradley counted among his friends such men as William Wilberforce and Thomas Scott, the Bible commentator. Bradley himself continued to attract attention as a preacher and published several more volumes of sermons. His son wrote of 'their singular simplicity and force, . . . the sustained dignity and purity of the language', and that 'their literary merits . . . will probably give them a lasting place in the literature of the kind.'[3] But perhaps more interesting are the comments recorded in George J. Davies's selected edition that Bradley's sermons were remarkable on account of the clearness of the divisions. A boy who heard Charles Bradley speak remembered and later wrote of 'the attractive style, the clear voice, the loving earnest way of applying his subject which was always divided and subdivided!'[4] It seems possible that Bradley's approach to his subject-matter had an equal effect on his son who also rigorously divided and subdivided his lectures.

He continued to reside at Clapham with some periods of absence until 1854 when the family moved to Cheltenham. His first wife having died in 1831, he married in 1840 one Emma Linton, and had by this second much younger wife another

[3] Article on Revd. Charles Bradley in *D.N.B.*, vol. ii, ed. Sir Leslie Stephen and Sir Sidney Lee (London, 1921), pp. 1073–4.

[4] *A Selection from the Sermons preached at High Wycombe, Glastonbury and St. James' Chapel, Clapham by the late Rev. Charles Bradley*, ed. with memoir by the Revd. George J. Davies.

equally large and yet more illustrious family. The eldest surviving son was Francis Herbert, the philosopher, and the youngest Andrew Cecil, the literary critic.

If Charles Bradley was a typical early Victorian father, his three famous sons were in many ways typical later Victorians. For this reason it is worth while to preface an inquiry into Andrew Cecil's life by a short description of the public lives of his famous brother and half-brother. George Granville Bradley first rose to eminence when he became headmaster of Marlborough in 1858, but before that he had aligned himself with the liberal reform spirit by signing in the winter of 1847–8, while a Fellow of University College, Oxford, a petition for a commission on the University. Other signatures include those of A. H. Clough, Matthew Arnold, and Baden-Powell. In 1870 he became Master of University College where he had been undergraduate and fellow. As Master he had a reputation for being a liberal at a time when Oxford reform was an almost national issue. He agitated for the removal of Greek as a compulsory requirement for an arts degree and consistently represented the reforming spirit in debate. In 1880, when a place fell vacant on the University Commission for which he himself had earlier campaigned, George Bradley took it up. In 1881 he published what is still one of the most widely used school text books, *Practical Introduction to Latin Prose Composition*, and in 1888 came the culmination of his career when on the death of Stanley, another member of the Oxford circle, he was appointed Dean of Westminster. He remained Dean until 1902 and after his death in 1903 was buried in the Abbey. His life is typical of those citizens who earn repute in their own time but oblivion in after years by a reforming spirit which brings about a way of life which will ensure that they are forgotten.

Francis Herbert Bradley, born on 30 January 1846, was never a prominent public figure. In fact, on account of ill-health and deafness and the philosophic train of his mind, he was, according to all records, something of a recluse. In 1865 he went up to University College, Oxford, where he failed like other prominent men at this period to obtain a first in *Literae Humaniores*. In

1870, contrary to his expectation, he was offered a Fellowship at Merton where he lived until his death in 1924. The kidney complaint from which he was never afterwards totally free first afflicted him the following year and probably helped to establish the pattern of his life. He had no students and did not lecture; but he published four important works: *Ethical Studies* (1876), *Principles of Logic* (1883), *Appearance and Reality* (1893), and *Essays on Truth and Reality* (1914). Published posthumously were *Collected Essays* (1935) and *Aphorisms* (1930). By means of his work he established himself as leader of the movement of Oxford philosophers grouped together as British Idealists. His philosophy has become 'old-fashioned' but his influence, it should not be forgotten, was more than contemporary. F. H. Bradley was one of the major influences on such a quintessentially modern writer as T. S. Eliot, and it was in Eliot's most aggressively modern period that the essay 'Francis Herbert Bradley' appeared containing such whole-hearted praise as:

> Of wisdom Bradley had a large share; wisdom consists largely of scepticism and uncynical disillusion; and of these Bradley had a large share. And scepticism and disillusion are a useful equipment for religious understanding: and of that Bradley had a share too.[5]

Little remains of the rest of Bradley's family; his letters tell us that his mother was ill for a long time before her death. (The family as a whole seems to have been dogged by ill-health and longevity.) There is record of a brother older than Andrew Cecil who was drowned in the Isis in 1866 while still a freshman at New College and of a sister who was playing championship tennis in the eighties at Wimbledon. This is not much and where only a little survives that little tends to display a family's serious side; as a corrective to this, we know that F. H. Bradley was prominent for sport at Marlborough College where he was educated and later was a close friend of Elinor Glyn, a scandalous romantic writer of the turn of the century. But the minutiae of family life are missing.

[5] T. S. Eliot, 'Francis Herbert Bradley' (1927), *Selected Essays* (London, 1932), quotation from 1961 edition, pp. 449–50.

Bradley's attitude to his family background is not known; he makes no reference to his father or his early childhood in his letters, not even when writing to Lady Mary Murray after the death of his mother. It is possible to read too much into this; Bradley was by then forty-eight years old, but there is no doubt that his family was not the strong formative influence on his life. Apart from the sister who nursed him in his long final illness, he was closest to Herbert, and it seems likely that this relationship, which lasted until the latter's death, was based on common Oxford interests. This is not to imply that Bradley was uninterested in his family; his letters have repeated references to his family's health and whereabouts: a sister in a carriage accident, holidays in West Malvern with Herbert, long visits to his sister and brother-in-law Ernest von Glehn in Taunton and Minehead. But it seems that it was the children of the first wife who continued in the evangelical spirit; the children of the second wife are more notable for a failure to conform to the family pattern. That there was some friendship between the two families is evident from the handwritten family magazine 'A Miscellany' which was edited by Edith and D. Bradley, two daughters of George Granville Bradley. To this magazine A. C. Bradley, who was their contemporary, was a regular contributor, and the surviving issues (Bodleian MS. Don. e 35, d 196) have among their contents a verse translation of a chorus from Aristophanes' *Clouds*, an original poem of little interest, and the first two chapters of a story called 'An Effort', all by Bradley. The story has a certain charm and its character can perhaps best be seen from the following extract:

> The scene will not be laid in England; why, I know not, for I have no idea what this story—if it may be so called—will be about. But one thing I know, and on that one thing I warn the readers of this magazine—and that thing is this. If you expect this story to be exciting or very interesting, you will find yourselves very much mistaken, for there will be little plot for you to get excited or interested in. But there is no use in saying this; for if you must read, you must.
>
> In a middle-sized room of a middle-sized house in the more than middle-sized city of Rome, you must look now. And this room you

will find it difficult to look very clearly at. For, if you will excuse my saying so, you are looking in in the evening time, and there is never a light to show you the room; and if there were you would not see much of it, for there is overspreading all, a cloud of sweet smoke fragrant—fragrant of tobacco.

Unfortunately the story does not proceed very far before the surviving copies run out—but at least by that time Bradley has roused enough interest for us to wish to read on.

Little or nothing is known of A. C. Bradley's early life beyond the barest facts. He was born at Cheltenham on 26 March in 1851. He was the youngest son. He was educated at Cheltenham College from 1864 where according to J. W. Mackail he had a good record both for games and work and, 'he had no enemies, but as many friends as he chose to make',[6] but even this latter statement is enigmatic. It might mean either that Andrew Cecil was a popular boy or, as seems more likely, a rather reserved child, but not disliked. In 1867 he won an exhibition to Balliol, which he took up the following year, immersing himself meanwhile, again according to Mackail, in the poetry for which he retained a life-long preference.

Shelley became his cynosure; Wordsworth and Keats, and in a lesser degree, Tennyson, became, and remained, stars in his firmament. It was the revolutionary side of the Romantic poets that most fully attracted him. It was but a step from this towards enthusiasm for the Italy of the Risorgimento and an introduction to the writings of Mazzini, for whom throughout life he retained an admiration that fell little short of worship.[7]

This picture is reinforced by Bradley's writing of Keats much later that 'he recalls one's youth to one'.[8] Significantly also he wrote in an article which he contributed to the *Oxford Undergraduates Journal*, of the gratitude which 'we students of poetry' felt for Rossetti's edition of Shelley. Moreover Bradley himself had a poem published in *Macmillan's Magazine*, then under the editorship of his brother-in-law, George Grove. Only the seventeen-year-old poet's initials were appended to the poem,

[6] J. W. Mackail, 'A. C. Bradley 1851–1935', *P.B.A.* xxi, p. 385.
[7] Ibid., p. 386.
[8] Letter to G. Murray, 23 Aug. 1896.

but his name appeared in full in the list of contributors. The poem itself, unlike the extract of fiction, gives us little cause to regret that there is not more of Bradley's early verse extant or that he did not continue as a creative writer. Here is the third of the five stanzas entitled 'A Sea-Shell':

> Not now, not now, sweet shell, some other day
> Tell me of sighings on the lonely shore,
> And seas that sob to birds that scream above;
> Tell me not now of earth grown weak and gray,
> Nor longing for the things that come no more,
> Nor any broken love.[9]

When at seventeen Bradley went up to Balliol, his mind had begun to take in those things which mattered most to him in later life, but Oxford was to help that mind take shape. There is little in Bradley's later works or life that does not show some mark from the years he spent as undergraduate and Fellow at Balliol. Nor was he alone in this; in fact the peculiar strength of Oxford's influence over Bradley must in part be attributed to the students who were his contemporaries, as well as to his superiors.

The Oxford to which Bradley went up in 1868 was in the midst of reform. The furore of the Oxford Movement in the 1840s and the scandal of *Essays and Reviews* published in 1860 were just dying down. The old Oxford, strongly clerical, reliant on privilege and influence, was gradually giving way to a new, which was to appropriate the most promising young minds in the country and develop them into the nation's leaders. Nowhere was this change more apparent than at Balliol, which was prominent for its liberalism and which housed, however uncomfortably, Benjamin Jowett, whose contribution to *Essays and Reviews*, 'On the Interpretation of Scripture', brought the convulsions which the publication of the book caused into his own college.

In 1862 Pusey put the ecclesiastical machinery of Oxford in motion against Jowett, but the case did not proceed. Jowett was left under an ecclesiastical cloud but free from formal condemnation from his University; and this was at a time when the ecclesiastical Oxford was giving way to the academic.

[9] Cf. Bibliography.

In the academic field, the publication in 1859 of both John Stuart Mill's *On Liberty* and Charles Darwin's *On the Origin of Species* brought about a new approach to secular study, which paralleled the new approach to theological study set out in *Essays and Reviews*. Instead of the old reliance on Biblical authenticity and the unquestioned acceptance of established gospel truths there was to be a rigorous questioning of all previously accepted fact. Not authority but inquiry was to be the watchword of academic works. The new approach met with a good deal of opposition especially since it attacked in regions where the Victorian mind was particularly sensitive: the literal truth of the Bible and the authority of the Church.

The intricacies of this development cannot be fully explored here but G. M. Trevelyan's summary of the position will perhaps suffice. Speaking of the earlier nineteenth century, he writes:

the advantages of Oxford and Cambridge were closed to half the nation by religious tests imposed in the interest of the Established Church, while the clerical and celibate character imposed on College Fellows, the almost complete supersession of the University by the individual Colleges, the close character of the elections to Fellowships, and the prevalence of absenteeism and sinecurism, rendered them incapable of meeting the demands of the new age, particularly in non-classical subjects, humane or scientific. Such impotence in the higher spheres of intellect and research must eventually have ruined the country in peace and in war, when matched against foreign rivals who valued scientific and educational progress. The timely reform of Oxford and Cambridge by Act of Parliament saved the situation.

This great work was accomplished in three stages, spread over a period of thirty years (1850–82). The impulse came partly from an intelligent minority in the Universities themselves, men like Jowett at Oxford and Henry Sidgwick at Cambridge, partly from the public demand that the national Universities should be open to all the nation. Great political interest was taken in academic questions during this epoch, partly because religious and sectarian questions were involved.[10]

The three separate stages were: the Oxford Act of 1854, which established the right of Parliament to legislate in University

[10] G. M. Trevelyan: *British History in the Nineteenth Century and after, 1782–1919* (London). Quotation from 1956 edition, pp. 355–6.

matters; the Test Act of 1871, which opened the University to Catholics and Non-conformists, and the later legislation of 1877–82, partly as a result of the Royal Commission, which freed the University from the stranglehold of the colleges. To this last movement Jowett was bitterly opposed. By this time he had become as renowned a reactionary as he had previously been a liberal.

This was the Oxford background in which A. C. Bradley found himself, but it was a smaller group, mostly of Balliol men, who were to shape him for the future. Jowett became Master of Balliol in 1870 but the fire in him was now dying down; the prophet of young Balliol was Thomas Hill Green, a man idolized in his time although now scarcely remembered outside specialist circles. This oblivion is in part due to the fact of his early death and consequent small output of work, his lack of advancement at Balliol, largely due to Jowett's opposition, and his overshadowing by the younger men whom he so much influenced, F. H. Bradley, R. L. Nettleship, and B. Bosanquet. Some record of his peculiar magnetism survives in a petition sent to him by Nettleship, both Bradleys, and others to join an essay society they had formed. Nettleship in the edition of Green's works which he and A. C. Bradley later edited wrote of the members of this society that they were

> Men who, having in them some strain of idealism, had found a difficulty in adjusting their lives to it; men in whom radicalism was seeking a meeting-point with loyalty or whose acceptance of a moral principle or a religious idea was crossed by a half-understood scientific theory or a half-disguised selfish impulse.[11]

And a manuscript draft, in Bradley's own hand, of the letter sent to Green elucidates the aims of the society. The most interesting of these, in the light of later views of A. C. Bradley as an academic totally unaware of a world outside his study, relates their

> earnest effort to bring speculation into relation with modern life, instead of making it an intellectual luxury, and to deal with the various

[11] M. Richter, *The Politics of Conscience. T. H. Green and his Age* (London, 1964), p. 161. The MS. draft in Bradley's hand and the actual letter sent to Green, 5 June 1872, are in Balliol College Library.

branches of science, physical, social, political, metaphysical, theological, aesthetic, as parts of a whole instead of in abstract separation.

And to T. H. Green these earnest young men wrote: 'We are all in one way or another your debtors, and look to you as the man who does more than anyone else in Oxford to teach men to think.'[12]

Writing to Gilbert Murray in July 1901 Bradley described himself delivering the Creweian Oration in Latin at Oxford:

That fiend Para[vicini] nearly killed me with anxiety by leaving a lot of the translation of the Creweian oration to the very last minute. It was horrible work reading it—the only downright fraudulent thing I have done, I think since I became a moral being (about nineteen).[13]

To Lady Mary Murray he wrote about the same oration that it was in 'Latin so exquisite I cannot construe it and am utterly ashamed to deliver it. Dear me, how Green would have chuckled to hear me.'[14] Add to these two the following: 'A. C. Bradley told a friend fifty years later that Green had saved his soul',[15] and something emerges of the profound effect that Green must have had on the young Bradley, that he at fifty and established in an Oxford Professorship should be so conscious of the moral attitude of a man who had been dead for twenty years.

Green's works survive; but his magnetism was not on account of his work of which the same Bradley who acknowledged Green as his spiritual saviour wrote: 'I think there is something not quite right.'[16] Green was a liberal in both university and national politics; he was sufficiently interested in non-academic politics to become an Oxford City Councillor, an action somewhat unusual for a don of the period. He believed in the Low Church and Liberal gospel of self-help; he thought that men should be educated to want the best things for themselves and not that legislation should force them to adopt moral attitudes. For this reason, Green and many of his followers were prominent in

[12] M. Richter, op. cit., p. 161.
[13] Letter to G. Murray, July 1901.
[14] Letter to Lady M. Murray, 14 June 1901.
[15] M. Richter, op. cit., p. 14.
[16] Letter to Lady M. Murray, 11 Dec. 1906.

Adult Education. Toynbee Hall and the South Place Ethical Society in London owe a good deal to the influence of Green on Toynbee and Bosanquet. He was, however, no unrealistic idealist—where he thought men were not wise enough to choose the best for themselves he was prepared with some reluctance to use legislation to help. He supported the Licensing Act of 1872 and was prominent in the anti-alcoholic movement of the late nineteenth century; it is further typical that he never drank alcohol himself, and meetings which he attended usually offered only coffee to other attenders in deference to Green's views. This because he felt not that the consumption of alcohol was evil in itself but that those who themselves could in fact drink moderately ought to be prepared not to drink at all if by so doing they could help those who could only drink immoderately or not at all, to choose the latter.

His views on this one matter indicate the sort of man he was, and this and his liberalism help to explain the extent and power of his influence. While Jowett was seeking to inform the young what paths they should follow in order to exploit their talent to the full and gain the right reward of that talent, Green was helping the young to help themselves in order that they might then do the same for others.[17]

In 1876 Bradley became a lecturer at Balliol having been a Fellow there since 1874. He had taken a Second in Classical Moderations and a First in *Literae Humaniores* and won the Chancellor's Essay Prize for an essay 'Utopia' in 1875.[18] By this time the conflict between Jowett the Master and Green and his young followers was quite marked. There are comments in the letters on the atmosphere at Oxford which seem to reflect the events of this period: 'it is so unwholesome to the body, and, as for the spirit, it is full of critical mediocrity.'[19] That Bradley took his stand firmly with the Green supporters is made clear not only by his later editing of Green's works but by the fact that he

[17] But cf. Sir G. Faber, *Jowett* (London, 1957), p. 357, for a totally contrary view of the position.

[18] This essay is unfortunately lost.

[19] Letter to G. Murray, Sept. 1894.

suffered, with Green, Jowett's disapproval. Richter sums this up: 'In the Master's view, Green as a tutor was apt to do more harm than good, and the same was true of A. C. Bradley and R. L. Nettleship.'[20]

The exact quality of Bradley's tutoring is not discoverable. Mackail, who knew him at Oxford, wrote that he was to the students 'an enigma, a veiled poet or a veiled prophet'.[21] The only indication of the attitude of undergraduates to Bradley the don is found in the rhymes:

I'm BR-DL-Y, and I bury deep
'A secret that no man can keep'
If you won't let the Master know it,
Or F-RB-S, I'll tell you,—I'm a poet.

and

I am MR. ANDREW BRADLEY
When my liver's doing badly
I take refuge from 'the brute'
In the blessed Absolute.[22]

The first of these rhymes was printed with some thirty others in *The Masque of Balliol* in Hilary Term of 1881 but the pamphlet was quickly withdrawn. Among the rhymes are the famous ones on Jowett and Curzon; these two on Bradley lack the vital accuracy of the other two, but they show a don, quiet and sickly (if not valetudinarian), given to the pursuit of Poetry and Philosophy. This is a picture which the letters bear out. Although the following extract from a letter to Lady Mary Murray refers to an earlier Oxford period it illustrates clearly the kind of young man

[20] M. Richter, op. cit., p. 152.

[21] J. W. Mackail, op. cit., p. 387.

[22] W. G. Hiscock, *Balliol Rhymes*, edited from the Rare Original Broadsheet with the Notes of J. W. Mackail, Lord Sumner, and F. A. Madan, together with a MS. from Christ Church Library (1939), pp. 5 and 28 respectively. The second line of the first rhyme according to J. W. Mackail is quoted from a poem which Bradley had published in *Macmillan's Magazine*. Bradley himself refers to this poem in a letter to Lady Mary Murray, 25 July 1908, and says it was published by George Grove thirty years before that 'even to a month I believe'. In fact the month was exact but not the year. It was forty years before, in 1868. The hypochondria hinted at in the second rhyme is well borne out by the letters.

Bradley was. He wrote sending Lady Murray a copy of a photograph of Mazzini:

> It is done from a photograph taken directly after Mazzini's death and sent to me then—forty one years ago. How I remember sitting in tears half the night after the telegram came and feeling a week after when the photograph came 'Nothing is here for tears'.[23]

Evidence of Bradley's interest in contemporary literature is found, even at this early date, in his review of Browning's *Inn Album*, contributed to *Macmillan's Magazine* in 1876. This lengthy and not very favourable review demonstrates well Bradley's critical skill, but more interesting still are two passages which make it clear that the Bradley of *Shakespearean Tragedy* was no sudden product of the Oxford Poetry chair. Here is the same carefully considered balance between substance and structure, and, even where not strictly relevant, the same interest in Shakespeare's characters, though here as later this is an aesthetic and not a purely psychological concern. He writes:

> You cannot possibly represent Falstaff, Iago, Cleopatra in critical prose, though it is well worth while to do what you can, because the attempt may help you to a more perfect imaginative appropriation of the character and the poetry.

And in a footnote further expands his idea of the essential unity of meaning and form:

> The mistake of supposing that the 'meaning' of a work of art can be adequately expressed in any other form than its own special artistic form is seen most clearly when attempts are made at putting the 'meaning' of a piece of music into words. The very word 'meaning' is misleading: for it commonly signifies something expressible in

[23] Letter to G. Murray, 27 February 1913. On the other hand, Norman Pearson, whose main contribution to Oxford life was on the river, wrote in a memoir of Balliol at this time: 'Another of my great friends was Andrew Bradley. . . . He was one of the most popular men in the college, an excellent cricketer, and passionately devoted to music. He took one of the best Firsts of his year in Greats and has held Professorships innumerable. There was an infectious light-heartedness about him in those days which made him a delightful companion; and though hard work and ill-health have tried him sorely in later years, the old fire is not altogether dead.' N. Pearson, 'Balliol as I Remember it', *Blackwoods*, clxxxvii (May 1910), pp. 633–42, at p. 636.

language, and in this sense music can hardly be said to have a meaning. It does not follow that we are to fall into the equal absurdity of saying that it expresses nothing at all.[24]

This is but a foretaste of the preoccupations of Bradley's criticism, which will be examined in more detail in the next chapter. It illustrates neatly Bradley's own confession in a letter to Murray at the time of writing his Oxford inaugural lecture, over a quarter of a century later: 'I know that everything I say really repeats one idea.'[25]

In 1880 Bradley contributed a chapter to *Hellenica*, a collection of studies of Greek culture edited by Evelyn Abbott. The essay 'Aristotle's Conception of the State' is his first publication in book form[26] and reflects the interest in philosophy which was then his major study. Nevertheless this essay demonstrates the basic attitudes which Bradley was to retain all his life. That Aristotle's *Poetics* were a profound influence on Bradley's conception of tragedy is widely accepted, but Aristotle's *Politics* and *Ethics* provide no less important a basis for Bradley's thoughts on tragedy. Expounding Aristotle Bradley said:

that man attains only for moments to some likeness of this divine perfection, we have already seen; but that he does so even for moments, and for a longer time can produce those activities of the moral life which are the victory of the divine element in him over his lower nature, is enough to place him at the head of earthly things.[27]

The emphasis is clearly different from that in the writings on tragedy but here we can see one of the sources of his interest in the role of man, which led Bradley to consider tragedy by means of its characters; and the same awareness of the highest potential in man and the need to use this potential to enrich the lives of others. The above statement is as good a justification of the role

[24] 'Mr. Browning's "Inn Album"', pp. 349–50.

[25] Letter to Murray, 8 Apr. 1901.

[26] Cf. Bibliography. As there is no means of locating all articles and contributions this bibliography is in all probability not quite complete (e.g. the omission of the essay mentioned in n. 18), but for the purposes of this book it will be taken as complete.

[27] *A.C.S.* in *Hellenica*, p. 199.

of Hamlet as will be seen anywhere in the writings of Bradley. This article also demonstrates Bradley's early mastery of language; the style which was to become his most powerful advocate is apparent even here. That the final flourish which caused so much scepticism in the twentieth century was essential to Bradley's modes of thought and expression is made clear by the fact that it occurs here long before Bradley was the established figure of whom such rhetoric was expected. He writes:

> That goodness is not abstinence but action; that egoism, to however future a life it postpones its satisfaction, is still nothing but selfishness; that a man does not belong to himself, but to the State and to mankind; that to be free is not merely to do what one likes, but to like what one ought; and that blindness to the glory of the 'world' and irreverence towards its spiritual forces are the worst of passports to any 'church' worthy of the name,—every new conviction of such truths is an advance towards filling up the gulf between religion and reality, and restoring, in a higher shape, that unity of life which the Greeks knew.[28]

J. W. Mackail was struck by the resemblance of these words to the final sentence of one of his Oxford lectures on poetry and wrote of the whole article as being of 'high value as the work not only of an original thinker and fine scholar, but of one who was already a master of style; a style unique in its combined precision and elasticity'.[29] Even remembering that this was written in an obituary by a friend it is hard to quarrel with the judgement.

Bradley was already, however, turning his attentions where possible to the study of literature on which he lectured to the Oxford Association for the Education of Women. He was the first don to do so before the founding of Lady Margaret Hall and Somerville College for which latter he retained an attachment to the end of his life,[30] and, again according to Mackail, this 'had a great deal to do with shifting the balance of his study and teaching

[28] Ibid., p. 241.

[29] J. W. Mackail, op. cit., p. 387.

[30] Letter to G. Murray, 11 Feb. 1921. 'I was just going to send (for Somerville) the largest donation I have ever made (thanks to the sale of my books—I mean the books I wrote), partly from attachment to Somerville and partly because women-teachers seem to be so badly paid.'

from philosophy to literature'.[31] In May 1881 he had an article published in *Macmillan's Magazine* (to which many Balliol and Oxford men of the period contributed and of which George Grove, A. C. Bradley's brother-in-law, was the editor) on 'Old Mythology and Modern Poetry'.[32]

The main thesis of this article is not so clearly followed as is usually the case even in these early writings of Bradley; but it seems that Bradley's point was that as the facts of the Arthurian and Greek legend had been successfully used by poets who no longer believed in the mythologies concerned, for readers who similarly did not believe, so the facts of the Christian religion would be able to serve in the near future when the Christian myths were no longer for the 'class of men who produce art and literature, the literal expressions of an absolute truth'.[33] The interest of the article lies not, however, in its main thesis but in the expression almost by the way of ideas which form an essential part of Bradley's aesthetic theory:

> It is surely the fact that deep and true ideas have a natural affinity to poetry which shallow and false ideas have not. But they ought to show it by *becoming* poetry; if they do not, their depth and truth are not poetic qualities at all.

and

> What we need for the purpose of imagination, if for no other purpose, is the power of detaching our minds from the special form in which our experience clothes itself, and of finding this experience in the shapes which other times have given it.[34]

These are ideas which are expounded again and again until they receive their definitive treatment in 'Poetry for Poetry's Sake' published in 1909 in the *Oxford Lectures*.

At about this time life at Balliol was becoming intolerable for Bradley and in the summer of 1882 he left Oxford. The precise details of why and upon what occasion Bradley left are difficult

[31] J. W. Mackail, op. cit., p. 389.

[32] Cf. Bibliography. In the same number of *Macmillan's Magazine*, Henry James's *Portrait of a Lady* was being serialized.

[33] *O.M.M.P.*, p. 46.

[34] Ibid., pp. 35 and 40.

to discover beneath the poetic phrases of obituary and the gentlemanly vagueness of academic biography. Richter, however, referred outright to 'Bradley's expulsion from Oxford'[35] and said of it:

On the basis of his ability and achievement, as well as his service, Bradley certainly deserved more from the College than this rude blow. Diverted from the teaching of philosophy into the Chair of English at Liverpool he later returned to Oxford as Professor of Poetry and became one of the most influential literary critics of his day.

This view is perhaps tinged with a little partisanship for the follower of Green, and *The Times* obituary's view of the situation is much less melodramatic.[36] According to this Bradley moved away from the Balliol set, was offered a post at Magdalen which he refused in order to follow his bent for literature, and went so far as to discuss with J. A. Symonds (Green's brother-in-law) the possibility of taking up writing as a career. The following extracts from a letter Green wrote to Bradley on 23 June 1881 cast more light on the position:

the persistency of the Master's opposition—not, it is needless to say, to you personally—but to that kind of teaching being given in the college in which you could be most useful . . . Whether you would do well to try for the Professorship of Literature at Liverpool, as I hear you have thought of doing, I cannot say. Enquire carefully about the climate.

The last sentence reflects the valetudinarian Bradley's concern for the air so well that it might almost be a sly joke. In a more serious vein Bradley replied:

It is troublesome to have narrow gifts and interests—if they cannot be made to bear fruit—and I know that the picking and rejecting it leads to must look like laziness or conceit. But every year I feel more keenly that it is vain to fight against nature and, for one with such a poor stock of energy, doubly vain . . . I would rather do a very little

[35] Richter, op. cit., pp. 152–3.

[36] *The Times*, 4 Sept. 1935, p. 14. Unfortunately *The Times* will not divulge the name of the writer of this obituary, or of any of the several articles on Bradley's works in *The Times Literary Supplement*.

to help the study of philosophy in Oxford than anything (outside writing) that could be in my power to do.[37]

His specific doubts about the Liverpool Chair were because it was for Modern Literature and History, but in the event a separate Chair of History was created while Bradley was in Liverpool. Another point which emerges from this letter is that the mere teaching of Literature, as opposed to writing, did not appeal to Bradley as much as the study of philosophy.

However, it came about in 1882 that he did become the first professor in the King Alfred Chair of Modern Literature and History at the University College of Liverpool which had been granted its charter the previous year. Few facts remain of his Liverpool days, but Professor McCunn, who was Professor of Philosophy at Liverpool while A. C. Bradley was there, is quoted in *The Times* obituary:

> He was generous in his response to literary associations in the city and neighbourhood, justly regarding this as not the least of the duties of a professor of a newly founded institution in a great community. . . . He had a rare faculty of enriching literary criticism by ideas, and a consummate art in penetrating comment and happy illustration. Few indeed have ever had so great a gift of saying weighty things in simple words while the fire and transparent sincerity of his character shone through every word of his exposition and criticism. . . . Nor was his philosophy without practical application. His political interests were keen and real. Citizenship was a word of much significance to him, and it was not only his students or colleagues who felt his departure from Liverpool to be an irreparable loss.[38]

Mackail gives the impression that Bradley was not happy in Liverpool, where he missed academic associates and friends, but the letters to Murray refer to several old Liverpool friends with some of whom he spent holidays for many years afterwards.

While he was at Liverpool he published another article in *Macmillan's Magazine*, this time a review of a book called *Natural Religion by the Author of Ecce Homo*, but the same basic ideas are

[37] Letter from Green to Bradley, 23 June 1881, and letter from Bradley to Green, 27 Sept. 1881. Both in Balliol College Library.

[38] *The Times*, 4 Sept. 1935.

still apparent: 'Before we can *realise* a philosophical truth most of us have to turn it into imagination.' Of religion he writes:

> It is not of such consequence as it is often assumed to be that the imaginative ideas which are vehicles to our religion should be *true*; it is of the utmost consequence that they should be good. They must be *inadequate* to the object of worship, but they need not be unworthy.[39]

Here Bradley is expounding a view of religion made possible only by the liberalism following the upheaval of *Essays and Reviews*; a view which interestingly enough is still expounded in the liberal press and still refuted vehemently.

Bradley's first major publication is dated Liverpool, April 1885. This is the posthumous edition of T. H. Green's works which Bradley edited with R. L. Nettleship, A. C. Bradley being responsible for the 'Prologomena to Ethics'. This work cannot be our concern here: all Bradley did was to divide into Books and Chapters, add an analytical table and some notes, and make the necessary corrections. Richter, writing over eighty years later when standards of editing have become much more exacting, thought that the works were 'very well edited'.[40] Apart from this Bradley's most important work from Liverpool is in the form of a lecture. This is 'The Study of Poetry' delivered in the Winter session of 1883 and published at Liverpool in 1884. Here is the first utterance of the authentic Bradley—appropriately made in the form of a lecture. This, his later inaugural lecture at Glasgow, that made even later as his Presidential Address to the English Association, and the most famous inaugural lecture as the Professor of Poetry at Oxford, all deal with one subject if from slightly different angles: the study of poetry as poetry. These four lectures constitute the best answer there is to the criticism that Bradley was unaware of the difference between art and life and will be considered together in a later chapter.

The only other publication by Bradley while at Liverpool is a contribution to the *Liverpool University College Magazine* of a review of his friend H. C. Beeching's edition of *Julius Caesar*. What is interesting about this short article is the use by

[39] *N.R.*, p. 156. [40] Richter, op. cit., p. 192.

Bradley of one of the phrases later used as a watchword by his enemies. Writing about the usual school edition of Shakespeare he says:

> When the average pupil and the average teacher find a play treated by the editor merely as a text for verbal interpretation and discussion, a hundred pages in length, they are tempted to forget that the play is anything beside this and they rise from the study of it without ever having studied it as the thing it is—a dramatic poem.[41]

Nearly fifty years later L. C. Knights told the Shakespeare Association of King's College, London that 'A Shakespeare play is a dramatic poem',[42] and ushered in a new era of anti-Bradleyan criticism, by means of a phrase which was Bradley's own.

There seems to be some indication that Bradley was not happy at Liverpool in the fact that in 1885 he was an unsuccessful candidate (in the company of Edmund Gosse, Edward Dowden, George Saintsbury, and J. Churton Collins) for the Merton Professorship in English Language and Literature. This was possibly due to the excessive amount of work. It was not until the session of 1883–4 that the Modern History Chair was created, reducing the work of Bradley's department by half; the administrative work must have been very heavy in a new department of a new university and the lecturing itself was on a subject new to Bradley as an object of academic tuition. In 1889 Bradley took over from Professor John Nichol as the Professor of English Literature at Glasgow—an appointment which met with mixed reactions. A magazine not strictly concerned with academic affairs heralded the appointment of Bradley with a sharp paragraph:

> The appointment by Lord Lothian of Mr. A. C. Bradley to the Chair of English Literature at Glasgow has given deep offence in Scotland and most assuredly it is an arrant job, for there were several gentlemen whose claims were far superior to those of Mr. Bradley, which indeed, rest on a very shadowy foundation for his merits are by

[41] Cf. Chronological Bibliography.

[42] L. C. Knights, *How Many Children had Lady Macbeth?* (Cambridge, 1933), p. 7.

no means widely known whereas some of the candidates had distinctly made their mark in literature.[43]

But this attitude to Bradley was not universal. Gilbert Murray, whose appointment to the Chair of Greek was condemned in the next paragraph of the same magazine, wrote in his autobiography 'to be condemned together with Bradley was a great distinction',[44] but this is possibly tinged with Murray's retrospective love and admiration of Bradley. John Nichol wrote of the choice of Bradley, 'I think the appointment a very good one, not only for Glasgow, but also for Scotland'.[45]

There is more material about Bradley's Glasgow days than any other. Bradley himself wrote of Glasgow in his letters to Murray and there survives an obituary appreciation of Bradley's teaching at Glasgow. Of his lectures given to classes of two hundred pupils it was recorded that they were

Written with infinite care and closely read. The control of his classes, to those whom he controlled, still offers a startling illustration of the victory of mind over matter. His intellectual influence, owing nothing to external circumstances, was overwhelming and permanent.

In Literature his inclination was towards creative and romantic rather than towards rationel and critical ages. And he directed his student

more to substance than to form and to appreciation, not criticism.[46]

These last two comments seem to be made in the light of a memory affected by the critical development of the years between and by Bradley's published work for, according to the Glasgow Syllabus, Bradley followed Nichol in lecturing on Elizabethan drama and poetry from Thomson to Byron, Chaucer, selected Romantic poetry, Tennyson, and Shakespeare but also on Addison and other eighteenth-century essayists and *The Vicar of Wakefield.*

[43] *Truth*, 1 Aug. 1889.

[44] G. G. A. Murray, *An Unfinished Autobiography*, ed. Jean Smith and Arnold Toynbee (London, 1960), p. 94.

[45] Professor Knight, *A Memoir of John Nichol* (Glasgow, 1896), p. 225.

[46] Excerpt from Minute of Meeting of the General Council of the University of Glasgow held on 30 Oct. 1935. A copy of this minute was sent to Balliol College Library where I was able to read it.

When an Honours class was instituted in 1893 Bradley lectured on Shakespeare, Addison, Fielding, and Goldsmith, the Waverley Novels, Shelley and Keats and Tennyson. While this shows a preponderance of romantic literature it must be remembered that as professor, Bradley could presumably choose to some extent on what he lectured and he chose to include some eighteenth-century writers.

At all events Glasgow seems to have received Bradley well. There is evidence that Bradley, together with Murray, was regarded in the light of a prophet. Lord Lindsay of Birker writing over fifty years later spoke of the 'wonderful impression . . . which A. C. Bradley and Gilbert Murray made on their students of the University of Glasgow'.[47] Bradley wrote to Lady Mary Murray: 'I met an Eton Master (McNaghten) who was reading G's book and pleased me by saying that G and I are the true gods.'[48] As Murray and Bradley were only together at Glasgow this impression was most probably formed on the basis of those days. Mackail wrote that compared with Liverpool he had 'much more enthusiastic classes, a wider scope, and an increasing body of friends'.[49] This seems to imply that Bradley was contented and even very happy to be at Glasgow. And Bradley certainly was happy in his friendship with Gilbert Murray and his wife of which Murray wrote, 'The close friendship of Andrew Bradley was one of the most precious influences of my life'.[50] But the impression received from the letters to Gilbert Murray which do not begin until 1892 is that this friendship was the only consolation for the dreariness of the place. Undoubtedly these letters reflect minor grumblings communicated to one of the few people Bradley felt would understand and should not be thought to reflect a total mood of such bitterness and despair as they sometimes suggest. In December 1897 Bradley wrote from Glasgow, 'this place is a howling wilderness' (he hated the cold), and the following

[47] Lord Lindsay of Birker, *The Place of English Studies in the British Universities and English Studies To-day*, ed. C. L. Wrenn and G. Bullough (1951), p. 169.

[48] Letter to Lady Mary Murray, 16 Aug. 1909.

[49] J. W. Mackail, op. cit., p. 389.

[50] G. Murray, *An Unfinished Autobiography*, p. 96.

March 'This blooming place is a weary waste without you'. In July 1899 he wrote from Kensington, 'I feel very sick about Glasgow. There is such [an] . . . atmosphere of trickery and littleness.' All this did not prevent him from writing much later to Lady Mary Murray, 'I wouldn't myself have missed my years in a Great business city, and I don't suppose you and G. would'.[51]

What seems to be the truth is that Bradley never really liked the establishment at Glasgow and probably felt something of an outsider despite the preponderance of Oxford men on the staff, and was already suffering from the varied ill-health which dogged the rest of his life and his correspondence. Moreover while he was at Glasgow he seems to have fallen in love with some quite inaccessible woman who later married someone else and this probably helped to accentuate the miseries attendant on the onset of middle age. Bradley was forty-eight by the time he left Glasgow.

Apart from the inaugural lecture discussed above Bradley published little work while he was in Glasgow. This is partly because he was editing the philosophical and literary remains of his friend Lewis Nettleship, who died in a climbing accident in the Alps. The first volume, which appeared in 1897, for which Bradley was totally responsible, is prefaced by a short life of Nettleship written by Bradley. This shows a very fair-minded approach to a subject who was a close friend of the writer and displays Bradley's ability in communicating an idea precisely; such a sentence as 'He would have winced to know it but he gave the impression of living on a height', makes the man very real to the reader.[52] After that much of Bradley's time must have been occupied with the preparation of his commentary on Tennyson's *In Memoriam* which appeared in 1901.[53] In 1891, however, Bradley published an address on *The Teaching of English Literature*.[54] This is interesting as it expounds Bradley's theories on education

[51] Letters to G. Murray, 31 Dec. 1897, Mar. 1898, July 1899; letter to Lady M. Murray, 12 Jan. 1920.

[52] *R.L.N.* i, p. xxxiv.

[53] This work was reissued in 1902 and 1930.

[54] This article is among the Bradley papers at Balliol College. I have found no copy of it elsewhere.

and elucidates his practice a little. He spares no consideration for the mechanical approach to literature: 'there is no good teaching but comes from enjoyment.'[55] He believed in the value of what became famous later as 'practical criticism':

> Our main object here is simply that the work should become to us what it was to the writer: an object unattainable, since (to take an instance) *Macbeth* can be to us what it was to Shakespeare only on condition that our minds become Shakespeare's mind; but yet an object on our approach to which depends the whole literary value of our study of *Macbeth* . . . No one ever lived himself thus into a work of accredited fame and yet found it dull. When we fail to care for such a work, it is simply because we have failed to make our souls live in its body.[56]

Having expounded his faith in the process, he proceeds to give an example of how it works. The example he uses is *Macbeth* Act I, scene i, the same as L. C. Knights was to use to expound a very similar method. The irony lies in the fact that L. C. Knights chose example and method to illustrate how wrong Bradley's method was.

Bradley seems to have held very unorthodox views on teaching. He opposed the use of literature as texts for the teaching of grammar and philology and held very idiosyncratic views on what works to teach children: 'This law always holds good, that what is peculiarly congenial to the teacher may be made congenial to the pupil though to most teachers and most pupils it would not be the best thing to choose', and 'A boy with a love for poetry will get more from the *Immortality Ode*, which he half understands, than from *Alice Fell*, which he is likely to think childish.'[57] He was, moreover, aware of the affliction which prevents readers of any age understanding poetry merely because they do not think it will bear any precise meaning on account of its peculiar form. All of this still seems very progressive and the whole is infused with the belief in his subject which Bradley always made apparent. Talking of the value of a good approach to literature he said, 'It aims at no mere means, but straight at the very end of

[55] *T.E.L.*, p. 7. [56] Ibid., p. 8. [57] Ibid., pp. 17 and 18.

education,—an eye that sees, an ear that hears and a heart that understands.'[58]

While he was at Glasgow Bradley gave the address on 'Inspiration' which he incorporated in *A Miscellany* in 1929. This address was also published separately in Glasgow in 1899 when it was presumably delivered. This will be considered later along with the other essays in *A Miscellany* but it is interesting to notice that it was delivered first in a Glasgow church although Bradley would appear to have had an abhorrence of organized religion.

For the rest Bradley's Glasgow days seem to have been passed in term time with evening lectures, theatre-going, music, and society, and in long vacations spent in London with his mother, at Oxford with his close friend Heberden at Brasenose, at Malvern with Herbert Bradley, or in the Alps again usually with Heberden. He seems to have seen Mrs. Patrick Campbell in *The Second Mrs. Tanqueray* which he praised to Murray. He took up golf and cycling, kept up a keen interest in politics both academic and national, and suffered from his usual indifferent health. In all this he seems not to have been very happy, but before he made his farewell speech at Glasgow he wrote to Murray, 'On Tuesday I give my prizes and reveal my dastardly intentions to my men, and for some reason I feel an utter traitor to them—They have been so nice and they have risen so well to W[illiam] S[hakespeare]—which is the first duty of man',[59] which suggests that his teaching was some consolation.

When he left Glasgow Bradley moved to London where he intended to devote himself to study. He was, however, proposed for the Oxford Chair of Poetry for which at first he showed no enthusiasm whatever. He wrote to Murray:

> I suppose its my duty to write about Shakespeare and the like for a good many years. I am tormented by the wish to philosophize—and again to think about politics . . . I am working more at last—I suppose I shall be elected at Oxford—and I wish I had any desire to lecture. Don't repeat it, but I feel ashamed of the business. In my heart I don't want it; I want the money and the pleasure of being at Oxford again.

[58] Ibid., p. 19.
[59] Letter to G. Murray, 25 Mar. 1900.

But I feel as if I had no message about literature and as if all the talk about it were mere idle voluptuousness.[60]

He was elected and the post offered him the opportunity to lecture as much as he liked on whatever subjects he chose. The outcome of his five years as Professor of Poetry was his two major works, *Shakespearean Tragedy*, published in 1904, and *Oxford Lectures on Poetry*, published in 1909. Whatever Bradley's initial hesitance in accepting the post there can be little doubt that it was this opportunity which enabled him to produce his best work. Apart from the Commentary on *In Memoriam* all his published work was originally delivered as lectures and even the Commentary arose out of his teaching work in Glasgow and Liverpool. It seems unlikely that he could have written anything as forceful without the initial stimulus of the lecture room audience.

The *Commentary on Tennyson's 'In Memoriam'* came out in 1901 and immediately a second edition was called for which entailed still more work by Bradley on the poem. The amount of work, revision, and research which went into this book is adequately described by Bradley's comment to Murray, 'Oh, how I loathe *In Memoriam*.'[61] The book is of little general interest, its appeal being exclusively to students of *In Memoriam*. The reason for this is explained by Bradley in the Preface: 'I have abstained almost wholly from "aesthetic criticism" chiefly because, although of course it interests me more than the kind of comment to which this book is restricted, I do not think the two kinds harmonise well.'[62] Bradley prefaces the Commentary proper by an Introduction dealing with the poem's origins, its composition, structure, and substance, the ideas it uses, the metre, and the debt to other poems. The most interesting comment to a student of Bradley as opposed to a student of Tennyson is made in the section entitled 'The Way of the Soul':

The ordinary reader does not indeed attempt to separate the poetic qualities of a work from some other quality that appeals to him; much

[60] Letter to G. Murray, 3 Feb. 1901. [61] Ibid., 15 Jan. 1902 (postmark).
[62] *T.I.M.*, p. ix.

less does he read the work in terror of being affected by the latter; but imagination and diction, even versification can influence him much as they influence the people who talk about them, and he would never have taken *In Memoriam* to his heart if its consoling or uplifting thoughts had not also touched his fancy and sung in his ears.[63]

The adequacy of the Commentary in fulfilling its function of exposition is well attested by the fact that it is still much used. Bradley, however, partly on account of some unfavourable reviews, seems to have doubted the value of the exposition:

Some of the reviews—with other things—have made me think that perhaps most people who are more or less fond of poetry do not *want* to do what I should call reading and understanding the poem—i.e. making the same process occur in themselves as occurred in the poet's head—but rather want what may be called the effect of the poem—i.e. something vaguer which is produced in them by reading the words. And if this is so I understand why commentaries annoy them so much. Perhaps too they are right so far as this, that there may be more imaginative activity in the vague process which the poem sets up in them than they would exert in the attempt to re-create the poet's process. I mean that it is hard to imagine as the poet did without losing something of the more general effect that one gets from one's first reading in which lots of detail is really not reproduced at all.[64]

And he never again devoted a whole work or even a whole lecture merely to elucidating the textual meaning of a work.

The content of Bradley's Oxford lectures will be examined in a later chapter. All that it is necessary to do here is to examine as far as possible the audience for whom they were designed and the reception with which they were met. In 1896 it first became possible to graduate at Oxford in English but in the years while Bradley was Professor of Poetry there were never more than five men taking Schools in English or more than twenty-one women. The majority of his audience would therefore not be specialists; indeed it was Bradley's responsibility to create his own audience, which according to the *Times Literary Supplement* review of *Shakespearean Tragedy*[65] he did with remarkable success. The only

[63] Ibid., pp. 36–7. [64] Letter to G. Murray, 22 Sept. 1901.
[65] *T.L.S.*, 10 Feb. 1905, quoted Chapter 1, p. 8.

other record there is of audience reaction is Bradley's own: 'The understanding seemed to be pleased as well as the kind masses.' and 'Was it not curious that the only face I saw in the theatre was my brother's—perhaps the only being I am afraid to lecture to. He said it was so long since he had been in church that he could not attend.'[66]

While Bradley held the Oxford chair he continued to live in London. His health seems to have continued poor and his interest in politics brought him continual worry. He seems to have formed a friendship at this time with Bertrand Russell and his wife and on one occasion went to see a Hauptmann comedy with them. This detail stands in interesting contrast to the usual picture of Bradley the solidly Oxford, non-theatre-going Victorian. While he was still giving the Oxford Lectures his *Shakespearean Tragedy* was published, which must have entailed quite an amount of work—there are thirty-one appendices and copious footnotes and the whole work must have needed much revision to make the lecturing style suitable for print. Bradley was, moreover, invited to give the Gifford Lectures at the University of Edinburgh in the winter of 1907–8 and spent a good deal of time preparing these. The Bradley who delivered the Oxford Lectures seems not to have been the Bradley envisaged by many of their readers. On the contrary he moved quite easily in London literary circles and deliberately avoided the role of college-confined don, which later generations have resolutely forced upon him.

In 1905, in accordance with a recently passed statute, Bradley's tenure of the Chair came to an end; he wrote to Murray: 'I am sorry to be ending at Oxford, but its really best for me, I think, and *much* best for Oxford to have the five year system.'[67] By this time Bradley seems to have become quite involved in the literary life of London. He helped to create the English Association which was formed in 1906. This Association was and still is predominantly concerned with the teaching of English and Bradley's part in helping the Association reflects his keen interest in the problems of education. When the London County

[66] Letter to G. Murray, 7 June 1901.
[67] Ibid, Sept. 1905.

Council proposed to build a monstrosity known as a 'Shakespeare's Temple', a monument to the bard and a house for the Arts combined, Bradley together with many others including J. M. Barrie, Sir Arthur Pinero, W. S. Gilbert, Gilbert Murray, and several earls wrote to *The Times* in protest. The Temple was never built.[68]

In 1907 Bradley was offered the King Edward VII Chair at Cambridge but he refused, presumably to devote more time to private study and writing. In 1907 and 1908 he delivered his Gifford Lectures, *Ideals of Religion*.[69] Bradley seems to have been dissatisfied with them. He wrote to Murray: 'I *can't* get on with my lectures. I say *nothing* of what I want to say. All that comes out is so stale to me that it makes me sick: and the real stuff seems to be too far inside me (supposing it exists at all) to get at.'[70] This is not the place, nor am I the person, to discuss what is really a philosophical work; especially as Bradley seems to have set about it in such a way as to exclude any hint of his personal beliefs and feelings. The lectures are critical in aim; they seem, understandably, to owe much to the philosophy of F. H. Bradley, and despite the intended exclusion of Bradley's personal creed, give some evidence of the broad shape of his philosophy. It would do Bradley a grave injustice to suggest that this work was written by a different part of himself from that involved in, for example, *Shakespearean Tragedy*; for throughout all of Bradley's work is apparent the same set of ideas. This is hardly surprising in view of the idealist philosophy which almost deified wholeness and unity; but it testifies to the way in which Bradley's philosophy had become absorbed into his life. It was not so much what he wrote about, as where he started from. It was therefore possible for

[68] R. Speaight, *William Poel and the Elizabethan Revival* (London, 1954), pp. 210–11.

[69] For some reason these were only published posthumously in 1940, being prepared for the press by Bradley's sister, Mrs. Ernest von Glehn. The Prefatory Note states 'Circumstances had prevented him from revising the lectures before his death' (p. vi), but it seems unlikely that he ever really intended to do so; circumstances could hardly have prevented him for twenty-eight years during which time he did prepare the much slighter *A Miscellany* for the press.

[70] Letter to G. Murray, 1907 (no more precise date).

R. W. Chambers when publishing a lecture on *King Lear* to refer in a footnote to a passage from *Ideals of Religion*. Indeed the passage referred to seems an admirable commentary on the basic problem of Shakespearian tragedy. Bradley wrote of mankind:

> Its first demand is for warmth and milk, and its last is for the Kingdom of God. And it is one and the same will that wants each. Can there be more astounding miracle than that, or a creation more contradictory than man, who being a pin-point desires, and is not his true self unless he desires, to be God?[71]

Is it not very nearly Hamlet's own summary of the predicament of man?

There is nothing to suggest that Bradley was an orthodox Christian and much to imply that he was not, but *Ideals of Religion* makes it apparent that he was intensely aware of religion in its fullest sense: 'Religion is release from evil because there is nothing in religion which is not divine as well as human';[72] and as intensely aware of the failure of man to live wholly religiously. This same awareness both of the ideal and of man's failure to attain it was always present in Bradley's mind and appears again in his criticism of *King Lear*. The criticism is frequently levelled against Bradley that he subdued Shakespeare to his own philosophy; what this philosophy was no one seems to be prepared to state unless a reference to Hegel or Aristotle can be called a summary; in fact there is evidence in all Bradley's philosophical writing that Shakespeare was a profound influence on his philosophy. The study of philosophy may have come before the formal study of literature but the literary instinct was strongest in Bradley.

> I was wise about poetry long before I ever read a word of philosophy, and in my proud stomach believe that any title I have to say anything about it comes from natural understanding of the way imagination works—a thing which most philosophers have not—and a natural love of metrical effect, which still fewer have.[73]

[71] *I.R.*, p. 262. Referred to in R. W. Chambers, *King Lear*. The First W. P. Ker Memorial Lecture Delivered in the University of Glasgow, 27 Nov. 1939 (published Glasgow, 1940), p. 31.

[72] *I.R.*, p. 284.

[73] Letter to G. Murray, 8 Apr. 1901.

It seems unlikely that Bradley could have been wholly deluded about something which mattered to him so much.

In all events after this he never wrote another work of philosophy. An article in the *Modern Language Review* of 1909 reflects Bradley's continuing awareness of Shakespearian problems and provides clear evidence that the criticism of the plays was conditioned by a knowledge of Elizabethan staging as well as a lively interest in contemporary theatre. Summing up his views on the locality of two early scenes in *King Lear* he writes:

> Shakespeare, if he imagined a place at all for I. ii (and I think it improbable that he did not), imagined the place of I. i. But it was not necessary for stage purposes to indicate a place and he may have known that the spectators would not trouble their heads about the matter. . . . In II. i, on the other hand, it *was* necessary to have a definite place, for the plot required that almost all the chief persons should meet at Gloucester's house in the country. So he put Edgar into concealment in his father's house, confident that the spectators would not ask the awkward question, how and when he got there. We, in studying the play, ask this question; and a stage-manager now has to ask it, because in our theatre everything happens somewhere in particular, and not on a bare platform as universal as the world. He would do best, I incline to think, to put I. ii where Pope put it, and to excise the indications of time.

The tone of this clearly suggests Bradley's dissatisfaction with the stage effects of his own theatrical experience, while his arguments and final suggestion are neatly practical.[74]

In 1910 he became a Fellow of the Royal Society of Literature and edited the first volume of *Essays and Studies* for the English Association of which in 1911 he became president. Also in 1910 he joined with some reluctance the British Academy Committee. 'I joined in a conditional sort of way in the end, but I really do not think it has any function except to celebrate centenaries and the like that don't properly concern the British Academy and if it tries to be a French Academy, I shall resign.'[75] None of the other obituaries mentions his being made a Fellow of the British

[74] 'The Locality of *King Lear* Act I Scene ii', pp. 239–40.
[75] Letter to G. Murray, 1 Nov. 1910.

Academy although the fact is recorded by the lecture 'Coriolanus' published by the Academy in 1912 and the fact that there is a British Academy obituary (this is only the case where Fellows are concerned).

When the war came Bradley turned his attention to writing about various issues; probably as a prominent literary man he was encouraged to do so but he undoubtedly would not have written anything which his conscience did not uphold. He contributed a preface to a book by J. A. Cramb, *Germany and England*, published in 1914, and gave a lecture subsequently published on 'International Morality'. This latter is interesting largely because of the obtrusion on the subject (really to do with the United States of Europe) of Bradley's preoccupation with the difference between art and life, aesthetics and morality. He says (as he so often said in various forms):

> Truth and beauty are not morality, nor yet mere means to it; they have an intrinsic value of their own. Moral goodness, therefore, though a large part of the best life, is not the whole. No; but it is the condition, the 'sine qua non', of these other parts. To discover truth, for example, is not a mere matter of natural gifts—it requires will, and a moral will.[76]

The war, however, was a shock to Bradley who had always, like so many academics of the late Victorian period, taken an interest in German culture. He was, he wrote to Murray, glad that England declared war: 'I was in mortal terror that we might stand aside', and added: 'It is infinitely sad to me to remember my enthusiasm over the attainment of German Unity in 1870.'[77] Mackail wrote in his obituary article, 'The strain of the war on him was great and he never quite recovered from it'.[78]

When war was declared Bradley was sixty-three and he had never been particularly robust. After the war his health declined further and in 1923 he became seriously ill with pneumonia from which he recovered, but he seems to have led only a half life after this until his death in 1935. His last communication to the Murrays was at Christmas in 1929 and before that his letters

[76] *I.M.*, p. 50. [77] Letter to G. Murray, Aug. 1914.
[78] J. Mackail, op. cit., p. 391.

had been confined after 1923 to annual greetings. In 1929 he published *A Miscellany* which contains several of the lectures which he gave after he finished as Oxford Professor. These were delivered at ever widening intervals of time in various places. Few of them display more than the relics of critical talent although the first essay 'The Reaction against Tennyson', first published in 1917, contains some perceptive comments on literary fashions, displaying Bradley's usual grasp of his subject and clarity of exposition.

Apart from his critical writing Bradley edited in 1917 a book by Edith Sichel,[79] a literary lady with whom Bradley was acquainted for a few years, and in 1924 he wrote the obituary article on Bernard Bosanquet for the British Academy. This is adequate biography but the voice behind it is now undeniably that of an old man. The comparison with the life of Nettleship, like Bosanquet an Oxford friend, is startling; the tone of this second biographical sketch is best illustrated in the comment 'He had many friends and I believe I speak for those who remain when I say that a day's visit to him left them happy, not only because of his affection but because a talk with him cleared their vision and strengthened their faith'.[80] The whole picture is faded and tired; only a memory of what has been can be recalled. This is in vivid contrast to the depiction of Nettleship who was much more alive, we feel, to Bradley, and is therefore to the reader.

Bradley's sister Marian von Glehn nursed him for the last ten years of his life although she herself was by no means young. When he eventually died at the age of eighty-four Bradley had to all intents and purposes been dead for five years. The life he had known had passed away; many of his old friends had been dead for so many years that they must have been largely forgotten; of his friends who, like the Murrays, survived, few lived near enough to visit him regularly. By 1935 his work was already a thing of the past. There were younger men, among them Mackail and M. R. Ridley, who admired Bradley's work, but the literary world as a whole had left him behind. His obituary in

[79] E. Sichel, *New and Old: Literary Remains*, ed. A. C. Bradley (London, 1917).
[80] *B.B.* (cf. Bibliography).

The Times is typically a little disapproving: 'Bradley approached the poets as thinkers and philosophers rather than as what they are first of all, creative artists, and had an imperfect apprehension of the practical and technical considerations to which the dramatist, and even the lyrist must have regard.'[81] The accuracy or otherwise of this statement is not our concern here; it is sufficient that it should have been written, and in an obituary.

Bradley was born a year after the publication of *In Memoriam* and died a year before the publication of T. S. Eliot's *Collected Poems*. It is perhaps no wonder that no generalization of his life and background should be adequate. His greatest work moreover was published only a little more than half way through this long life and apart from this one work he did little else to attract the attention of the reading public. The man he was to those who knew him can no longer be recovered and the type of man he was, 'That shy, gentle, refined, subtle, hypersensitive, entirely moral, almost other-worldly personality, at once donnish, a little old-maidish, and extraordinarily winning . . . with his frail figure and tender smile',[82] is particularly open to misunderstanding and satire.

Indeed Bradley's biography can offer little to the student except perhaps a corrective to the most inaccurate inferences from his works. Bradley *did* go to the theatre. If he was an Oxford don it was only for a short while, and when he could choose he lived in London. If he was a Victorian, he was also an Edwardian and a Georgian. In short he was a man as little capable of being summed up by a short tag as any.

[81] *The Times*, 4 Sept. 1935, p. 14. Leading obituary of the day.

[82] J. D. Wilson, *The Fortunes of Falstaff* (Cambridge, 1943.)

3

CRITICAL PRINCIPLES

BEFORE considering the influence of Bradley's Shakespearian criticism it is necessary to understand something at least of the basis of that criticism, especially as the aesthetic and critical principles which underlie his work are found best expressed in other works than *Shakespearean Tragedy*. In doing this it will be seen that far from restricting his interests to Shakespearian tragedy he was interested in the aesthetic experience as such, though particularly as manifested in Shakespeare. Bradley was academically trained as a philosopher and his interests were always truly philosophical; he was more interested in why than in how something worked. He was also more interested in synthesis than analysis. He prefers, for example, to discuss *Hamlet* as tragedy and tragedy as poetry. This does not mean that he was unaware of the peculiarities either of the individual play or the dramatic art as such; but these were not the aspects which he chose to emphasize in *Shakespearean Tragedy*. Subsequent chapters will deal with Bradley's judgements on individual issues but in order to see these in their proper light it is necessary temporarily to forget this aspect of Bradley and concentrate on his general principles and the reasons why he considered poetry worthy of so much of his attention.

> Of course, I do not suppose that a poet regards his poem as a piece of philosophy dressed up in metaphors and set to dance to a metre; that Shakespeare, for instance, was as tedious as his critics.[1]

This is A. C. Bradley conducting his own defence in a place where unfortunately it is unlikely to be heard. This quotation from his inaugural lecture at Glasgow illustrates clearly how well aware he was of the pitfalls of criticism; they were pitfalls into

[1] *P.L.*, p. 20.

which he like most critics was to stumble from time to time. The fame of Bradley's Shakespeare criticism has eclipsed even a minor interest in his general aesthetic criticism. In the latter, Bradley repeatedly draws attention to the dangers of ignoring the essential wholeness of poetry. In the former, like many other critics, he is sometimes guilty of overlooking the complete work in the pursuit of detail.

This unawareness of Bradley's aesthetic theory cannot wholly be laid at the door of misfortune; Bradley seems to have been very reticent about his aesthetic criticism. He published 'Poetry for Poetry's Sake' (1901), shortly after its delivery, as a separate book and later incorporated it into the *Oxford Lectures*, but the remainder of his general aesthetic criticism survives only as printed by the bodies to whom the original lectures were delivered. *The Study of Poetry* (1883) was published in Liverpool; *Poetry and Life* (1889) in Glasgow and the *Uses of Poetry* (1912) in London by the English Association. Furthermore in the preface to *Shakespearean Tragedy* Bradley almost deliberately invites misunderstanding. Of the lectures he says:

> I should, of course, wish them to be read in their order,[2] and a knowledge of the first two is assumed in the remainder; but readers who may prefer to enter at once in the discussion of the several plays can do so.[3]

Thus he invites the reader to hasten past the discussion of Shakespearian tragedy in general towards a description of the particular plays, and to read about the characters without reading why this is a worthwhile approach to Shakespeare. Reasons for this reticence are not easy to discover: it seems, however more likely that Bradley doubted his ability to make clear what he wanted to say on the philosophy of art than that he doubted the value of saying it. Something of Bradley's conviction as to the value of general aesthetic criticism and the difficulties which arise from any discussion of it appear in the long letter he wrote to Gilbert Murray while preparing 'Poetry for Poetry's Sake'. He acknow-

[2] *S.T.* pp. ix–x
[3] *S.T.*, p. vii.

ledges the likeness of this lecture to the Glasgow lecture and continues:

What I am aiming at is to be called Poetry for Poetry's *Sake*. Many of these things come into it but I want it chiefly to be about substance and form. This brings up all the troubles there are and I am sometimes quite desperate, though I don't think its difficult to dispose of any *theory* of mere form that I have ever seen. I want to say something about this because I think the cant of purely artistic value and purely literary value does a lot of harm to literature and because I don't think the people who *feel* on the other side can mostly put their position. . . . In one sense I am bound, I think, to 'idealise' the matter. That is, I must take poetry to be what it is to *me*, and God knows it's hard enough to make out what that is.[4]

Another possible reason why Bradley did not collect his general aesthetic criticism, for example into his final work *A Miscellany*, is that he felt the repetition of the same theme with variations had little value. He may have felt that in 'Poetry for Poetry's Sake' he had effectively summed up all he had to say, though if this is so it leaves his later *Uses of Poetry* as a pale reflection of old ideas and this is not the impression gained while reading it. Possibly Bradley considered these four particular essays merely as the baffled attempts of one poetry reader to theorize from his experience and as such not worthy of publication as a definitive treatment of the subject. There is a remark in a letter to Murray which suggests that Bradley did at one time contemplate writing such a work. He said of 'Poetry for Poetry's Sake', 'I think I shall print it as it stands, but I should like to make a small book out of it later'.[5]

Nothing ever came of this 'small book' possibly because of pressure of other work and possibly because the subject proved too large. The fact remains that the aesthetic contained in these four lectures provides an excellent introduction to Bradley's criticism of Shakespeare and other writers.

Behind all Bradley's criticism lies an essential creed; faith in the powers of the imagination.

When a man is indifferent to the necessities of those below him,

[4] Letter to G. Murray, 8 Apr. 1901. [5] Ibid., 7 June 1901.

when he is unkind and selfish to those about him, even when he commits a crime, the reason is often—nay, commonly—not that his heart is unusually hard but that he does not know what he is doing. His imagination does not act.[6]

Bradley's theory of poetry must always be seen in its true relation to imagination. Poetry would enlarge the imagination, imagination is the only guide to the reading of poetry. The process is reciprocal.

It will be seen from the above preliminary remarks that Bradley was concerned with the reading rather than the writing of poetry. The psychology and philosophy of the creative process in the poet were only subjects of interest to him when this process is repeated in the mind of the reader, which Bradley believed must happen in all true reading of poetry. When 'the poem becomes to the reader what it was to the writer. He [the reader] has not merely interpreted the poem, he has recreated it. For the time being his mind has ceased to be his own, and has become the poet's mind.'[7] In the first lecture that he wrote on the general nature of poetry Bradley set out his theory of the study of poetry more explicitly.

We should study poetry simply for its own sake; we should study it because the exercise of the imagination is intrinsically valuable; we should study it because it satisfies one of the highest and deepest wants of our nature; or, since this want is the same want that brings poetry itself into the world, we should study it in order to reproduce in ourselves more faintly that which went on in the poet's mind when he wrote.[8]

Twenty years later he repeated this basic idea, elaborating on it a little. Reading poetry, we must, Bradley said,

recreate the poem by repeating the mental acts in which it existed. And, so far as we can do this, you will observe, we re-live in ourselves a section of the poet's life; not 'the weariness, the fever, and the fret', the life where perhaps he was no better than ourselves, but the life of genius, in which he was greatly if not immeasurably, our superior.[9]

[6] *S.P.*, p. 16.
[7] *P.L.*, p. 21.
[8] *S.P.*, p. 6.
[9] *U.P.*, p. 3.

This idea was not an original one, although the stress Bradley laid on it is perhaps unusual. Dowden, Bradley's greatest recent predecessor in the field of Shakespearian criticism, describes the aim of reading: 'to come into the presence of the living mind of the creator.'[10] And, although the point cannot be pressed, this view of poetry owes something perhaps to the cult of the hero or great man reflected in much of Victorian life and letters.

This sympathy with the genius of the poet is not the only result of a true reading of poetry; the reader is also made more aware of the whole of the created world—'it is the effect of poetry, not only by expressing emotion, but in other ways also, to bring life into the dead mass of our experience, and to make the world significant.'[11] This increased awareness of life, by affecting the reactions of the reader, gives poetry its best claim to moral value. The sympathy of the reader is awakened by the presentation of the poetry and simultaneously his imagination sees embodied in poetic form various aspects of life which must have something to teach him. This is perhaps best expressed by Bradley himself in *The Study of Poetry*:

> To refine a man's intellect and feelings is not to make a man better directly, but it gives him a greater chance of becoming better . . . A man who has once seen the hideousness of ingratitude in *King Lear* . . . has a better chance than he had before of checking the beginnings of such things in himself.[12]

If Bradley seems here to be teetering on the brink of the Victorian conception of edifying literature his conception of the moral worth of literature and the relationship of the arts to the whole man is no more Victorian than that of Dr. Leavis. The imaginative process mediating between the poetry and the value of it is repeatedly stressed in Bradley; it is wilfulness on the part of the present-day reader to ignore what Bradley emphasized so often as central to the poetic experience.

> No doubt one main reason why poetry has poetic value for us is that it presents to us in its own way something which we meet in another

[10] E. Dowden, *Shakspere: a Critical Study of his Mind and Art* (1876), quotation from 1889 edition, p. 5.

[11] *P.L.*, p. 10.

[12] *S.P.*, p. 16.

form in nature or life and yet the test of its poetic value for us lies simply in the question whether it satisfies our imagination; the rest of us, our knowledge or conscience, for example, judging it only so far as they appear transmuted in our imagination.

The claim made for poetry is that it, like the other arts, is the channel of a higher *truth* than we otherwise possess.[13]

For Bradley this was sufficient, but he could only go on to consider the effect which the imparting of this 'higher truth' had on the reader. The value of poetry lay in the imparting of this higher truth; the moral, social, psychological uses were extraneous to the essential experience.

I believe that, though the value of poetry is much increased by its uses, it has a value of its own, which it would still possess if it were perfectly useless; and, further, that its usefulness in contributing to ends beyond itself depends on its first fulfilling its primary purpose which is nothing but itself.[14]

It was in his last work of aesthetic criticism that Bradley wrote that. In all his works there is evident a preoccupation with discovering the exact nature of the 'primary purpose which is nothing but itself'.

Bradley made no extravagant claim for the readability of poetry; in fact he opened his inaugural lecture at Liverpool with a characteristically unpretentious estimate of the entertainment value of poetry: 'If poetry *is* an amusement I think we must agree with the majority that, except for a man here and there, it is a kind of amusement perhaps rather refined but certainly rather flat.'[15] On the other hand, poetry was not for Bradley first and foremost a subject of study: 'There is no use whatever in reading poetry if we do not appreciate it, and we may be sure we do not appreciate it if we do not enjoy it . . . *Evangeline* is not so good as *Hamlet*: but *Evangeline* enjoyed is worth fifty *Hamlets* unenjoyed.'[16] Bradley emphasized, however, the value of discipline in the true enjoyment of poetry:

though in really reading poetry, our feeling of pleasure is involved, we certainly do not seek it, we have not our eyes on it at all, nor in any

[13] *O.L.P.*, p. 7. [14] *U.P.*, p. 2. [15] *S.P.*, p. 5. [16] Ibid., p. 21.

way on ourselves, not even on our activity as such. We absorb ourselves in the emotional sounds, images, thoughts, and the like. We surrender ourselves to them. And if we will not do so we miss both them and the pleasure that attends them.[17]

It may seem from the above quotation that Bradley's idea of discipline in the reading of poetry was merely another way of expressing a belief in a surrender to imagination. If there is little emphasis on the hard work attendant upon reading poetry this is not because Bradley had no time for research but because he felt that there was sufficient emphasis on this aspect of reading and that the imaginative processes were in danger of being overlooked. 'I think there is, for students, more need of warning against absorption in this kind of knowledge [i.e. of scholarship and research] than of encouragement to it.'[18]

It was absorption in scholarship that Bradley was arguing against, not scholarship itself, and the same lecture provides plenty of evidence as to Bradley's awareness of the necessity for hard work in reading works of genius. 'There is no play of Shakespeare's which can be really appreciated without a good deal of exertion', and 'Every moment of our reading it [a Shakespeare play] ought to be a moment not of laziness but of tension.'[19]

If Bradley made high claims for poetry the very highest were reserved for tragedy (and thus for Shakespeare). Even in the earliest lecture on poetry there is something of Bradley's preoccupation with the theory of this particular poetic form:

[In tragedy] in the like freedom from accident and detail, we see completely what we had seen by snatches before, not the mere outside of man's life which hardly lets the meaning through, but the soul of it making a body for itself, passion working out its true effects, and the moral forces of the world—not thwarted or uncertain, as the lying appearance of things shows them—but as a just and irresistible doom.[20]

This is only a short preview of Bradley's theory of tragedy but it contains germs of the essential ideas which Bradley was later to expound most fully in 'Hegel's Theory of Tragedy' in *Oxford Lectures on Poetry* and 'The Substance of Shakespearean Tragedy' in *Shakespearean Tragedy*.

[17] *U.P.*, p. 8. [18] *S.P.*, p. 24. [19] Ibid., pp. 17 and 23. [20] Ibid., p. 9.

As it is almost impossible to understand Bradley's view of tragedy without reference to his principal influence any summary of Bradley's views must begin with a summary of Hegel's philosophy which is in fact provided by Bradley himself in an essay 'German Philosophy and the Age of Wordsworth' published in *A Miscellany*:

> Everything finite, for him, whether it be natural or human, is more or less deeply touched with imperfection and with conflict; when it feels, with pain; when it is also rational, with sorrow and moral evil.
>
> Man is not, indeed, by nature evil in the full sense of that word; but he is not by nature what he should be, and in that sense he *is* evil. He has to become good; and he can become good only by making himself so. For goodness is free activity, acts of will issuing in outward deeds; and though you can give a man a thing, to talk of an act being given to him, by Nature or anything else, is to talk pure nonsense.
>
> Life and freedom . . . are not merely *merited* by conquest, they *are* conquest; and conquest implies a foe. Without evils, then, no moral goodness.[21]

Whether or not this is faithful to Hegel is not our concern here; what matters is that it is what Hegel represented to Bradley. In 'Hegel's Theory of Tragedy' Bradley considers more particularly how the Hegelian philosophy of tragedy can be adapted to become more relevant to Shakespeare; thus defining at the same time his own and Hegel's theory. He sums up the latter:

> The essentially tragic fact is the self-division and intestinal warfare of the ethical substance, not so much the war of good with evil as the war of good with good.
>
> It is the nature of the tragic hero, at once his greatness and his doom, that he knows no shrinking or half-heartedness, but identifies himself wholly with the power that moves him, and will admit the justification of no other power.
>
> The end of the tragic conflict is the denial of both exclusive claims. It is not the work of chance or blank fate; it is the act of the ethical substance itself, asserting its absoluteness against the excessive pretentions of its particular powers.[22]

[21] *A.M.*, pp. 134–5. [22] *O.L.P.*, pp. 71–2.

Bradley disagreed with Hegel; or rather he sought to modify his tragic theory in order to make it more relevant to Shakespearian drama. Bradley laid more emphasis on the 'spiritual value' on both sides of the conflict, whether that was political or social or solely within the hero's mind. The spectator's horror at the evil resulting from the collisions was therefore greater and correspondingly so was the relief at the reconciliation of this conflict.

'Reconciliation' was to Bradley the aim of all tragic drama. Why this is so emerges clearly from any of his descriptions of the working of tragedy (whether the idea of reconciliation is mentioned or not). And most clearly perhaps in his most abstract study—that of Hegel's theory.

> We might then simply say that, as the tragic action portrays a self-division or intestinal conflict of spirit, so the catastrophe displays the violent annulling of this division or conflict. But this statement . . . would represent only half of Hegel's idea, and perhaps nothing of what is most characteristic and valuable in it. For the catastrophe . . . has two aspects, a negative and an affirmative, and we have ignored the latter . . . which is the source of our feelings of reconciliation, whatever form they may assume. And this will be taken into account if we describe the catastrophe as the violent self-restitution of the divided spiritual unity. The necessity which acts and negates in it, that is to say, is yet of one substance with both the agents. *It* is divided against itself in them; they are *its* conflicting forces; and in restoring its unity through negation it affirms them, so far as they are compatible with that unity. The qualification is essential, since the hero, for all his affinity with that power, is, as the living man we see before us, not so compatible . . . But the qualification does not abolish what it qualifies. This is no occasion to ask how in particular, and in what various ways in various works, we feel the effect of this affirmative aspect in the catastrophe. But it corresponds at least with that strange double impression which is produced by the hero's death. He dies, and our hearts die with him; and yet his death matters nothing to us, or we even exult. He is dead; and he has no more to do with death than the power which killed him and with which he is one.[23]

[23] Ibid., pp. 90–1.

This process; the division of the ordered world against itself, neither part solely nor wholly good, but both under the circumstances inexorably inimical, the catastrophe in which the individual, to the loss of the whole, is destroyed, and the final feeling of relief and content that moral order, despite the cost, has once more asserted itself, was central to Bradley's theory of tragedy but its restatement in the discussion of each of the individual tragedies demonstrates how fully it also expressed his experience of the tragic art.[24] Whatever Bradley's theory on tragedy, however, it can never be understood completely in isolation from the particular plays from which he evolved it. To Bradley tragedy was really Shakespeare's tragedy; the Greeks, the French, the other Jacobean writers are only referred to as they throw light on Shakespeare. The culmination of Bradley's aesthetic and his theory of tragedy was his work *Shakespearean Tragedy*.

The most important questions about literature were, for Bradley,

> What is the substance of a Shakespearean Tragedy, taken in abstraction both from its form and from the differences in point of substance between one tragedy and another? . . . What is the nature of the tragic aspect of life as represented by Shakespeare? What is the general fact shown now in this tragedy and now in that? . . . What is Shakespeare's tragic conception, or conception of tragedy?[25]

and these questions he sought to answer in the first lecture of *Shakespearean Tragedy* on 'The Substance of Shakespearean Tragedy'. By methods typical of Bradley he gradually builds up a picture of what Shakespearian tragedy is; by analysing its basic features in turn, modifying at each stage the composite

[24] Cf. index to *S.T.* for an indication of how widespread are references to 'reconciliation'. Looking up the references will moreover indicate how diverse are the expressions of this feeling in the different plays. The essay on *Antony and Cleopatra* yields a further point on how Bradley felt with regard to this sense of 'reconciliation'. 'We are saddened by the very fact that the catastrophe saddens us so little; it pains us that we should feel so much triumph and pleasure.' *O.L.P.*, p. 304.

[25] *S.T.*, p. 5.

result. The method is almost scientific, and in accordance with best scientific practice Bradley had set out his method as well as his aim at the opening of the book:

> Our one object will be what . . . may be called dramatic appreciation; to increase our understanding and enjoyment of these works as dramas; to learn to apprehend the action and some of the personages of each with a somewhat greater truth and intensity, so that they may assume in our imaginations a shape a little less unlike the shape they wore in the imagination of their creator.[26]

On the subject of method he is even more explicit.

> the prime requisite here is . . . a vivid and intent imagination. But this alone will hardly suffice. It is necessary also, especially to a true conception of the whole, to compare, to analyse, to dissect. . . . readers often shrink from this task, which seems to them prosaic or even a desecration. They misunderstand, I think. They would not shrink if they remembered two things. In the first place, in this process of comparison and analysis it is not requisite, it is on the contrary ruinous, to set imagination aside to substitute some supposed 'cold reason'; and it is only want of practice that makes the concurrent use of analysis and of poetic perception difficult or irksome. And, in the second place, these dissecting processes, though they are also imaginative, are still, and are meant to be, nothing but a means to an end.[27]

Here is an expanded description of the same process of which Bradley wrote earlier; 'an analysis which never ceases to be also imaginative vision, and a vision which sees in their relations and their movement the objects of analysis.'[28]

The results, however much the reader may disagree with them, are as vividly set out and as cogently defended as the aims and methods. The best illustration of this is to quote at length Bradley's conclusion to his lecture on the substance of Shakespearian tragedy in which he arrives painstakingly at some idea of what is the essential nature of tragedy.

> Tragedy . . . is the exhibition of . . . convulsive reaction [to evil]; and the fact that the spectacle does not leave us rebellious or desperate

[26] Ibid., p. 1. [27] Ibid., p. 2. [28] *P.L.*, p. 21.

is due to a more or less distinct perception that the tragic suffering and death arise from collision, not with a fate or blank power, but with a moral power, a power akin to all that we admire and revere in the characters themselves. This perception produces something like a feeling of acquiescence in the catastrophe, though it neither leads us to pass judgment on the characters nor diminishes the pity, the fear, and the sense of waste, which their struggle, suffering and fall evoke.

Nor does the idea of a moral order asserting itself against attack or want of conformity answer in full to our feelings regarding the tragic character. We do not think of Hamlet merely as failing to meet its demand, of Anthony merely sinning against it, or even of Macbeth as simply attacking it. What we feel corresponds quite as much to the idea that they are *its* parts, expressions, products; that in their defect or evil *it* is untrue to its soul of goodness, and falls into conflict and collision with itself; that, in making them suffer and waste themselves, *it* suffers and wastes itself; and that when, to save its life and regain peace from this intestinal struggle, it casts them out, it has lost a part of its own substance,—a part more dangerous and unquiet, but far more valuable and nearer to its heart, than that which remains,—a Fortinbras, a Malcolm, an Octavius. There is no tragedy in its expulsion of evil: the tragedy is that this involves the waste of good.[29]

Bradley knew better than to think that he had found a simple solution to the question—'tragedy would not be tragedy if it were not a painful mystery'[30]—but he could not allow this to defeat him without first having tried to solve its riddle or at least to come to terms with the fact of its insolubility.

We remain confronted with the inexplicable fact, or the no less inexplicable appearance, of a world travailing for perfection, but bringing to birth, together with glorious good, an evil which it is able to overcome only by self-torture and self-waste. And this fact or appearance is tragedy.[31]

That the presentation of this essential tragedy was the most interesting feature of Shakespeare to Bradley is undeniable; but it would be wildly unjust to assume therefore that Bradley was quite unaware of any other aspect of Shakespeare. The

[29] *S.T.*, pp. 36–7. [30] Ibid., p. 38. [31] Ibid., p. 39.

chapter following this in *Shakespearean Tragedy* is concerned with the 'construction' of the plays; lectures in *Oxford Lectures on Poetry* discuss 'Shakespeare the Man' and 'Shakespeare's Theatre and Audience'. There are lectures on *Antony and Cleopatra*, *Coriolanus*, the Falstaff plays, and finally on Feste and other jesters. His letters reveal an even wider interest in Shakespeare: '*Measure for Measure* is a very strange play. It seems to have the same air of aloofness and contempt that is even stronger in *Troilus and Cressida*', he wrote to Murray, giving the lie to the theory that Bradley could only read Shakespeare as though it were biography. There is at one stage a long exposition of a theory of Shakespeare's marriage, reference to 'Mrs. Benson as Rosalind', the purchase of a concordance to Shakespeare, and to Schubert used as background music for *Two Gentlemen of Verona*.[32]

The essay on 'Keats' Letters' in *Oxford Lectures on Poetry* further reveals another aspect of Shakespeare which interested Bradley. 'In quality—and I speak of nothing else—the mind of Shakespeare at three and twenty may not have been very different.' Of 'negative capability' he says: 'That is not a description of Milton or Wordsworth or Shelley, neither does it apply very fully to Keats; but it describes something at least of the spirit of Shakespeare.'[33] It would be overstating the case if like J. Middleton Murry we thought that Bradley had anticipated him in his theory of a unity of soul between Keats and Shakespeare; but the likeness of the two was valuable to Bradley because it helped him to understand better the essential spirit of both poets; and it was this essential spirit with which he was concerned.

There is apparent throughout Bradley's criticism a sameness of approach, a similarity in the findings. Despite varied subjects what impresses the reader is how little Bradley's position in regard to these subjects varies. The reason for this is not difficult to understand. Bradley was thirty-one when he became Professor at Liverpool; he had been up till then concerned with philosophy

[32] Letters to Murray, 15 July 1897, May 1898, 12 Feb. 1899, and Jan. 1906, respectively.

[33] *O.L.P.*, p. 238.

as a teacher. But he records in a letter to Murray: 'I was wise about poetry long before I ever read a word of philosophy.'[34] He began his literary career with his critical faculties already matured by long use. He seldom wrote, moreover, on any subject which he had not read from his youth. The poets whom Mackail cited as his chief delights are the poets on whom he writes. The letters reveal wide reading of other works among them those of George Eliot, W. B. Yeats, Dickens, and 'Everyman',[35] but his reading only rarely appears in the lectures and then only to cast light on a more familiar subject. It would oversimplify to say that Bradley only lectured when he had made up his mind on the subject, but he certainly did not use the lectures to help shape his thoughts; his thoughts had been shaped long before. The lectures were a communication of the speaker's considered views. What Maud Bodkin wrote of his criticism of tragedy is true of all his writings; 'the attempt of one eminent critic to render his own deeply pondered experience of tragic drama'.[36] The progress in Bradley's work is not that of a sharpening critical insight; after the fumbling which can perhaps be noted in the first lecture 'The Study of Poetry', Bradley had found not only his critical position but also a medium for expressing it. After this the progress is only chronological; the only change is one of decay in the final works when Bradley was an old man. The period during which Bradley held the Oxford Chair of Poetry undoubtedly saw him produce his finest work; the stimulus of the audience, the leisure to correct and revise, and the fact that at fifty Bradley could fairly be thought to be at the height of his powers contribute to this fact. But it can in no wise be accounted for by a theory that Bradley had at last found a successful critical method; he was as always using natural gifts, trained no doubt by long periods of reading, but as Bradley himself wrote, none the less natural: 'natural understanding of the

[34] Letter to Murray, 8 Apr. 1901.

[35] Letters to Murray, 4 Oct. 1899, 20 Jan. 1902, 21 Apr. 1899, and 5 Aug. 1901, respectively.

[36] M. Bodkin, *Archetypal Patterns in Poetry* (London, 1934), quotation from 1951 edition, p. 20.

way imagination works—a thing which most philosophers have not—and a natural love of metrical effect which still fewer have.'[37] This is a high claim and it does not cover all that went into Bradley's criticism, but it explains the peculiar strength and unity in everything he wrote.

[37] Letter to Murray, 8 Apr. 1901.

4

BRADLEY THE VICTORIAN

Shakespeare made in the image of a Victorian intellectual.

THERE is nothing to prove that this Victorian intellectual was Bradley but the context makes it clear whom S. L. Bethell had in mind; so saying he sums up a widely held view of Bradley's Shakespeare: 'a sadly diminished and distorted figure'.[1] Some qualification usually modifies the description. Critics in general have been shy of labelling Bradley a Victorian; maybe because they recognized that the Queen had been dead two years when *Shakespearean Tragedy* was published. Even so, diverse comments on Bradley show the strong tendency of modern critics to class him with the Victorians where, they feel, he belongs:

Victorian critics (including Bradley)[2]

The nineteenth century psychological interpretation as summed up, say, by A. C. Bradley (*Shakespearean Tragedy*).[3]

'Victorianism', the critics seem to feel, sums up Bradley's approach; what exactly did 'Victorianism' mean in terms of Shakespeare criticism? J. W. Draper wrote:

The early nineteenth century had bowdlerized Shakespeare; the later nineteenth century Victorianized him. It let its own feelings and predispositions be its guide in determining character and theme: democracy ruined King Claudius; and feminism ruined the passive Ophelia, without restoring the shrewd and independent Olivia; Iago ceased to be a realistic Renaissance petty officer and became an inhuman monster; and most of the plays were so thrown out of focus

[1] S. L. Bethell, *Shakespeare and the Popular Dramatic Tradition* (Westminster, 1944), p. 53.

[2] T. J. B. Spencer, 'The Tyranny of Shakespeare', *B.A.* (1959), pp. 153–71, at p. 165.

[3] R. Langbaum, 'Character v. Action in Shakespeare', *S.Q.* viii (1957), pp. 57–69, at p. 59.

that critics, though they still repeated the shibboleths about Shakespeare's truth to nature, no longer found in him the illustration of any fundamental truths or principles of conduct, and so could point to no significance or theme. Thus his comedies, without meaning or guiding truth-to-life, became mere farces, and his tragedies ranting and unmotivated melodrama, sustained only by exquisite, but inappropriate, poetry. So the age largely understood Shakespeare, and so its critics and actors largely depicted him. Indeed, the very priests of the sacred temple reduced their divinity, in their own image, to that of a fourth-rate godlet; and, to all-important matter of interpretation, the precise historical method given to text and sources was rarely, if ever, systematically applied. Meanwhile, exact scholars were extending their activities to include the Elizabethan theater, its construction, its business organization, and its stage conventions; and from this last approach, especially in the hands of Professor Stoll early in the present century, came the first significant broadside against romantic Shakespeare interpretation, which had been running its course through the works of Lamb, Dowden, Professor A. C. Bradley, and the rest.[4]

This is not an isolated example of twentieth-century distrust of the Victorian period although it may be a little extreme.[5] The inclusion of Bradley moreover as an example of a Shakespeare critic who 'reduced [his] divinity . . . to . . . a godlet' because he 'found in him [no] illustration of any fundamental truths or principles of conduct' and thought the 'tragedies ranting and unmotivated melodrama', reveals how far away from Bradley's writings criticism of Bradley had moved in order to label him simply 'Victorian'.

It is this same impulse that causes the proliferation of such

[4] J. W. Draper, *The Humors and Shakespeare's Characters* (Durham, N.C., 1945), pp. 4–5.

[5] The desire to push Bradley back in time began very early, as the following shows: 'I have just been reading your introduction to the little shilling Shakespeare book [*Shakespearian Criticism* 1916]—it is jolly good. I am amused to find (by inference) that I belong, with you, to the twentieth century, while old Bradley is decently buried in the nineteenth. Serves him right. I don't know how it is, he interests me all the time, and all the time he irritates me. I believe it's the religious strain in him. Come to think of it, he treats the text exactly as preachers treat the Bible. Twist it to get the juice out.' (Letter from Walter Raleigh to D. Nichol Smith, 20 Jan. 1918; *Collected Letters* (1926), p. 473.)

labels as: 'the sober A. C. Bradley',[6] 'an elderly Victorian gentleman';[7] the last, incidentally, refers to a work published when Bradley was fifty-four, the writer of the reference, John Dover Wilson being sixty-nine. The Victorian aura accompanies Bradley's image almost throughout; sometimes to the detriment of critical accuracy. Lord David Cecil, for example, relying on an assumption that Bradley was a Victorian and therefore prim and mealymouthed, wrote of his estimate of *Antony and Cleopatra*: 'He . . . finds the moral atmosphere unpleasant, lacking in nobility.'[8] It was in fact this remark which prompted J. D. Wilson's defence:

> It took some pluck in 1905 for an elderly Victorian gentleman to echo with enthusiasm Dolabella's cry 'Most sovereign creature!' and to write 'Many unpleasant things can be said of Cleopatra; and the more that are said the more wonderful she appears.' When, therefore, in the freer air of a generation later, Lord David Cecil dismisses the lecture with the remark that Bradley seems to find 'the moral atmosphere unpleasant' he seems a little unfair and more than a little misleading.[9]

There have been other critics who, accepting Bradley's Victorianism, sought to turn it into a virtue. P. N. Siegel wrote twelve years later than his fellow American J. W. Draper:

> Bradley's *Shakespearean Tragedy* came after nearly a century of analysis of Shakespeare's characters and of attempts to extract aesthetic and ethical systems from his plays. Although much of this is worthless romantic impressionism, German pedantry, and Victorian moralizing, the work of such men as Coleridge, Hazlitt, Schlegel and Dowden furnished valuable critical insights that Bradley used in his book, which culminates the tradition.[10]

[6] R. W. Chambers, 'The Jacobean Shakespeare and *Measure for Measure*', *B.A.* (1937), p. 57.

[7] John D. Wilson, New Cambridge Edition of *Antony and Cleopatra* (1950), p. xvii.

[8] Lord David Cecil, *Antony and Cleopatra*. Fourth W. P. Ker Memorial Lecture delivered 4 May 1943, Glasgow (published 1944, and collected later in *Poets and Storytellers*, London, 1949.)

[9] Cf. n. 7 above.

[10] P. N. Siegel, *Shakespearean Tragedy and the Elizabethan Compromise* (New York, 1957), pp. viii–ix.

Compared with Draper's historical survey this demonstrates a genuine attempt to find a place for Bradley in the development of Shakespearian criticism. For undoubtedly such a place had to be found. Some critics like Siegel saw Bradley at the end of the Romantic line; H. Levin, for instance, wrote: 'Coleridge, following A. W. Schlegel as usual, and followed by Bradley as usual',[11] and Albert Gerard in an article on *Othello* sums up the opposition: 'Romantic critics, from Coleridge to Bradley.'[12] 'From Coleridge to Bradley', the summary reverberates through twentieth-century criticism, isolating the whole of nineteenth-century criticism between the two great masters who stood at its either end.

But is this summary essentially true? On a factual level Bradley's *Shakespearean Tragedy* missed the nineteenth century by four years and the Victorian era by two, but such a narrow margin can hardly be said to prove Bradley a twentieth-century Edwardian. If Bradley did not exist for criticism before the publication of *Shakespearean Tragedy*, he had existed as a man for over fifty years. If 'Victorianism' existed then it was undoubtedly under its shadow that Bradley was formed. The critics he read predominantly were those of the earlier nineteenth century; he illustrates the typical late Victorian reliance on the Romantic period. But to say all this is still not to prove that he belongs to that encapsulated period of the past known as 'the Victorian era'.

If Bradley was the last of the Romantic critics he was, as D. J. Palmer says, also a modern: 'Bradley displays a temperament that we recognise as academic and he stands at the beginning of the era in which almost all the major criticism of Shakespeare has come from the Universities.'[13] If S. L. Bethell in 1944 saw Bradley as the culmination of the Victorian critics,[14] John Palmer in 1945 classed him, with Murry and Hudson, as a modern critic.[15] J. D. Wilson in 1943 called him 'the greatest of modern

[11] H. Levin, *The Question of Hamlet* (New York, 1959), p. 143.

[12] A. Gerard, '"Egregiously an Ass": The Dark Side of the Moor. A view of Othello's Mind', *S.S.*, x (1957), pp. 98–106, at p. 98.

[13] D. J. Palmer, 'A. C. Bradley', *C.S.* ii. 1 (Winter 1964), pp. 18–25, at p. 18.

[14] S. L. Bethell, op. cit., p. 63.

[15] J. L. Palmer, *The Political Characters of Shakespeare* (London, 1945), p. 308.

Shakespearian critics'.[16] M. R. Ridley who knew Bradley personally was more explicit and energetic in the denial of Bradley's romantic Victorianism: 'It is the fashion now to write Bradley off as a "Romantic", as distinct from the virile and no-nonsense school of the day. Why a razor-edged mind, a wide range of exact knowledge, and a cool austerity of presentation are specifically Romantic is not apparent.'[17]

That Bradley cannot be confined solely to the Victorian era, even if his place is indubitably in the past, is confirmed by references to Bradley's place in a much longer line by D. A. Traversi, for although in his text he writes of 'the great tradition of the nineteenth century—running from Goethe and Coleridge to Bradley's *Shakespearean Tragedy*', in his Author's Note acknowledging his debt to earlier Shakespeare critics he recognizes a much longer line, the 'great line of authors ... from Dryden to Bradley'.[18] And other critics have coupled Bradley's name with those of other non-romantic critics: 'Aristotle–Bradley', 'Johnson–Bradley', and perhaps less surprisingly 'Morgann–Bradley'.[19] Modern critics, who are devotees of Bradley, naturally enough feel with H. B. Charlton that he is 'the greatest Shakespearian critic of our time',[20] for to such people Bradley is still a living force. The impartial testimony of a critic and editor may, however, carry more weight: 'Bradley's *Shakespearean Tragedy* is still an important guide in interpretation, and those who fancy that recent "historical or objective" criticism has outmoded his method should read Alfred Harbage's *As They Liked It*.'[21]

Perhaps the most telling fact is the large number of critics

[16] J. D. Wilson, *The Fortunes of Falstaff* (Cambridge, 1943), p. vii.

[17] M. R. Ridley, 'On Reading Shakespeare', *B.A.* (1940), p. 12.

[18] D. A. Traversi, *An Approach to Shakespeare* (London/Glasgow, 1938), quotation from 2nd ed. 1957, p. 1, and 'Author's Note'.

[19] 'Aristotle–Bradley' in S. M. Matthews, 'Othello and the Dignity of Man', *Shakespeare in a Changing World* (London, 1964), p. 137; 'Johnson–Bradley' in M. R. Ridley, op. cit., p. 13; 'Morgann–Bradley' in H. Jenkins, 'Shakespeare's History Plays, 1900–1951', *S.S.* vi (1953), p. 13.

[20] H. B. Charlton, 'Falstaff', *J.R.L.B.* xix (1935), pp. 46–89, at p. 58. First delivered 14 Nov. 1934.

[21] P. Alexander, *The Complete Works of Shakespeare* (London/Glasgow, 1951), p. ix.

usually held to be peculiarly modern who have acknowledged a debt to, or admiration of Bradley. R. S. Bridges, a forerunner of the historically aware cynical school of modern criticism is deferential to Bradley throughout his essay, *On the Influence of the Audience*. Of *Othello* he writes: 'It is just as Mr. Bradley points out'; of *Macbeth*: 'His admirable account of this play'; and where he does disagree about an interpretation of *Hamlet* he adds: 'if I do not agree, I see that Mr. Bradley can easily prove me to be mad.'[22] Clearly Bridges did not consider Bradley as the last bastion of that Victorian over-reverence to Shakespeare which in this very essay he was doing so much to overthrow.

Bridges, writing in 1906 and moreover a friend of Bradley's, may be accounted to be too near to the object to see it in 'historical' perspective; but Bridges's attitude is echoed by later critics and most notably Professor Wilson Knight who in the 1949 edition of his *Wheel of Fire* claims Bradley as the founder of his own technique.

> Though Bradley certainly on occasion pushed 'character' analysis to an unnecessary extreme, yet it was he who first subjected the atmospheric, what I have called the 'spatial', qualities of the Shakespeare play to a considered, if rudimentary, comment. Indeed, my own first published manifesto concerning my general aims in Shakespearian interpretation . . . defined those aims as the application to Shakespeare's work in general of the methods already applied by Bradley to certain outstanding plays. It was, and is, my hope that my own labours will be eventually regarded as a natural development within the classic tradition of Shakespearian study.[23]

Plainly Bradley cannot be glibly confined to his period, if indeed any clear picture of his period remains after the diverse classifications seen above. Perhaps the most important aspect of this historical labelling is whether it is thought that being of his

[22] R. S. Bridges, *On the Influence of the Audience* (London, 1906), quotations from private edition printed for Stanley Morrison (New York, 1926), pp. 19, 13 n., 20 n., respectively.

[23] G. Wilson Knight, *The Wheel of Fire* (London, 1930). Quotation from prefatory note to the 1949 edition, p. v.

period invalidates the criticism of Bradley. Dame Helen Gardner thought not:

> Each generation asks its own questions and finds its own answers, and the final test of the validity of those answers can only be time. Johnson, Coleridge, Bradley, all tell us things about *Hamlet* which are consistent with the play as we read it. A critic of today cannot hope for more than that his questions and answers will seem relevant, and will continue to seem relevant to others who read and ponder the play.[24]

This tolerant attitude allowing each critic to make his own way into the canon is not universally shared and Bertram Joseph wrote an article which among other things sets out to prove that *Shakespearean Tragedy* should not be read today because it was written over sixty years ago:

> There is no need to discredit him as a critic, or his critical methods as such, in order to show that he is outmoded. For that is really what is wrong with him, if there be anything unequivocally wrong. What satisfied his own time, and still satisfies those whose minds were formed before the war of 1914, no longer rings true to our experience of human malice and prejudice since that year. And we have found, too, that it is possible for decent people to behave with horrifying brutality and stay decent, while an ability to produce and appreciate sublime art can live in one mind, with elements of the morality of a ruthless barbarian.
>
> Bradley's Shakespeare is inadequate for most of us younger than fifty, who find that we cannot ignore what historical research tells us of Shakespeare's own age, with its glimpses of experience so like our own, and so unlike that of the nineteenth century.[25]

If, therefore, a critic is to stand or fall according to the relevance of his period to the readers some importance must attach to the process of assigning each critic to his proper period. It seems, however, from the above that it is possible to confine some critics within 'a proper period' more easily than others. Mr. Joseph's writings are a typical product of the 1950s, shouldering the burden of a guilt-ridden and frightened post-war world with a sense of moral duty which would do credit to any Victorian.

[24] H. Gardner, *The Business of Criticism* (Oxford, 1959), p. 51.

[25] B. Joseph: 'The Problem of Bradley', *U.E.* v (1953–4), pp. 87–91, at p. 88.

Mr. Joseph writes as though human malice and prejudice were born into the world in 1914; it seems as though he cannot have read *Othello*. In fact, if carried to its logical conclusion, Mr. Joseph's advice against reading Bradley can only be extended to include advice against reading Shakespeare, whose mind also was formed before 1914.[26]

In fact the real argument against Bradley, the Victorian, as Mr. Joseph points out elsewhere in the article, is not that he belonged to a period now outdated but that he belonged to a period other than Shakespeare's which made insufficient attempts to understand that period historically. Mr. Joseph would go so far as to say that Bradley was deliberately unscholarly in order to preserve his blinkered Victorian Shakespeare; his argument is tortuous but it embodies much of what seems to be generally accepted but rarely stated.

Bradley knew quite well what he was about. He realised that he was interpreting Shakespeare in the light of a later age, for people to whom much would have been distasteful and even trivial if shown as it appeared to the renaissance.... And he was no less completely aware of the position he was adopting when it came to appreciating Shakespeare the dramatic artist. Bradley knew that in the last resort the naturalistic attitude to the verse could be exposed as untenable. Yet he chose to show that it was possible to interpret Shakespeare's characters as thinking and acting in a way which was consistent with what the late nineteenth century assumed to be the truth about human behaviour, and with what naturalism insisted was the correct method of portraying this on the stage. To give this consistent interpretation of Shakespeare, Bradley had to ignore what he knew about the past whenever it introduced an element of inconsistency.[27]

This seems to portray a Bradley of almost inhuman intellectual control. A critic, able to do the right thing, which, indeed, he

[26] In fact this view of an essential relation between world affairs and Shakespeare is shared by a much more recent critic. Maynard Mack in his *King Lear in our Time* (1966) wrote: 'After two world wars and Auschwitz, our sensibility is significantly more in touch than our grandparents' was with the play's jagged violence, its sadism, madness and processional of deaths, its wild blends of levity and horror, selfishness and selflessness, and the anguish of its closing scene' (p. 25).

[27] B. Joseph, op. cit., p. 87.

recognized, but choosing not to do it and pursuing this wrong course with steadfastness: and the aim of all this discipline and contortion was merely consistency. It illustrates, however, the perfect twentieth-century picture of Bradley; a man whose mind was obviously too astute to make the errors it does, and yet, obviously and repeatedly, making them. The more usual cause to which this is attributed is, of course, Bradley's period. 'Bradley is not without his weaknesses', wrote Kenneth Muir:

> though they are mostly those of his age and not peculiar to himself. The catalogue he gives of Shakespeare's faults, for example, seems now as presumptuous as Johnson's similar list in his great Preface . . . There is not one of these accusations [Muir offers as example the objection to the short scenes in *Antony and Cleopatra* and the gnomic passages in *King Lear*] which would be supported by a competent modern critic, at least without many qualifications. And this fact is not, of course, due to the superiority of modern critics, but rather to the fact that the conventions of the Elizabethan stage are now better understood and appreciated.[28]

To this last statement there can be no objection; it is not surprising that the most consistent critics of Bradley have been the most prominent scholars in the fields of historical, psychological, and theatrical studies; E. E. Stoll, L. L. Schücking, L. B. Campbell, J. W. Draper, and others. Other critics of Bradley, however, have objected that his view of Shakespeare was coloured by his period, for example Professor Francis Johnson, who gathers up the traditional criticisms of Bradley and sets them all in the framework of Bradley's period.

> Twentieth-century criticism takes its departure from the extremely influential lectures and essays of A. C. Bradley; whose brilliant psychological analysis of the character of Shakespeare's plays in terms of the familiar psychology of the nineteenth century was profoundly satisfying to his own generation. But Elizabethan scholars soon voiced two principal objections to Bradley's conclusions which although they did not invalidate many of his points yet called for their modification in several details—

[28] K. Muir, 'Fifty Years of Shakespeare Criticism: 1900–1950', *S.S.* iv (1951), pp. 1–25, at p. 3.

(1) Bradley had often overlooked the essential difference between persons existing in real life and those existing only in a play and for that reason necessarily portrayed in accordance with the accepted dramatic conventions of the time . . .

(2) [They] emphasised the need for explaining the dramatic criticisms of Shakespeare and his fellow playwrights in the light of Elizabethan psychology.[29]

This is all true enough but open to a simple and irrefutable answer, *de te fabula*, which has, in fact, been voiced in Shakespeare criticism:

Poor Bradley has been accused by modern critics of monumental crimes, chief among them being a habit of giving a psychological background for the characters in terms of his own or his period's conception of morality. The amplitude, privacy and irrelevance of the moral, political, and religious theories by which Heilman supports—nay, determines his reading of *King Lear* make his distinguished predecessor seem like a beginner.[30]

Heilman is cited here because of the nature of the article but what Keast says is true to a certain degree of all critics to whom it is not given to be 'not of an age' even should they subsequently prove to be 'for all time'.

However general the conditioning of critics by their period, unless each individual critic can prove that his particular period has something to offer to criticism then the first objection remains valid; unless Bradley can convert what would otherwise only narrow his view into a means for examining with especial searching some aspect of Shakespeare, then he was indeed only Victorianizing Shakespeare.

C. H. Herford in a survey of Shakespeare criticism 1893–1923 (unfortunately undated but probably published in 1923) put forward the unusual view that Bradley has something positive to

[29] F. R. Johnson, 'Shakespeare and Elizabethan Psychology', *English Studies Today*, ed. C. L. Wrenn and G. Bullough (London, 1951), p. 112.

[30] W. R. Keast, '"The New Criticism" and "King Lear"', *Critics and Criticism: Ancient and Modern*, ed. R. S. Crane (1952), pp. 108–37 at pp. 118–19. This article was first published in *M.P.* (1949).

offer Shakespearian criticism merely because his approach was unhistorical.

> Pr. Bradley disclaimed any attempt to deal with the recognised preoccupation of Shakesperean scholarship—with 'his life and character, the development of his genius and art.' *Shakespearean Tragedy* was nevertheless an indirect contribution of the first importance to the study, at least, of his genius, and his art, and implicitly of his 'character' also. The current doctrine, rapidly hardening into dogma, that Shakespeare, like lesser men, can be interpreted only through the historic conditions in which he wrote, went by the board. Bradley's instrument of interpretation was the intuitive insight of a trained, alert, and kindled imagination . . . with a methodical precision which reflected the more scientific temper of the Elizabethan scholarship of his own time.[31]

This is a point rarely made about Bradley's obviously unhistorical study; but in fact he was not writing before, but just after the birth of modern academic scholarship. The Furness Variorum edition was begun in 1871, Sir Sidney Lee's *Life* was published in 1898, and although Jaggard's *Bibliography* was not published until 1911 the work must have been begun long before that. Swinburne's parody of the New Shakespeare Society demonstrates that even as early as 1880 there was some scepticism as to the value of dry research. Bradley's own works provide many examples of mistrust of the growing research industry. 'Research, though toilsome, is easy; imaginative vision, though delightful, is difficult', he wrote in his essay 'Shakespeare's Theatre and Audience', and added: 'We may be tempted to prefer the first.'[32] That Bradley was so tempted and occasionally succumbed is illustrated by the unpublished and unpublishable papers in the Balliol Library which include a notebook full of Shakespeare words beginning with 'a', their purpose quite obscure. Other research found its way into print and some of it has stood later scholars in good stead. His essay 'Scene-endings in Shakespeare and in *The Two Noble Kinsmen*' is cited with respect by Kenneth

[31] C. H. Herford, *A Sketch of Recent Shakespeare Investigation*, 1839–1923 (London, n.d. ?1923), p. 32.

[32] *O.L.P.*, p. 362.

Muir in his article on the play in the *Shakespeare Survey*, an unimpeachable organ of specialist research.[33]

The Index to *Shakespearean Tragedy* will provide further evidence of Bradley's use of research and reveal that Bradley was to a certain extent aware of the limitations of his time. 'Stage directions, wrong modern', is followed by five references, four of them to one scene in *King Lear* and one to the rapier scene in *Hamlet*. The accuracy or otherwise of Bradley's findings is not at issue here; the interest lies in the fact that he should have so thoroughly questioned current practice. The index abounds in references to romantic and later critics, but, although there are not perhaps so many as modern scholars would think necessary, there are also references to earlier playwrights, Peele, Greene, Heywood, and Marlowe. There is a reference 'Scot on Witchcraft' which leads us to a long discussion of contemporary views of witches as used by Shakespeare and a quotation from Reginald Scot's *Discovery* (1584). If all this still does not amount to a historical approach to Shakespeare this is because, as Herford points out, Bradley was deliberately offering as an alternative to the academic approach, an essay in 'dramatic appreciation'. That he was doing this because he was assured of its value as an approach to Shakespeare is undeniable, but he was probably also prompted by the knowledge that his peculiar gift was for imaginative reading. There seems to be little grounds for thinking that he wrote as he did merely because as a Victorian he could see no alternative. The general assumption is that being a Victorian is the worst handicap possible for a Shakespeare critic; whether Bradley was or was not a Victorian becomes therefore a question of paramount importance. The alternative is to accept that Bradley was Victorian and to ask how much in fact this helped or hindered him.

Critics who have been concerned to make a controversial point have often sought to add the authority of a weighty name to their argument. M. D. H. Parker, writing of the relationship of Shakespeare's idea of justice to that of St. Thomas Aquinas

[33] K. Muir, 'Shakespeare's Hand in *The Two Noble Kinsmen*', *S.S.* xi (1958), pp. 50–9, at p. 59.

and St. Augustine, at one point supports her argument with an interesting parallel. She quotes from St. Augustine's 'Confessions' a passage including 'whatever is is good', and comments: 'This might indeed be a paraphrase of Bradley's dictum that evil in Shakespeare lives only by virtue of good, and in destroying good destroys itself.'[34] It is not relevant to this critic's argument to point out the importance of this parallel in terms of the controversy over Bradley's peculiarly Victorian attitude to Shakespeare. Miss Parker's concern is with Shakespeare and to back her claim that Augustinian ideas were current in the late Elizabethan era she points out the number of translations made at that time. Equally significant to the study of Bradley is the parallel fact that Miss Parker herself uses a translation of St. Augustine made by Pusey, an elder contemporary of Bradley's at Oxford. Whether Bradley had read Pusey's translation or not hardly matters although it seems likely that he would have done; whether Bradley consciously developed his conception of Shakespearian tragedy with the help of St. Augustine matters equally little although again it seems likely that Bradley turned whatever he had read to good use. What is of interest is that Bradley's period, scoffed at for its narrow Victorianism, should have provided a translation of a medieval work used in the best tradition by a modern scholar to illustrate Shakespeare's relation to the ideas of his own time.

That Miss Parker should find parallels between Shakespeare's conception of justice and St. Augustine's is interesting because elsewhere another critic has found a similarity between Bradley's conception of evil and its inherent goodness and Aquinas's theory on the same subject. In a footnote to his discussion of *Macbeth* W. C. Curry quotes A. C. Bradley:

> That which keeps the evil man prosperous, makes him succeed, even permits him to exist, is the good in him (I do not mean only the obviously 'moral' good). When the evil in him masters the good and has its way, it destroys other people through him, but it also destroys *him*.[35]

[34] M. D. H. Parker, *The Slave of Life: A Study of Shakespeare and the Idea of Justice* (London, 1955,) p. 219.

[35] *S.T.*, p. 35.

This, says Mr. Curry, 'might have been taken from Thomas Aquinas'.[36] This is not the place to argue the accuracy of the parallel, but the fact of its being made at all adds substance to the idea that Bradley's theories (for whatever reason) are not so remote from the ideas accepted by Shakespeare's contemporaries as some critics would suggest.

Ivor Morris in an article on Fulke Greville almost loses sight of his subject in his eagerness to write of Bradley and the likeness of his tragic vision to Greville's. He wrote:

> Some minds have been able to react totally and uninhibitedly to the impressions of Shakespearian tragedy, and have combined the gifts of analysis and imagination—the disintegrating and the plastic powers—to a significant degree. The best of them was Bradley's; and it is here suggested that the reaction of such an intellect to the multifarious impressions of Shakespearian tragedy offers the most direct means of gaining an idea of its tragic vision. It is also suggested that the idea thus gained bears some resemblance to the tragic vision of Fulke Greville.[37]

There is no suggestion in the article that Bradley used Greville's ideas to help him formulate his own; no inquiry into how far Greville's tragic vision reflected that of his contemporary, Shakespeare; in fact the article seems to be no more than an examination of an odd literary coincidence. Certainly Greville's name is not among those Elizabethan dramatists mentioned by Bradley in *Shakespearean Tragedy*, nor do the letters uncover an avowal of profound debt to Shakespeare's contemporaries. The parallelism for which Morris makes a very plausible case cannot be accounted for either by Bradley's academic research or by any proven relationship to the same source, Shakespeare. If there is a reason for the coincidence it must be this latter, but, whether it is or not, does not seriously affect the point that it is possible to come to conclusions about tragedy very similar to

[36] W. C. Curry, *Shakespeare's Philosophical Patterns* (Baton Rouge, 1937), quotation from 1959 edition, p. 233.

[37] I. Morris, 'The Tragic Vision of Fulke Greville', *S.S.* xv (1961), pp. 66–75, at p. 72.

those of Bradley without the advantages or disadvantages of his historical background. Whatever else the likeness proves it must considerably weaken the theory that Bradley's criticism was the product of his age alone.

If the parallelism of Bradley's theory and those of a Jacobean dramatist reveals how easy it is to overrate the importance of historical background in the development of ideas so does the likeness of Bradley's results to those of peculiarly historical critics. P. N. Siegel pointed out in a footnote:

> Bradley had shown how Shakespearean tragedy included the mediaeval view of tragedy in its depiction of the striking calamity culminating in death which overtakes a man of high estate, but went beyond it; Farnham shows how this historically came to be. Miss Campbell's own valuable scholarship in Elizabethan psychology does not contradict Bradley, as she thinks, but rather supplements and re-inforces him . . . in speaking of error and sin, is not Miss Campbell reaffirming Bradley's insistence upon moral responsibility which she had denied? And is not the tragic flaw which Bradley finds in Shakespeare's heroes of 'a fatal tendency to identify the whole being with one interest, object, passion, or habit of mind' similar to Miss Campbell's view of Shakespeare's tragic heroes as 'slaves of passion' and does not his perception that all of Shakespeare's heroes are 'torn by an inward struggle' agree with her account of their 'turbulence of soul created by passion'?[38]

This may seem to be an oversimplification of the history of modern criticism but its value here lies in that very simplicity. The wide range of tortuous methods often hides from readers the essential sameness of the results. In one way Miss L. B. Campbell and Prof. A. C. Bradley represent two poles as far removed as possible from each other; yet if as P. N. Siegel suggests there is little difference in the Shakespeare they portray, they must have more in common than is apparent beneath the exteriors of a modern American academic and a Victorian Oxford don. It may be too much to hope for, but since what they have in common is related to Shakespeare surely it reflects how far the criticism

[38] P. N. Siegel, 'In Defence of Bradley', *C.E.* (Chicago, 9 Feb. 1948), pp. 250–6, at p. 252 n.

of both is true to the subject, so that, indeed, the results ought to be the same.

A. P. Rossiter also considered Bradley's views in relation to those of the theories of the Elizabethan and Jacobean period and especially in relation to Sir Philip Sidney. The criticism of Bradley which emerges is not really coherent, but the central argument is very interesting because of the use of Bradley in a context, which did not really call for it, by a critic who certainly was not a blind Bradleyite. Rossiter wrote:

> He [A. C. Bradley] labours to believe that the gods *are* just: that a moral principle re-establishes itself at the end of *King Lear*; and yet he writes: 'to assert that he deserved to suffer what he did suffer is to do violence not merely to language but to any healthy moral sense'. On the next page he says: 'Let us put aside the ideas of justice and merit . . .'; and I have used Sidney's tragic principles as an approach to Shakespeare, because it seems to me that what Shakespeare had to do was to put aside those ideas, in order to become a Shakespearian, not an Elizabethan, *tragedian*: or writer of genuine tragedy not 'moral-tragicall' Histories.[39]

The idea that Shakespeare was compelled to write in contradiction to the ideas current at his period is an unusual one and has value therefore on that account; how far it is helpful to an understanding of Shakespeare is not really the issue here. What is of interest is that Rossiter should write of Bradley together with Sidney; Rossiter was probably making an unconscious comparison of the two methods of criticism, the aesthetic and the historical. Rossiter tried the historical method and found it wanting, and saw in contrast the value of the aesthetic reading, however imperfectly formulated he found it in his example, Bradley. What Rossiter does not say is that Bradley benefitted from his exclusion of historical considerations in his criticism of Shakespeare because by doing so he avoided the assumption that Shakespeare was simply an 'Elizabethan tragedian'.

Bradley lived at the latest time when it was possible to write Shakespeare criticism without a heavy ballast of research material,

[39] A. P. Rossiter, *Angel with Horns, and other Shakespeare Lectures* (Cambridge, 1961), p. 260.

or at the very least, a reputable record of research behind one. From the early twentieth century onwards, the way to consider Shakespeare has been in terms of the psychological, philosophical, and medical treatises of his time, sociological surveys of the possible audiences, and architectural studies of theatrical limitation; whatever the writer wants to say, he will somewhere have to substantiate his view by a detailed account of its likeness to the view held by one of Shakespeare's contemporaries or forebears. Parker, Morris, and Rossiter are not exceptions to the general rule. When Bradley wrote he was able to ignore the findings of historical research; his success as a critic does not depend on his ignoring this aspect of Shakespearian study, but it depends on his being able to pursue a critical method for which he felt he was peculiarly fitted, and which he considered to be highly relevant to the general understanding of Shakespeare. Menon expresses the point naïvely: 'After performances of Shakespeare's plays I have overheard people who had never read criticism pass remarks strongly reminiscent of Bradley. Bradley needs no further corroboration.'[40] 'Overheard people' are not a reliable test for critical analysis but Bradley would have appreciated the point; *Shakespearean Tragedy* is really an account of Bradley's trained reaction to the text; it is a testimony to Shakespeare and to Bradley's success at delineating the reaction to Shakespeare, that the critic and playgoer should agree.

The fact is that now a writer would have to have some extrinsic claim to attention in order to be able to write a long critical work on Shakespeare based only on one educated man's reading of the text. The late Victorian period was sympathetic to this type of criticism largely because it was used to no other. Literature was still regarded only as a pastime and pleasure even if it was expected to be also morally improving; it was not yet regarded as the raw material of the academic profession. Of the three Chairs Bradley held, he was first holder of one, and second of the other, and the last, the Chair of Poetry at Oxford, was then, as now, considered primarily as an embellishment to

[40] C. Narayana Menon, *Shakespeare Criticism: an Essay in Synthesis* (London, 1938), p. 51.

learning. Professionalism in criticism was only just emerging. D. J. Palmer in his book *The Rise of English Studies*[41] analyses the birth of academic criticism and takes as the hero of his story Walter Raleigh, who followed Bradley at Liverpool, Glasgow, and finally at Oxford. After the 1920s it is difficult to find a work of Shakespeare criticism which has been accorded serious critical attention which is not the product of a professional attitude to literature. Before 1900 even the most serious writers of criticism were the product of amateurism (Dowden, a professor at Trinity College, Dublin, and Moulton, an American Professor, are two rare exceptions). Of the critics who were Bradley's immediate predecessors referred to in the index of *Shakespearean Tragedy*, Hales was a Methodist minister, and his work significantly modestly entitled *Notes and Essays on Shakespeare*, Mrs. Jameson was a well-to-do widow, and Swinburne an eccentric poet. Sir Sidney Lee's book published in 1898 was a self-conscious attempt at thorough research but the tone as well as the content of his preface is significant.

> Aesthetic studies of Shakespeare abound, and to increase their number is a work of supererogation. But Shakespearean literature, as far as it is known to me, still lacks a book that shall supply within a brief compass an exhaustive and well-arranged statement of the facts of Shakespeare's career, achievement, and reputation, that shall reduce conjecture to the smallest dimensions consistent with coherence and, shall give verifiable references to all the original sources of information. After studying Elizabethan literature, history, and bibliography for more than eighteen years, I believed that I might, without exposing myself to a charge of presumption, attempt something in the way of filling this gap, and that I might be able to supply, at least tentatively, a guide book to Shakespeare's life and works that should be, within its limits, complete and trustworthy.[42]

The first sentence defines the true academic approach, the second the courtesy and modesty of the amateur. The description of this monumental volume as a 'guide book' is typical of the Victorian writer and the sort of reader he would expect.

[41] D. J. Palmer, *The Rise of English Studies* (London, 1965).

[42] Sir S. Lee, *A Life of William Shakespeare* (1st edn., London, 1898), quotation from rev. ed. 1915, pp. ix–x.

By the time Bradley's *Shakespearean Tragedy* was published this amateur attitude was dying so fast that it could no longer be taken for granted. One reviewer welcomed *Shakespearean Tragedy* with all the fervour of one who sees the old way threatened. 'Professor Bradley's book is popular in aim. He desires to propagate a familiarity with Shakespeare's work.' There is jubilance in the tone and the reason why becomes obvious when the reviewer continues:

> The first lecture, perhaps the least good in the book, is suspiciously like a sop thrown to the 'Dons'. It consists of a generalisation with regard to the *substance* of Shakespearean Tragedy in the abstract, a subject which would never occupy the attention of any one except a professional academic critic. And indeed it is not a matter of great importance, even for such an one, that the 'tragic fact' should be accurately defined.[43]

This it seems is a wilful misreading of Bradley's intentions, a distortion of his appeal, but beneath the distortion there is considerable truth. *Shakespearean Tragedy* is hardly 'popular in aim' but that it is intended more for readers than specialists is made evident by the comment in the Preface. 'Many of the Notes will be of interest only to scholars, who may find, I hope, something new in them.'[44]

In fact Bradley's work stands between the truly Victorian belletristic criticism and the truly modern academic research. Bradley was an enthusiastic poetry reader before he was a student much less a don, and his sympathies lay, as he said, 'with the crowd who somehow feel better for reading poetry though they have bad ears and confused minds'.[45] He was also, however, twice a Professor, a man classically educated at Oxford and capable, as certain papers in *A Miscellany* show, of the most painstaking research. Whatever the relationship of Bradley to his period in other respects, in this respect alone it offered him a unique opportunity. He was hampered by the conventions neither

[43] R. Y. Tyrrell, 'Tragedy' (review of *Shakespearean Tragedy*), *Academy*, lxviii. (11 Mar. 1905), pp. 229–31, at p. 230.

[44] *S.T.*, p. viii.

[45] Letter to G. Murray, 8 Apr. 1901.

of the old nor the new criticism; his life offered him the opportunity both to develop as a Victorian gentleman of private means and as a professional academic in industrial cities. Criticism had not yet hardened into a profession but it was developing, at least in the form of specialist students, a discipline of its own.

In other ways too, his Victorian background may not have been only a hindrance to Bradley. Bradley was witnessing in a totally different way the end of an age of certainty much as Shakespeare must have been in the late sixteenth century. Critics have castigated Bradley for secularizing Shakespeare and it certainly reflects not only the strongly agnostic temper of his mind but also his critical background that he should do so. Bradley's period was one in which it was impossible to take for granted either for oneself or one's hearers the basic truth or the external happenings of the Christian religion; consequently Bradley strove to express for himself, and others, a concept of the absolute which did not rely on a personal God. Although modern critics may find his work threaded through with references to Christian thinkers and Christian dogma the fact remains that if Shakespeare *was* writing a Christian drama it was not exclusively Christian. Bradley was, because of the times in which he lived, peculiarly fitted to recognize the truths in Shakespeare which although they could be expressed in Christian terms are not in fact so expressed within the plays. Modern critics stress how Bradley failed to recognize the Christian temper of the Elizabethan era: K. Muir, for instance, writes: 'Bradley rightly stressed the secular nature of the Elizabethan drama; yet . . . it was after all written for the most part by Christians for Christians.'[46] Such critics seem to forget equally how Christian was Bradley's own background. The late Victorian period may have seen the birth of scepticism but it also saw a flourishing of the Christian religion to which the large number of churches surviving to the modern period present ample testimony. Generally accepted Christianity and private doubt characterized Bradley's period as they did Shakespeare's.

In other ways too Bradley's period shows resemblance to Shakespeare's. In all such generalizations about period every

[46] K. Muir, 'Shakespeare and the Tragic Pattern', *B.A.* (1958), p. 158.

remark contains almost as much falsehood as truth; but since critics have relied so heavily on Bradley's Victorianism it seems only right to redress the balance even if by means which are not necessarily more accurate. Shakespeare wrote at the end of a long reign and so did Bradley; Elizabeth meant to the majority of Elizabethans something very similar to what Victoria meant to most Victorians; a symbol of the established order. Because of religious upheaval Shakespeare's period was very much aware of religious issues; so was Bradley's. Shakespeare's age saw the beginning of a century of important scientific discovery which was helped forward because of its own keen inquiry into fundamental issues; the same is true to a certain extent of Bradley's period.

Bradley's philosophical background was, moreover, not the impediment to a true understanding of Shakespeare that some critics have thought. The British Idealist belief in a Reality which embraced in proper proportions all Appearance, linked the whole of the created world in a way not so totally different from the concept of the great chain of being; order was in both cases of paramount importance, the part always subservient to the whole. It was the influence of Hegel and Aristotle as accepted by the Victorian world, which gave Bradley his conceptions about tragedy, but these bear a remarkable resemblance to the conceptions embodied in Elizabethan plays; and this in part is due to the likeness of the philosophical structure behind both. Bradley wrote:

> Consider, for instance, in the most abstract way what a great tragedy does, and what kind of insight comes to us unconsciously from it. It takes certain characters some of whom rise far above the common level in power or in beauty. It places them in a certain set of circumstances and in certain relations to one another, such circumstances and relations as tend to elicit the forces of character in a given direction and with perilous energy. And the direction is one which must lead to conflict. Such a situation . . . exhibits, not in a theory but in the shape of a struggle at which the spectator holds his breath, the fundamental contradiction of human nature, or the fact that man is at once infinite in capacity and limited in achievement. Infinite: for the tragic

hero is so identified with some passion or some object that it becomes to him the whole world. Limited: because he is in truth but one organ, so to speak, of a spiritual life much wider than himself. Because he is the first, because he has poured the infinity of his being into a single channel, he shows us human nature at its greatest tension, what is sublime in man. Because he is the second, a part and not the whole, the limitless assertion of his being brings him into conflict with the elements of the spiritual organism to which he belongs; and in the convulsion of this conflict he succumbs to the forces of the whole, which to preserve itself destroys him, and which yet exhibits its own energy nowhere more clearly than in his boundless passion. According to this view (which is of course a very general and also a partial view) the origin of a tragic action lies in the division of a moral whole against itself.[47]

This passage has been quoted at length because it illustrates not only Bradley's heavy dependence, especially in the expression of the latter part of the passage, on the accepted philosophy of his period but also the debt in his thought to Shakespeare. The description of man as 'infinite in capacity and limited in achievement' is an obvious parallel to Hamlet's statement and has its counterpart in much of Elizabethan philosophy. It illustrates furthermore the wide divergence between Bradley's philosophy of tragedy and the Elizabethans; if their view of the macrocosm was very much similar, they had no such common ground in their understanding of the microcosm. If the two conceptions of order have much in common they are expressed in a widely different context.

It would be unwise to contort either the Elizabethan idea or Bradley's in order to fit one into the mould of the other. What is valuable in Bradley's theory is largely what is different from the Elizabethan; the fact remains, however, that, in some ways at least, the philosophical background of Bradley's age was not so remote from that of Shakespeare's, that its differences could not be critically both valid and interesting.

It would be pointless, and beyond the scope of this book, to press these comparisons further, but the fact remains that such

[47] *P.L.*, p. 10.

comparison can and ought to be made to stand against the universally accepted theory that Bradley was a Victorian and therefore incapable of understanding Shakespeare's age. A more accurate way to say this would be that the modern age sees certain things in Shakespeare which Bradley because of his period was unable to see. There is nothing to tell us how much more the one view is true to Shakespeare than the other.

Seeing Bradley purely in terms of his period only ensures that we miss a good deal of what he is saying. Bradley no more than anyone else is a typical product of his age; his age no more susceptible than any other to facile generalizations. If Bradley was at Oxford under Jowett in the 1870s, in March 1905 he went to see a Hauptmann comedy with Bertrand Russell and his wife.[48] It may be more convenient to a critic to stress the former but the resulting picture is only partially true and can only lead to misconceptions. If a historian stresses what appear to be the formative influences on a man's life to the point of ignoring the man as a whole, the picture which emerges will be lifeless and, more important, historically inaccurate.

While anti-Bradleyans have eagerly labelled the founder of their movement 'Victorian' his followers have seldom made any reference to his biography and background. This fact is surely significant. Those critics who found the universal acceptance of Bradleyan ideas a constricting evil were seeking to confine the evil and the easiest way to do so was to put him back in his period. If the name 'Bradley' was supposed to stimulate eager agreement, the word 'Victorian' was the most efficient counterblast.

Miss L. B. Campbell's objection to Bradley amounted to something more comprehensive and thoughtful than a mere label but the opening paragraph of her article 'Bradley Revisited: Forty Years After' sums up usefully the motives of the most ardent anti-Bradleyans:

More than forty years ago, in 1904, Professor A. C. Bradley published his *Shakespearean Tragedy*. It was a mighty book, taking Shakespearean criticism again into the realm of the universal and the

[48] Letter to G. Murray, 20 Mar. 1905.

significant. I well remember the enthusiasm of my teachers when they read it, for I was at an age when I wondered at their excitement. . . . So great was their enthusiasm that, to explain Shakespeare they took to explaining Bradley, and they oriented all Shakespeare studies to the new sun. But the young scholars of the first decade of the twentieth century are those who now attend the Old Guard dinners of the Modern Language Association, and it is as dangerous in scholarship as in politics to stop thinking new ideas and reconsidering old ones. . . . Among Shakespearean scholars there are still many who regard the dicta of Bradley as having been brought down to the people from Sinai, and who demand that each new interpretation be tested by whether it can be reconciled with what Bradley says. It seems to me that the time has come to re-examine Bradley's book in the light of what we have learned during these forty years.[49]

The impulse comes not so much from distrust of Bradley's methods and disagreement with his results as from annoyance that his works should be accepted without question. The reaction that stems from this kind of feeling, however natural that may be, is not likely to be very critical. Bradley writing of Tennyson was well aware of the force and critical irrelevance of literary reaction.

To care for his poetry is to be old-fashioned, and to belittle it is to be in the movement. . . . The Mid-Victorian, a figure amply proving the creative energy of Georgian imagination, is supposed to have been blind to Tennyson's defects, though the actual surviving mid-Victorian rarely hears a sane word about them which was not familiar to him in his youth. And—what really matters—the antipathy to these defects seems in some cases to have so atrophied the power of enjoyment that Tennyson's weakest poems and his best meet with the same indifference or contempt, and a reader will remain unmoved by lines which, if he were ignorant of their authorship, he would hail with delight.[50]

Allowing for the differences between reaction to poet and critic this is a remarkably accurate forecast of what happened to Bradley. Bradley has been in many ways the Tennyson of twentieth-century criticism; he has supplied a personification of an era

[49] L. B. Campbell, 'Bradley Revisited: Forty Years After', in *S.Ph.* xliv (1947), pp. 174–94, at p. 174.

[50] *A.M.*, pp. 2–3.

which never existed so clearly as in the mind of a later generation concerned only to move away from the past. Critics who have written of Bradley have mentally included him in the same old-fashioned group as Mrs. Jameson, Dowden, and Swinburne, and although they are seldom mentioned by name, the same vague old-fashioned aura embraces them as well. Bradley is a name for all that is old-fashioned, worn out, and unsatisfactory in criticism; it is testimony to Bradley's previous power and fame as a critic that his name should have been chosen to represent the age.

When critics write that Bradley is a Victorian the historical truth of this description is not important; the term does not express Bradley's period but the attitude of the modern critic to his significant predecessor. This is the reason why criticism is so uncertain about what exactly is Bradley's period. The date of publication of *Shakespearean Tragedy* is at odds with the critics' preconceptions as to Bradley's great antiquity. J. D. Wilson's odd description of a man younger than himself as 'elderly' is typical. To the modern critic Bradley can never have been young and vital and a leader of the reaction; he must symbolize the old and the outworn.

This attitude to Bradley was necessary while he was, in Lord David Cecil's phrase, 'just not contemporary'. He goes on to make the following interesting observation:

> Have you ever noticed, when looking at a photographic group taken twenty years ago, that it is impossible to judge which women were well dressed, for all the clothes look equally grotesque; whereas in a group taken forty years ago some were clearly charming? The same phenomenon is true of literature. During the early years of the present century people were in such violent revolt against that Victorian view of life so perfectly expressed by Tennyson, that Tennyson's stock went rushing down. Now that the Victorian age is thoroughly behind us, Tennyson's reputation is once more rising.[51]

In the world of criticism Bradley is now emerging from the

[51] Lord David Cecil, *Hardy the Novelist* (London, 1943), quotations from 1960 reprint of 2nd ed., pp. 11–12. This provides an interesting comment on Bradley's earlier prognostications about Tennyson; c.f. *A.M.*, p. 4.

reaction which he and all that his period represented suffered in the name of progress. Bradley the Victorian has served his purpose; Bradley the Shakespeare critic can now be reinstated.

There are signs that this process is now well established. Bradley's major shortcomings, most of them attributed to his period, are accepted and it is possible for later critics to make use of Bradley as they would make use of Coleridge and their own contemporaries. Period is no longer a total barrier, but just as Coleridge is seen as an imperfect help because of the human limitations of his time so is Bradley. The point is that these imperfections are now seen in a more critical light.

More recent Shakespeare criticism has come to accept Bradley's age with a greater equanimity than earlier writers, nearer to the giant, Victorianism, could afford; this does not, however, mean that the assumption now is that Bradley's age was the best possible for the interpretation of Shakespeare. A certain amount of disagreement with one's predecessors is essential, as J. D. Wilson wrote of Bradley: 'I have myself made bold to criticise him here and there; for if one had nothing new to say, why write . . . at all?'[52] What the later twentieth century has had to say that was not said before has depended largely upon a realization of the Christian elements in Shakespearean tragedy. The cry now is that Bradley's Elizabethan drama was over-secular. P. N. Siegel in 1957 explained his aim in his book *Shakespearean Tragedy and the Elizabethan Compromise* in terms of this particular revision of Bradley:

> *Shakespearean Tragedy*, despite the scorn cast on it some years ago by those who would read the tragedies solely as poems not as dramas, retains today its vitality as a classic. . . . However, the work of recent critics and scholars, notably G. Wilson Knight and S. L. Bethell has shown Christian overtones in the tragedies of which Bradley was unaware or only dimly aware. By examining the Christian humanist basis of the tragedies I have sought to rectify the inadequacies of Bradley's description of Shakespeare's tragic vision and to reinterpret the four great plays he discussed.[53]

By 1964 this idea has almost hardened into accepted fact.

[52] J. D. Wilson, *What Happens in 'Hamlet'* (Cambridge, 1935), p. vii.

[53] P. N. Siegel, op. cit., p. ix.

D. J. Palmer in his article on Bradley also defends Bradley from the more usual criticism and then adds that he underestimated the Christian aspect of Shakespearian drama. He wrote:

> No use . . . to demand historical perspective from Bradley, the scholarship of his day could not have put him in possession of even the average modern undergraduate's knowledge of Elizabethan stage conventions and Renaissance conceptions of tragedy. . . . As a rule however Bradley's investigation of character and action does not often contradict what evidence literary history can throw upon Shakespeare's tragedies because he approaches the subject at a different level. Perhaps his most general offence against the historical perspective is his underestimation of the Christian element in the plays. Shakespeare did not write religious drama but the influence of Christian doctrines is much more apparent and pervasive than Bradley allowed.[54]

This comment seems to be open to several objections, first that it underestimates Bradley's historical knowledge of the Elizabethan period (and overestimates that of the average modern undergraduate) but most important that the defence which Palmer makes in the first case is equally applicable in the second: 'he approaches the subject on a different level.' The fact is that Palmer like every critic is subject to the fluctuations of fashion. It is as impossible for him to disentangle himself sufficiently from the certainty that Bradley underestimated the Christian nature of the plays as it was for earlier critics to see clearly why Bradley's criticism was not substantiated by historical research.

Irving Ribner in his book also follows the general pattern:

> Bradley could lead his readers only to a Shakespeare without positive belief, to a conception of tragedy merely as the posing of unanswerable questions and to a moral system in the plays which is upon close analysis not moral at all. Such a tragedy as Bradley found in Shakespeare could have been written only in the secular Renaissance of nineteenth-century historians, and not in the Renaissance which more recent scholarship has revealed to us.[55]

Ribner is here seeing Bradley's defects as a critic in terms of his failure to appreciate the non-secular Renaissance which the

[54] D. J. Palmer, 'A. C. Bradley', *C.S.* ii. 1 (1964), pp. 18–25, at p. 21.

[55] Irving Ribner, *Patterns in Shakespearean Tragedy* (London, 1960), p. 3.

modern academics have unearthed; but his expression of the point in terms of the nineteenth century and more recent scholarship is surely significant; Ribner is more concerned with the historical background of the various critics than he is with the historical background of Shakespeare.

In the same year as Ribner's work appeared J. Lawlor wrote:

> Nothing in the Shakespearian universe that I know of offers any contradiction to the truths of the Christian religion. But his province as a dramatist, the distinctive scope and purpose of his 'poesy' is in the last resort 'deeds and language such as men do use'.[56]

That Lawlor should thus be writing against the general trend not so much self-consciously as a crusader but quite unobtrusively is more easily understood if the tone of the whole book is remembered. In his whole work, which covers the four great tragedies, *Henry IV* and *Henry V*, Lawlor makes no references to G. Wilson Knight, F. R. Leavis, L. C. Knights, C. F. E. Spurgeon, and only refers in a footnote to H. Granville-Barker. There are, however, several references to Bradley; Lawlor, it appears, stands aloof from the fashions of his day.

In many ways he was perhaps wise, for now there are signs of a reversal in the trend; Barbara Everett in 1960 published an article which sought to counteract the new mystical *King Lear*. Bradley, she said, had maintained the proper tragic poise, modern 'mystical' criticism had overturned it. The position as she sees it is less simple: 'It is obviously impossible to decide, simply, whether or not *King Lear* is a "Christian" play'.[57] What her article in fact amounts to is a defence of Bradley's reading of *King Lear*, a reaction against 'The New King Lear'; as defence of Bradley becomes more popular it seems likely that, for some critics at least, this will constitute looking again at the Christian Shakespeare. Palmer, because his criticism depends so heavily on fashion, is by nature already old fashioned. By the time a way of thought has become a recognized trend, reaction is imminent and the trend outdated.

[56] J. Lawlor, *The Tragic Sense in Shakespeare* (London, 1960), p. 175.

[57] B. Everett, 'The New King Lear', *C.Q.* ii. 4 (1960), pp. 325–39, at p. 332.

5

BRADLEY: THEORIZING ACADEMIC

THE Victorian Bradley had other attributes besides his historical period, although they can almost always be related to what the twentieth century has thought of his period. As a Victorian, Bradley has stood for the twentieth century not as a figure of robust family pride and patriotism, but as a quiet unworldly academic. J. D. Wilson's description of him as 'That shy, gentle, refined subtle hypersensitive, entirely moral, almost other-worldly personality, at once donnish, a little old-maidish, and extraordinarily winning . . . with his frail figure and his tender smile',[1] would find little opposition in the critical world; John Bayley writing when living memory of A. C. Bradley must be rare called him 'humane and bookish'[2] and what the obituary in *The Times* has to say of him does not contradict the description. Of Bradley's university teaching *The Times* wrote:

> Bradley displayed a singularly attractive, vivacious, swift, and keen intellect, and though neither physically nor intellectually an orator—indeed, too subtle for that—he was an effective and winning lecturer, with the natural charm, lightness, and thrilling note of a delightful bird.[3]

Nor is there anything in the letters to show that Bradley was much different than these two generalizations imply.

What is important, however, is not the truth of the description or general acceptance of Bradley as a quiet unworldly academic critic but the effect such an idea has had on the twentieth-century

[1] J. D. Wilson, *The Fortunes of Falstaff* (Cambridge, 1943), p. 13.

[2] J. Bayley, *The Characters of Love. A Study in the Literature of Personality* (London, 1960), p. 140.

[3] *The Times*, 4 Oct. 1935, p. 14: Obituary, 'A. C. Bradley'. This obituary although it speaks rather harshly of Bradley's criticism, was the leading obituary of the day—there were five others.

attitude to his criticism. The best-known result of this picture of Bradley is the conviction widespread in modern criticism that Bradley never went to the theatre. K. Muir illustrates a typical attitude; the way in which he says that Bradley's criticism ignores the stage is as telling as the fact that he does so:

> Bradley, with all his critical insight, missed something in his ideal theatre of the mind, that his valet might have got in the gallery of the Lyceum. It is worth noting that the alleged theatrical weaknesses of the play have been analysed most effectively by Bradley himself who yet seems to have had little experience of the play in the theatre.[4]

The opposition of Bradley to his valet in the Lyceum gallery is telling; Bradley is regarded as a little effete and cut off from all the rich realities of life—although there is no reason why this should be true. Even more telling is the phrase 'seems to have had little experience of the play in the theatre'. Where does this impression come from? Muir is unlikely to have known Bradley, or anyone who knew whether or not he had indeed seen the play. In fact, the text of *Shakespearean Tragedy* would have told him (admittedly in a footnote) that Bradley did see at least one performance of *King Lear*, and the comment:

> I am not denying that it is a great stage-play. It has scenes immensely effective in the theatre; three of them—the two between Lear and Goneril and between Lear, Goneril, and Regan, and the ineffably beautiful scene in the Fourth Act between Lear and Cordelia—lose in the theatre very little of the spell they have for imagination[5]

seems to indicate a record of at least one performance having this impression on Bradley. Another reference to *King Lear* is found in his article 'The Locality of *King Lear* Act I scene ii', which also, but unfortunately without precise reference, gives the impression of being the result in part of theatrical experience (cf. Chap. 3, p. 43). True or otherwise, Muir's remark is hardly critical and in fact it is only an embroidery preceding his inquiry into Bradley's criticisms of the stage-worthiness of the play.

[4] K. Muir, ed., *King Lear*, Arden edition (London and Cambridge, Mass. 1952), p. xlviii.

[5] *S.T.*, pp. 292 and 247 respectively.

Muir begins by stating, 'Most of the improbabilities mentioned by Bradley would not be noticed in the theatre, and they cannot therefore detract from the effectiveness of *King Lear* as a stage play',[6] and having summarized Bradley's objections answers them in a footnote one by one. Some of Muir's answers, however, only prove the strength of Bradley's objections; according to Muir, Bradley finds that 'Cordelia does not reveal Kent's identity to the gentleman, in spite of the promise of III. i.' to which Muir's defence of Shakespeare is, 'Perhaps Shakespeare changed his mind.'[6] Apart from the fact that Bradley's criticism is not phrased in this way at all—what he says is: 'Why does Kent so carefully preserve his incognito till the last scene? He says he does it for an important purpose, but what the purpose is we have to guess.'[7] —Muir's answer comes nowhere near the essential point regarding the dramatic effect of such inconsistencies. Although other of Muir's arguments have more weight than this, it is indicative of his attitude to Bradley's objections that they should be summarily dismissed in a footnote. The remark in the text about the valet in the Lyceum is supposed to be sufficient answer; and to many readers it probably has been, although Muir's approach bears much more resemblance to Bradley's than it does to that of any member of a gallery audience.[8]

The more general criticism, that Bradley had analysed the plays in terms of a reading rather than a performance, is much more weighty, and perhaps the best objection to the argument about *King Lear*'s fitness for the stage is that Bradley should never

[6] K. Muir, ed. cit., pp. xlviii–l. [7] *S.T.*, p. 258.

[8] More recent criticism is more objective in its estimate of this aspect of Bradley, but there persists the same note of superiority: 'the identity of true tragedy was established in a century that never forgot Lamb's claim that Shakespeare's tragedies ought not to be performed. Bradley, it is true, did not share Lamb's conviction, and treated the stage with far greater respect; yet in *Shakespearean Tragedy* he speaks constantly of the book and addresses the reader. I do not claim any special insights in the essays that follow, and they are of course the result of a close study of the text; but I hope it will appear that that study, an imaginative one by necessity, is governed by an imagination trained to think of the stage. At least it will be seen that I write of the play and the audience.' (Nicholas Brooke, *Shakespeare's Early Tragedies*, 1968). Yet would it not, nowadays, be more realistic to recognize that the greater number are readers of Shakespeare, and not members of an audience?

have been seduced by the example of his predecessor Lamb into entering the discussion at all. Granville-Barker's reply to Bradley is instructive on this issue. He wrote:

> Bradley's argument is weighty yet—with all deference to a great critic—I protest that, as it stands it is not valid. He is contending that a practical and practised dramatist has here written a largely impracticable play. . . . Ought we moreover to assume—as Bradley seems to—that a play must necessarily make all its points and its full effect, point by point clearly and completely scene by scene, as the performance goes along? Not every play, I think. For the appreciation of such a work as *King Lear* one might even demand the second and third hearing of the whole which the alertest critic would need to give to (say) a piece of music of like calibre.[9]

With this, Bradley could only have agreed; the objections he himself makes to the dramatic fitness really amount to the one objection that a reader of the play is puzzled by inconsistencies instead of moved by the dramatic whole. For Bradley who had a very active and highly trained imagination it was probably easier to reconstruct the dramatic whole in the mind's eye, especially at a time when stage performances were more spectacular than dramatic. It is furthermore instructive that Granville-Barker, himself a producer, should treat Bradley's objections with respect; another producer elsewhere records some agreement with Bradley's view of *King Lear*:

> These arguments [that *King Lear* is not good on the stage] are founded on a deep appreciation of its fiery quality and passionate impact, and more than once they have been associated with a complete approval of Bradley's assessment of the play as a work to be deemed one of the greatest artistic creations of all time.[10]

Both Granville-Barker and Szyfman, just quoted, agree with the mild academic about the producer's difficulties in conveying the hugeness of effect in *King Lear* on the stage. Bradley's reading

[9] H. Granville Barker, *Prefaces to Shakespeare* (London, 1958), quotation from 1961 reprint, p. 264.

[10] H. Szyfman, '*King Lear* on the Stage: A Producer's Reflections', in *S.S.* xiii (1960), pp. 69–70.

was not, then, so far removed from an experience of a performance as some other academics have thought; the mistake he made was to preface this reading by a tabulated inquiry into minor deficiencies in the play's structure which, as Muir said, in all likelihood go quite unnoticed on the stage.

Dover Wilson makes a further point in respect of Bradley's reliance on a reading knowledge of the play as opposed to a theatrical involvement in it. He wrote in *What Happens in 'Hamlet'* of Bradley's account of the cause for the two months' interval between Act I and Act II of that play.

> Dr. Bradley's words illustrate a fallacy that impairs a good deal of his Shakespearian criticism, brilliant and subtle as it is, viz., the fallacy of regarding separate episodes of the play, especially episodes early in the play, in the light of his knowledge of the whole.[11]

This is irrefutable but it raises two further questions; how far is it possible in the case of a play as well known as *Hamlet* to read the beginning without the consciousness of the end, and if possible, is it desirable? Was Bradley in fact trying to give an account of what happened in *Hamlet* in historical, chronological terms?

The answer to the first point must depend largely on the individual critic, and the outcome of the discussion is not really relevant to a study of Bradley except in so far as it will be part of an answer to the second point. Bradley was, as he said, trying to further 'dramatic appreciation' of the tragedies discussed. Although it is against Bradley that the accusation of confusion of art and reality is most often levelled, in fact Bradley in his interpretation sees more clearly than Dover Wilson the difference between understanding a fiction and following a train of events. Dover Wilson's method does not allow sufficiently for the dramatist's power to suggest the end in the beginning, to create a unified vision of the whole, to involve the audience in a dramatic suspense which does not rely on the outcome of events. Bradley in trying to evaluate the dramatic experience was using all the means possible and, surely, one of the most useful and most accessible of those means is to understand the part in terms of the

[11] J. D. Wilson, *What Happens in 'Hamlet'* (Cambridge, 1935), p. 94.

whole. Dover Wilson's analysis of *Hamlet* is interesting reading for itself, like a newspaper account of a criminal intrigue, but it does not even attempt to explain the artistic effect of the play; the question of *Hamlet*'s powerful hold on any audience is never raised. Wilson's objection to Bradley's method looks like another facet of the general objection that Bradley's criticisms disregarded the stage; but on examination it seems that Bradley's criticism of the play is truer to the total effect of the drama even if less accurate in terms of details than Wilson's account.

Bernard Spivack takes the criticism that Bradley disregards the theatre even further and says that Bradley's criticism penetrates the play and leaves the problem where he found it:

> After demonstrating how impossible it is to accept Iago's motives literally, he breaks out into the emptiness on the other side of the play and builds his own interpretation in the void. His criticism weaves for Iago a psychological wardrobe out of invisible thread and then says: Behold now, how suitably he is clothed. But stare as much as we can and with the greatest good will in the world, we still look on the naked problem.[12]

Spivack is making no reference to Bradley the man locked in his isolated study, but stripped of such biographical irrelevance, what he is saying amounts to very much the same thing; that Bradley's criticism takes insufficient notice of the play as drama. Because it is so stripped it has more critical weight; and is not easily answerable within the confines of this book. All that can be done here is to suggest that Spivack's method is no more infallible than Bradley's. Bradley according to Spivack weaves Iago's motives out of 'invisible thread', but not even Bradley could weave them out of nothing. According to his own lights and however distorted by the prejudices of his period and background Bradley's interpretation of the play is based on the play itself. Spivack's interpretation, enlightening as it is, is based on a lengthy study of pre-Shakespearian drama. In a book of over four hundred and fifty pages, over three hundred are devoted to

[12] B. Spivack, *Shakespeare and the Allegory of Evil* (London and New York, 1958), p. 246.

material quite other than the play itself. To an impartial observer it might seem that Spivack's criticism is more applicable to himself than to Bradley. Of the two readings Bradley's must surely be more accessible in the theatre, truer to the dramatic experience than Spivack's, although the latter is possibly more illuminating as history of the drama.

In the case of each of these objections it has been seen that it is at least possible to consider Bradley's interpretation as true to the play; the fact remains that critics do not consider it so and M. R. Ridley's comment is perhaps relevant here: 'Though Bradley himself never forgot that Shakespeare was writing for a theatre, and his own theatre, it is dangerously easy for the reader of Bradley to forget this.'[13] Another of Bradley's disciples made the same point. In his lecture, 'The Elizabethan Shakespeare', Dover Wilson wrote of A. C. Bradley that he is:

> one of the greatest of Shakespeare's critics, yet at the same time apt to be misleading to readers who follow his penetrating curiosity into the very viscera of a tragedy and overlook his constant warning that these matters are often irrelevant as far as the theatre is concerned.[14]

R. M. Smith writing of H. Granville-Barker sets him off against Bradley as a critic of whom he writes: 'Bradley may be said to have written the standard philosophical interpretation and character analysis from the point of view of the scholar examining minutely the tragedies within the four walls of the library.'[15] The confusion of which Ridley speaks is here evident: Smith speaks of Bradley writing from the 'point of view of the scholar' which of course Bradley was, but as appears from the rest of his comment Smith infers from this that Bradley is only concerned with Shakespeare as a source for study. Bradley was in fact attempting something quite different; as his Introduction indicates, he was seeking to refine the reader or audience's reaction

[13] M. R. Ridley, *Shakespeare's Plays: A Commentary* (London, 1937), p. 7.

[14] J. D. Wilson, 'The Elizabethan Shakespeare', *B.A.* (1929), p. 7. This warning was given in Bradley's lifetime while he was still a Fellow of the British Academy and entitled, even if unable, to attend.

[15] R. M. Smith, 'Granville-Barker's Shakespeare Criticism', in *S.A.B.*, xxiv (1949), pp. 291–3, at p. 291.

to Shakespearian tragedy by means of analytical criticism. Or alternatively he was communicating his own reaction to Shakespearian tragedy, which had indeed been 'enriched by the products of analysis', and he was doing this by means of a process as precise and scholarly as that of any scientific treatise. Any aesthetic criticism must seek to analyse and explain the aesthetic experience; this does not mean that the writer considers the work of art solely as an object of intellectual searching.

If Bradley's experience of Shakespearian tragedy consisted in his own imaginative recreation of the play this in many ways was at his time a good thing. Ribner, for example, complains of Bradley:

> The theatrical tradition in which Shakespeare worked was different from the nineteenth-century naturalist theatre which has so profoundly affected the drama of our own time. A weakness of Bradley's work, great and perceptive as it undoubtedly was, was that he read Shakespeare's tragedies in terms of such a naturalist stage.[16]

Edward Gordon Craig, Harley Granville-Barker, The English Stage Society, and William Poel were only just emerging when *Shakespearean Tragedy* was produced. Bradley's letters illustrate how sympathetic he was to the evolution of a less naturalistic drama. In the same letter he praises Granville-Barker's performance in *Candida* at the Royal Court and disparages Beerbohm Tree's *Tempest*.[17] His support of Gilbert Murray's translations from the Greek further illustrate that his conceptions of drama were not confined to late Victorian naturalism. At the same time his period offered him little opportunity to enjoy any other form of Shakespeare production. If Bradley did see productions of *King Lear* (as seems more than likely) one of them was probably that of the Lyceum with Lear played by Henry Irving whom G. B. Shaw described:

> His slowness, his growing habit of overdoing his part and slipping

[16] I. Ribner, *Patterns in Shakespearian Tragedy* (London, 1960), p. 3.

[17] Letter to G. Murray, Dec. 1904. The actual reference to Tree is coloured by a reference to an unknown personality. The passage reads 'Went with Sh. to Candida which I would have enjoyed (i.e. going with Sh.) even if to see Tree's Tempest', but the meaning is quite clear.

in an imaginative conception of his own *between* the lines (which made such a frightful wreck of Lear), all of which are part of his extraordinary insensibility to literature.[18]

The dramatic productions of the period were so unsatisfactory that one writer was of the opinion:

> For those who prized the authentic Shakespeare there was more of genuine revelation, more substantial and satisfactory mental pabulum in the subtleties of romantic criticism, and in particular of A. C. Bradley's studies of the tragedies, than in the frequently crude simplifications of romantic spectacular production.[19]

A critic can only see the performances his age offers; if he is dissatisfied with them he can only re-create for himself the drama as he would wish it presented. He cannot be blamed for the deficiencies in production either of his age or his imagination; neither is likely to be equal to the dramatic experience as Shakespeare intended it. On the other hand, the second alternative is likely to yield a view of Shakespearian tragedy not otherwise possible. No stage performance can be perfect, and it can carry in each instance only one interpretation of a given aspect of the play; the imaginative re-creation may lose in not taking into account the imperfections which a stage and actors impose on a play, but at least it can carry several interpretations at once. Moreover, the play may have been written to be seen on the stage but it was conceived in the imagination. As Kenneth Muir remarked, there is no standard to measure the accuracy of either audience or study reaction: 'What the groundlings or even the "judicious" thought in Shakespeare's day may be as far from a complete, a Shakespearean, understanding of *Macbeth* as the speculations of an Andrew Bradley.'[20] No doubt Bradley's name is chosen for one extreme as the 'groundlings' are for the other; what remains, however, is an observation on the permanent

[18] C. St. John, ed., *Ellen Terry and Bernard Shaw: a Correspondence* (1931), quotation from reprint of 3rd edn., 1949, p. 47.

[19] M. St. Clare Byrne, '50 years of Shakespeare Productions 1898–1948', in *S.S.* ii (1949), pp. 1–20, at p. 9.

[20] K. Muir (ed.), *Macbeth*, Arden edition (London/Cambridge, Mass., 1951), p. lxii.

mystery of a 'Shakespearian understanding' which must be attempted by any means possible.

Most twentieth-century critics including those who castigate Bradley for taking insufficient notice of the limitations of the stage are themselves scholars and students, more interested in the library or lecture room than the theatre. As Dover Wilson in the introduction to the New Cambridge edition of *Othello* shrewdly pointed out in discussing Leavis's criticism of Bradley: 'The burden of this article by an academic journalist like the present writer is that Bradley, academic bookman, was incapable of understanding Shakespeare's portrait of a man of action.'[21] They are, however, specialist students of literature; probably specialists in the study of Shakespeare and the drama of his period. The objection to Bradley is often that he was too little a specialist in these subjects. The feeling is that Bradley was too preoccupied with philosophy and brought to the plays a system of thought which in reality had nothing to do with them. This idea, like the idea that Bradley was totally unaware that the stage was the medium for drama, probably arose from the very nature of Bradley's criticism. Where other critics have confined their studies to the specific[22] and made only very general conclusions on particular points usually judicially placed at the end of the work, Bradley sought to account for the essential experience behind Shakespearian tragedy. Because Bradley thought, as he said in his Introduction, that the plays had much in common, he considered it more practical to consider these aspects first:

before coming to the first of the four tragedies, I propose to discuss some preliminary matters which concern them all. Though each is individual through and through, they have, in a sense, one and the same substance; for in all of them Shakespeare represents the tragic

[21] A. Walker and J. D. Wilson (eds.): *Othello*, New Cambridge edition (Cambridge, 1957), p. lii n.

[22] Cf. T. R. Henn, *The Harvest of Tragedy* (London, 1956), p. 282 n.: 'Apart from A. C. Bradley's dicta, I have only read a single attempt at formulation (of tragedy &c.)', citing M. Harris, *The Case for Tragedy* (1932). If this seems to exclude discussions like those of F. L. Lucas and U. Ellis-Fermor this is because these critics are concerned with the form and structure of tragedy rather than an evaluation of the aesthetic experience involved.

aspect of life, the tragic fact. They have, again, up to a certain point a common form or structure. This substance and this structure which would be found to distinguish them, for example, from Greek tragedies, may, to diminish repetition, be considered once for all; and in considering them we shall also be able to observe characteristic differences among the four plays.[23]

It seems unjust, however, to infer immediately from the fact that these come first that Bradley started from the generalization and made the particular fit in with the pattern.

Such inference has, however, been made. A. P. Rossiter wrote:

> Can he arrive at a conception of Shakespearian Tragedy? The easy way is 'a priori' not to arrive *at*, but to arrive *with* one ready-made; to start with previous notions derived from the Greek, from Aristotle (or from Bradley whom many still mistake for a pseudonym for Aristotle).[24]

True enough Rossiter does not here indict Bradley of this offence, though the mention of his name may indicate a connection. He continues, however, quoting G. B. Shaw:

> 'Pooh! Cambridge! If you had been educated at Oxford you would know that the definition of a play has been settled exactly and scientifically for two thousand six hundred and sixty years.' As I was not educated classically, I find that unacceptable.[24]

Bradley, of course, was educated at Oxford; where Rossiter was educated he does not say, but he was a lecturer at Cambridge. The fact is not altogether irrelevant. Cambridge, which, in the world of philosophy, bred Sidgwick and then Bertrand Russell, was always strongly suspicious of Oxford which fathered Hegelian Idealism. Bradley was conspicuously an Oxford man with its typical philosophical bent; his brother was the foremost Idealist philosopher, he himself published an article on Aristotle, and proclaimed his affiliations in the title of one of his publications. When as time went by a school of criticism emerged at Cambridge it was inevitable that they should be equally suspicious of the criticism which Oxford philosophy had fostered. It would oversimplify

[23] *S.T.*, p. 3.

[24] A. P. Rossiter, *Angel with Horns and other Shakespeare Lectures* (London, 1961), p. 253.

to say that F. R. Leavis's objections to Bradley for example were explicable merely in terms of his university but something of the opposition seems to have been transposed into the critical field. Oxford stood for the ancient precepts and in the twentieth century Cambridge stood for modern scientific inquiry. Rossiter does not say so but there is evident in his remark a vague feeling that as Bradley came from Aristotelian Oxford his ideas must have been lifted wholesale from Aristotle.

Rossiter is not alone in this idea that Bradley can be summed up in terms of his philosophic influences: an American scholar wrote: 'In contrast to Bradley's Hegelian approach, Kittredge united the empiricism of a scientist with the sympathetic insight of a poet.'[25] What is interesting here is not only the summary of Bradley's approach with one adjective but the description of Kittredge which says little which is not equally true of Bradley. The feeling here is that Bradley was a Hegelian (an indisputable fact) and that he could not therefore have been either of the other two things.

Hegel and Aristotle; to these two have been attributed the greater part of Bradley's criticism and to his reliance on them the worst of his errors. The debt to Hegel has already been examined and indeed it was a considerable debt; so was the debt to Aristotle—but as was seen in Chapter II this was not a simple debt to the precepts of the *Poetics* but due to the profound influence of Aristotle on Bradley's education. The way in which the influence of these two philosophers worked on Bradley is apparent from any intelligent reading of *Shakespearean Tragedy*. There are very few overt references either to Hegel or to Aristotle. The only acknowledgement of an outright debt to Hegel comes in the description of a comparison of the Witch scenes in *Macbeth* with the first book of the *Iliad*.[26] He twice mentions Aristotle, once to disagree with him. He deliberately avoids discussing the idea of 'conflict' in tragedy in Hegelian terms:

The frequent use of this idea in discussions on tragedy is ultimately

[25] K. Myrick, 'Kittredge on Hamlet', in *Shakespeare 400: Essays by American Scholars*, ed. J. G. MacManaway (Detroit, 1964), pp. 219–34.

[26] *S.T.*, p. 348.

due, I suppose, to the influence of Hegel's theory on the subject, certainly the most important theory since Aristotle's. But Hegel's view of the tragic conflict is not only unfamiliar to English readers and difficult to expound shortly, but it had its origin in reflections on Greek tragedy, and as Hegel was well aware, applies only imperfectly to the works of Shakespeare. I shall, therefore, confine myself to the idea of conflict in its more general form.[27]

Bradley begins his discussion of the substance of Shakespearean tragedy by avowing his intention of avoiding critical help.

> In approaching our subject it will be best, without attempting to shorten the path by referring to famous theories of the drama, to start directly from the facts, and collect from them gradually an idea of Shakespearean Tragedy.[28]

And this is in effect what he does. That the resulting picture bears strong resemblance to the pictures of tragedy painted by earlier theories is hardly surprising; the fact of tragedy would, ideally, account for some overlapping in ideas, and further, Bradley, as an academic, was well aware of alternative theories especially those of Hegel and Aristotle.

Where critics have misunderstood Bradley's debt to these philosophers of tragedy they have done so because they do not recognise how far Bradley had rethought each idea in terms of his own composite theory. This is most clearly seen in critics' discussions of the 'tragic flaw', which one critic discusses as 'the Aristotle–Bradley doctrine of the "tragic flaw" '.[29] This sentence illustrates the failure of some critics to recognize the difference between Aristotle's theory and Bradley's; a failure which has led other critics to find inconsistencies in Bradley which do not exist. E. E. Stoll, for example, wrote of Bradley's statement of tragic heroes 'we do not judge': 'A fine and proper but rather remarkable thing for Mr. Bradley to say, for in all the heroes he finds a flaw and an imperfection even in Cordelia.'[30] The opposition of the two statements which Stoll sets up is in fact not

[27] *S.T.*, p. 16. [28] Ibid., p. 7.

[29] G. M. Matthews, 'Othello and the Dignity of Man', in *Shakespeare in a Changing World*, ed. A. Kettle (London, 1964), pp. 123–45, at p. 137.

[30] E. E. Stoll, *Shakespeare and other Masters* (Cambridge, Mass., 1940), p. 71.

totally relevant to Bradley's criticism; it stems from Stoll's acceptance of what is now an old-fashioned view of Aristotle's conception of *hamartia*. There is anyway nothing in Bradley's theory to suggest that Aristotle's conception of *hamartia* is in any way relevant to Shakespeare; and if there is some reliance on Aristotle's conception Bradley's use of the word 'flaw' would come much closer to the accepted modern 'error of judgement' rather than to the old-fashioned 'moral weakness' to which Stoll seems to refer. It is worthwhile perhaps to summarize Bradley on this point and then to examine it again in the light of Stoll's statement. The third section of the Lecture 'Of the Substance of Shakespearean Tragedy' is devoted wholly to the tragic character, its exceptional qualities and the 'tragic trait' which leads to the catastrophe. In the heroes Bradley says:

> We observe a marked one-sidedness; a predisposition in some particular direction; a total incapacity, in certain circumstances, of resisting the force which draws in this direction; a fatal incapacity in certain circumstances of resisting the force which draws in this direction; a fatal tendency to identify the whole being with one interest, object, passion or habit of mind. This it would seem, is, for Shakespeare, the fundamental tragic trait.
>
> In the circumstances where we see the hero placed, his tragic trait, which is also his greatness, is fatal to him. To meet these circumstances something is required which a smaller man might have given, but which the hero cannot give. He errs, by action or omission; and his error, joining with other causes, brings on his ruin.[31]

The remark 'we do not judge' comes from a later section in the same chapter: 'When we are immersed in tragedy we feel towards dispositions, actions, and persons such feelings as attraction and repulsion, pity, wonder, fear, horror, perhaps hatred; but we do not *judge*.'[32] Bradley is here talking about something totally different from the theoretical makings of a tragic hero; he is analysing the effect of tragedy on the audience. Whether his analysis is correct or not is not at issue here, but this statement can only be seen in contradiction to the conception of the hero's 'flaw' if like Stoll we consider that such a flaw must be a moral

[31] *S.T.*, pp. 20, 21. [32] Ibid., pp. 32–3.

weakness. If, for example, *Othello* is a tragedy where a noble Moor falls to his doom because of jealousy then our emotions at the catastrophe must be affected by some kind of moral judgement, for, in essence, that is what the tragedy will have been about; if, on the other hand, the play is seen in Bradley's terms as depicting a noble character whose very nobility in the circumstances in which he was placed led him to the error of judgement which caused his downfall then moral judgement will no more affect our emotions at the catastrophe than they do in the case of domestic tragedy caused by an unavoidable accident. Stoll, it seems, although he does not say so, is accepting an 'Aristotle–Bradley doctrine' of the 'tragic flaw' which is certainly not true to Bradley and probably not true to Aristotle either.

If Stoll illustrates a typical misunderstanding of Bradley on this issue then Ribner demonstrates a not unusual failure to read the text at all. He wrote:

> Bradley's particular use of *hamartia* led him to a static conception of Shakespearian Tragedy. He measured Shakespeare's plays against a single dramatic formula which he could find exemplified only in *Hamlet*, *Othello*, *Lear* and *Macbeth*. But Shakespearian Tragedy is not a static phenomenon. To exclude such plays as *Romeo and Juliet*, and *Titus Andronicus* . . . or such plays as *Richard III* or *Julius Caesar* . . . is an evasion of the issue.[33]

In fact Bradley only excludes these plays for the reason which he gives; the reasons may not seem adequate to Ribner but he cannot fairly substitute his own without making some reference to his author's idea on a subject where his view must be more relevant than any one else's. Bradley wrote in the Introduction to *Shakespearean Tragedy*:

> Much that is said on our main preliminary subjects will naturally hold good, within certain limits, of other dramas of Shakespeare besides *Hamlet*, *Othello*, *King Lear* and *Macbeth*. But it will often apply to these other works only in part, and to some of them more fully than to others. *Romeo and Juliet*, for instance, is a pure tragedy, but it is an early work, and in some respects an immature one. *Richard III* and *Richard II*, *Julius Caesar*, *Antony and Cleopatra*, and *Corialanus* are

[33] I. Ribner, *Patterns in Shakespearian Tragedy* (London, 1960), p. 11.

tragic histories or historical tragedies, in which Shakespeare acknowledged in practice a certain obligation to follow his authority, even when that authority offered him an undramatic material. . . . There remain *Titus Andronicus* and *Timon of Athens*. The former I shall leave out of account because, even if Shakespeare wrote the whole of it, he did so before he had either a style of his own or any characteristic tragic conception. *Timon* stands on a different footing. Parts of it are unquestionably Shakespeare's . . . but much of the writing is evidently not his, and as it seems probable that the conception and construction of the whole tragedy should also be attributed to some other writer, I shall omit this work too from our preliminary discussions.[34]

Ribner might well have quarrelled with Bradley's reasons for omitting all but four tragedies, but he does not do this nor does he take account of the fact that many critics of Shakespearian tragedy have confined their attention to these four plays.[35] Not only does Ribner ignore the reason why Bradley has not included these plays in his account, but he omits an extension of his basic idea of the hero's 'tragic trait' to include some of the tragedies which Ribner says he wilfully ignores:

the fatal imperfection or error, which is never absent, is of different kinds and degrees. At one extreme stands the excess and precipitancy of Romeo, which scarcely, if at all, diminish our regard for him; at the other the murderous ambition of Richard III. In most cases the tragic error involves no conscious breach of right; in some (e.g. that of Brutus or Othello) it is accompanied by a full conviction of right.[36]

What Ribner's criticism amounts to is very similar to what A. P. Rossiter wrote in general terms; he is levelling against Bradley the accusation that he did not 'arrive at a conception of Shakespearian Tragedy' but followed 'the easy way . . . "a priori": not to arrive *at*, but to arrive *with* one ready-made'.[37] His idea that Bradley's conception of *hamartia* (of which he speaks as though it were the whole of Bradley's theory of tragedy) is

[34] *S.T.*, pp. 3–4.

[35] e.g. L. B. Campbell, *Shakespeare's Tragic Heroes* (1930); C. J. Sisson, *Shakespeare's Tragic Justice* (1962); E. E. Stoll, *Art and Artifice in Shakespeare* (1933).

[36] *S.T.*, p. 22.

[37] A. P. Rossiter, *Angel with Horns* (London, 1961), p. 253.

'a static conception' is not easy to understand, but the complaint of the second half of the comment about the exclusion of certain plays leads the reader to think that Ribner was accusing Bradley of having an idea of Shakespearian tragedy applicable only to his chosen plays. Firstly, of course, Bradley did write fully of *Antony and Cleopatra* and *Corialanus* in very much the same terms as he wrote *Shakespearean Tragedy*; secondly Ribner tries to have it both ways. If Bradley's criticism of *hamartia* amounts to 'measuring Shakespeare's plays against a single dramatic formula' then there is no reason why he could not so measure all of Shakespeare's plays. Surely the very fact that Bradley recognizes that his theory in its entirety is only applicable to the height of Shakespeare's tragic achievement indicates that Bradley is deducing the formula from the text and not subduing the text to the formula.

C. J. Sisson in his book *Shakespeare's Tragic Justice* offers some explanation as to why criticism has come to talk of 'Bradley's tragic flaw', and he also attempts to see Bradley's conception of tragic error in terms of his whole theory of tragedy:

> We have been long familiar with A. C. Bradley's more complex version of the theory of 'hamartia' which made of it a key . . . to disclose the hidden sources of reconciliation to tragic conclusions in the heart of the reader of Shakespeare's tragedies. As Bradley applied the theory, it gained persuasiveness from its presentation in his classical book upon *Shakespearean Tragedy*, from the mind and the imagination of a subtle and philosophic critic who from every quarter illuminated the dramatic poems upon which he was engaged. He was careful not to press too closely his survey of the tragedies in the direction of syllogisms with a constant major premise. Yet that premise remains dominant in the concept of the tragedy of character with an operative 'tragic flaw' or 'fatal flaw' to use the terms in general usage, though they are a perversion of the Greek word and concept of 'hamartia'. For my part, I have never been able to find comfort in this concept, even if I had been able to assent to it . . . Aristotle's argument, indeed, a piece of special pleading, countered Plato's attack upon poetry on ethical grounds with an appeal to a higher court of aesthetic principles, as Bradley well knew.
>
> But even if we could accept a directly ethical basis for tragedy we should be hard put to it when we apply the principle of the 'tragic

flaw' to Shakespeare's tragedies. This indeed is coming into increasingly general agreement of late . . . Aristotle's *Poetics* themselves, along with Bradley, have been subjected to a searching criticism which repels all destructive moral analysis of tragic heroism in Greek and Shakespearian tragedy alike.[38]

This embodies a much more serious criticism of Bradley's whole theory of tragedy than any expressed dissatisfaction at the particular theory of *hamartia*. Sisson, like the critics previously discussed, implies that Bradley brought his ready-made system of tragedy to bear on Shakespeare; 'as Bradley applied the theory' implies that the inquiry into the nature of tragedy was merely for Bradley a case of applying a set of given rules, rules given in fact, according to Sisson, by Aristotle. Like Stoll, moreover, he assumes that Bradley makes the once common but no longer critically accepted interpretation of the term *hamartia*. Though Sisson does not say so this may well stem from an idea that Bradley read Aristotle in S. H. Butcher's translation; in fact he probably read Aristotle in the original Greek and was in any event capable of making his own interpretation of the individual terms; and it appears from 'The Substance of Shakespearean Tragedy' that Bradley's definition of the 'tragic flaw' bears no resemblance to any use of the term to denote moral weakness. Sisson does not take this into account largely because he assumes as it appears from his statement that Bradley's ideas are derived directly from Aristotle. This leads Sisson into the idea that Bradley's theory of tragedy is ethical whereas in fact, Bradley never considers the possibility of a moralistic interpretation. He twice explicitly discusses the idea of the essential and excessive 'goodness' of the hero.

Shakespeare never drew monstrosities of virtue; some of his heroes are far from being 'good'.

The tragic hero with Shakespeare, then, need not be 'good', though generally he is 'good' and therefore at once wins sympathy in his error. But it is necessary that he should have so much of greatness that

[38] C. J. Sisson, *Shakespeare's Tragic Justice*, lectures delivered at the Shakespeare Institute, Stratford-on-Avon, 1955 (London, n.d. [1962]), pp. 7–8.

in his error and fall we may be vividly conscious of the possibilities of human nature.[39]

If the hero is 'good' then, as the above quotation shows, Bradley thought that this was not so that the tragedy could bear an ethical meaning but so that the audience should feel 'sympathy' for him.

Sisson, convinced of the truth of his reading of Bradley in terms of Aristotle's *Poetics*, reads the rest of Bradley's criticism in these terms. As he is one of those critics who find mystical significance in, for example, *King Lear*, he understandably finds Bradley's more balanced view of the tragedy less than satisfactory. Sisson writes of Bradley's interpretation of *King Lear*:

> There is no subject upon which Bradley is more guarded, and more inconclusive, than the question of poetical justice. Yet through a maze of words it would seem that his conception of dramatic principles, as applied to *King Lear*, is offended by the gross disproportion between cause and effect in the catastrophe of this tragedy. He agrees that we may not measure the consequences of flaws in character in precise proportion to their results, and the logic of tragedy is not the logic of justice. Yet for him, here in *King Lear*, the vast sway of moral equilibrium in the universe is wanting and there is consequently aesthetic dissatisfaction.[40]

There is nothing in this summary which would not find a correspondence in Bradley; but the summary does not take into account the context of the remarks. Bradley was analysing the reasons for general dissatisfaction with the play when he wrote as above. Bradley was not here writing of his own personal reaction to the tragedy but rather attempting to understand the general view. That Sisson misunderstood this led him later on in the same chapter to say:

> We have long ago learned to recognise in its action and development a theme which might justify the title 'The Redemption of King Lear' in place of 'The Tragedy of King Lear' pointing to a happy ending of deeper truth than Tate's or that desired by Bradley.[41]

[39] *S.T.*, pp. 20 and 22. [40] C. J. Sisson, op. cit., p. 78.
[41] Ibid., p. 88.

Sisson gives no indication of being aware of the source for the new title of *King Lear* and this is surely because he quite ignored the side of Bradley's argument on the subject of *King Lear* which produced:

> Should we not be at least as near the truth [as we were in talking of the 'malicious' 'pessimistic' justice of the play] if we called this poem *The Redemption of King Lear* and declared that the business of 'the gods' with him was neither to torment him, nor to teach him a 'noble anger' but to lead him to attain through apparently hopeless failure the very end and aim of life? One can believe that Shakespeare had been tempted at times to feel misanthropy and despair, but it is quite impossible that he can have been mastered by such feelings at the time when he produced this conception.[42]

Sisson seems to be here committing the very fault which by implication he imputes to Bradley; he starts with his theory of what Bradley said and then finds fault with Bradley along the lines of that theory; much as he said Bradley started with a theory and found fault with Shakespeare. It may seem presumptuous for anyone to suggest why Sisson should write as he does, but the possible reasons for it are relevant here. Sisson writing on 'tragic justice' was probably conscious of the danger of falling into a moralistic definition of justice in tragedy; it was therefore probably a considerable help to him to isolate the moralistic view and set his own view against it. As the numerous references to Bradley show, Sisson was very aware of *Shakespearean Tragedy* and probably felt strongly the contrast between his almost otherworldly concept of tragedy and Bradley's sane and balanced view.

As I hope has been apparent Sisson's view of Bradley's *Shakespearean Tragedy* is a very partial one; indicative more of what Sisson thought Bradley said than what he said in fact. This is not uncommon and is perhaps easily explained. Critics of the 1950s are aware of Bradley and remember him from their youthful reading of *Shakespearean Tragedy* or even perhaps only from a teacher's summary; when in a critical work they turn again to Bradley it is to a Bradley coloured by a vaguely remembered

[42] *S.T.*, p. 285.

reading further distorted by layers of critical opinion. They look, therefore, for a Bradley they have long assumed to exist and find texts to support their assumption. Sisson's Bradley was obviously a moralist, repeating in more persuasive forms the ancient theories of Aristotle; a philosopher looking to the text only for confirmation of his philosophy rather than a literary critic. And it is this Bradley of whom Sisson writes rather than the Bradley evident in *Shakespearean Tragedy*.

Sisson cites P. Alexander as evidence of the modern rejection of both Bradley and Aristotle but in fact Alexander is much more sympathetic to Bradley's standpoint than Sisson implies. Alexander opens his book *Hamlet: Father and Son* by avowing, 'I still think Bradley's method genuinely critical and illuminating';[43] and he then considers Bradley's position at some length and concludes by examining his discussion of *hamartia*. This discussion is really not conducted in terms of Bradley's criticism but as a preliminary explanation necessary to Alexander's book; Alexander, however, thought fit to discuss *hamartia* by considering Bradley's theory for reasons which he states: 'Every modern critic who talks of the tragic flaw is, if he has considered the matter seriously, a student of Bradley.'[43] He then considers some of the objections to the theory and asks, 'Has Bradley given the doctrine of "hamartia" some turn that relieves it of the objections . . . urged against it? . . . how then does he overcome the difficulty about the lack of correspondence between the flaw and the catastrophe?'[43] Alexander explains this by referring to Bradley's reliance on Hegel:

> Bradley's elaboration of the Hegelian thesis has had a strong attraction for scholars and men of letters. Yet it shows no respect for the virtues of men; the best are doomed because not wholly perfect.
>
> Bradley in his zeal to reconcile us to the facts of tragedy offers us a conclusion to which only a profound pessimism could possibly reconcile us.

That Bradley had no more intention than Hegel of maintaining a pessimistic doctrine is clear from his work as a whole; mingling with

[43] P. Alexander, *Hamlet: Father and Son* (Oxford, 1955) (first delivered as the Lord Northcliffe Lectures at University College London in 1953), pp. 48–55.

his main thesis are currents of thought from a different source; many of his most characteristic utterances flatly contradict the premises on which his argument rests.[44]

Alexander, it seems here, overestimates the place that the concept of a 'tragic flaw' had in Bradley's theory of tragedy. It is significant that nowhere in his theory of tragedy does Bradley use the term *hamartia* and he only once uses the word 'flaw'. What Bradley was concerned with was the fact and results of the tragic conflict, not the mechanics of its coming about. Alexander seems to realize this when he continues:

> he found more things in Shakespeare than were allowed for in Hegel's philosophy. Bradley, although he is the most thorough exponent of the doctrine of 'hamartia', indeed just because he makes so determined an effort to provide for it a philosophical and psychological basis, has to keep looking beyond it to interpret the tragedies. He is divided between Hegel and Shakespeare.[44]

Finally he concludes that Bradley was not really a supporter of the 'tragic flaw' concept at all.

Alexander it seems is making a public criticism of his impression of Bradley. It seems as though he started out with the generally accepted view of Bradley as a critic convinced of the moral failure of Shakespeare's heroes and then as he examined the view was gradually convinced of how little relation this idea had to what Bradley in fact said. It is true, as Sisson said, that Alexander rejects the concept of *hamartia*, but it is not true that he rejects Bradley and Aristotle on that account. He was seeking to correct the view that Bradley's critical theory depended on acceptance of a 'tragic flaw' in the hero; this task is more difficult than he realized. There is more wilful ignorance of the actual ideas of Bradley than Alexander accounted for; Sisson even having read Alexander's account prefers to maintain a view of Bradley as moral critic finding fault with all the heroes.

Alexander is not alone in rejecting the idea that Bradley's criticism depends on the idea of *hamartia*. Morris Weitz wrote:

> Bradley . . . has been mistaken for an exponent of hamartia, even

[44] Ibid.

by himself! For, in spite of his ostensible emphasis on the tragic flaw, Bradley also turns the flaw into virtue by making it the source of the hero's greatness.[45]

Weitz offers no evidence to support his theory that Bradley considered himself an exponent of *hamartia*; and makes no reference to the fact that if this is so there is very little stress on this aspect of his theory of tragedy and much more emphasis on other aspects, for example, the final reconciliation. Despite this weakness, however, Weitz's remark is interesting because he alone of the critics discussed makes reference to the fact that for Bradley the flaw and the greatness were one and the same thing. Weitz does not continue to say what surely should be said that the isolation of the flaw and its resulting tragic consequences was inherent not only in the hero's greatness but in the circumstances which surrounded him. This omission of Weitz's (it must be remembered that his book *Hamlet and the Philosophy of Criticism* contains a detailed analysis of Bradley's criticism) illustrates once more the misunderstanding of Bradley which arises because insufficient attention is paid to what he said. Is it possible that this arises because a critic feels that, as he has read the work once and knows the critical feeling on the subject, he is already well acquainted with the substance of Bradley's work?

In her book *Shakespeare's Tragic Heroes*, Miss L. B. Campbell came to quite a different conclusion concerning Bradley's criticisms of Shakespearian tragedy. She wrote there:

Professor Bradley began his analysis of Shakespeare's conception of tragedy by a discussion that implicitly accepted Aristotle's *Poetics* as the base for differentiation. He questioned the medieaeval idea of tragedy . . . as inadequate to explain Shakespeare in full and he specifically affirmed that 'the tragic world is a world of action and action is the translation of thought into reality'. He concluded 'The tragic suffering and death arises from collision not with fate or blank power but with a moral power, a power akin to all that we admire and revere in the characters themselves'. It is this conception of tragedy as action

[45] M. Weitz, *Hamlet and the Philosophy of Criticism* (London, 1965), p. 295.

and of the plot of tragedy as a statement of metaphysical belief that has so much interested later critics.[46]

Having made this reference to Bradley in the Preface she continues her study proper without referring to him again.

Seventeen years later she no longer saw him as a critic who held such straightforward views on the constituents of tragedy and, herself interested in the psychology of the characters, turned her attention to Bradley's views on this subject. She now thinks Bradley sees character as the centre of the action:

he by definition makes a tragic hero set the tragic circle in motion while he is morally responsible and then proves that he must have been morally responsible when he set the forces of destruction at work or else he could not have been a tragic hero.[47]

This is a summary of the second section of the lecture 'The Substance of Shakespearean Tragedy'. Its very tone, however, indicates that it is not an impartial summary, as will be seen by a comparison of Miss Campbell's statement with Bradley's words:

The calamities of tragedy do not simply happen, nor are they sent; they proceed mainly from actions, and those the actions of men.

The 'story' or 'action' of a Shakespearean tragedy does not consist, of course, solely of human actions or deeds; but the deeds are the predominant factor. And these deeds are, for the most part, actions in the full sense of the word . . . acts or omissions thoroughly expressive of the doer,—characteristic deeds. The centre of the tragedy, therefore, may be said with equal truth to lie in action issuing from character or in character, issuing in action.

The dictum that, with Shakespeare, 'character is destiny' is no doubt an exaggeration, and one that may mislead (for many of his tragic personages, if they had not met with quite peculiar circumstances, would have escaped a tragic end, and might even have lived fairly untroubled lives); but it is the exaggeration of a vital truth.

Bradley concludes his argument on this topic by considering

[46] L. B. Campbell, *Shakespeare's Tragic Heroes: Slaves of Passion* (Cambridge, 1930), quotation from 1961 paperback edition, p. v.

[47] L. B. Campbell, 'Bradley revisited: Forty Years After', in *S.Ph.*, xliv (1947), pp. 174–94, at p. 178.

three factors which would appear to contradict the above statements; mental aberrations, the introduction of the supernatural, and the intervention of accident and chance. Of the first he says:

> these abnormal conditions are never introduced as the origin of deeds of any dramatic moment. Lady Macbeth's sleepwalking has no influence whatever on the events that follow it. Macbeth did not murder Duncan because he saw a dagger in the air: he saw the dagger because he was about to murder Duncan.

Of the second which he considers more seriously he says:

> It forms no more than an element, however important, in the problem with which the hero has to deal, and we are never allowed to feel that it has removed his capacity or responsibility for dealing with this problem. So far indeed are we from feeling this, that many readers run to the opposite extreme, and openly or privately regard the supernatural as having nothing to do with the real interest of the play.

Of the third factor he says:

> this operation of accident is a fact, and a prominent fact of human life. To exclude it *wholly* from tragedy, therefore, would be, we may say, to fail in truth. And, besides, it is not merely a fact. That men may start a course of events but can neither calculate nor control it, is a *tragic* fact . . . On the other hand, any *large* admission of chance into the tragic sequence would certainly weaken, and might destroy, the sense of causal connection of character, deed, and catastrophe. And Shakespeare really uses it very sparingly.[48]

It seemed worth while to quote at length from Bradley's argument on this subject to emphasize the most obvious difference between what Bradley says and what Miss Campbell claims he says. This is apparent in the omission from Bradley's discussion of the words which are basic to Miss Campbell's argument: 'morally responsible'. What Bradley is saying is that the action in a tragedy issues from character and not character distorted by insanity, or subject to supernatural powers or the workings of chance. What is, furthermore, interesting, is that Miss Campbell could have made her point about the circular nature of Bradley's argument without introducing the question of moral responsi-

[48] *S.T.*, pp. 11–15.

bility at all. More than this, she complains on the same page that 'Bradley ignores the Elizabethan acceptance of these abnormal states of mind as resulting from the unchecked domination of passion over reason and hence confuses cause and effect',[49] which appears like a complaint that Bradley overlooks the hero's moral responsibility for his actions. Despite the fact that Miss Campbell, following, no doubt, the dictates of then accepted ideas about what Bradley stood for, complains of his misunderstanding the 'moral responsibility' of Shakespearean heroes, she is herself much more of an exponent of the moralist's view of tragedy, which Sisson for example, sought to lay at Bradley's door. Her concluding remarks amply illustrate this:

> Bradley by discussing the three 'additional factors' in tragedy—abnormal conditions of mind, the supernatural, and accidents—only to prove that they were not really factors at all because none of them served to remove the moral responsibility of the characters for their actions was proving something irrelevant. Lady Macbeth's sleep-walking was not the source of any tragic act. True but it is an important part of the tragedy because it is part of her punishment.[50]

Miss Campbell does not claim that Bradley falls into his moralistic errors because of his dependence on Aristotle or Hegel; in fact she offers no reason for what she considers to be his wildly irrelevant reading of Shakespeare apart from his general ineptitude. Her criticism of Shakespeare illustrates a further relation of the twentieth-century critic to Bradley; a need to use his criticism as a whetstone so implicitly accepted that there is no explanation of or interest in the reasons why Bradley went wrong. Miss Campbell probably assumed that the burden of Bradley's argument was to prove the 'moral responsibility' of the hero because she associates him as a critic with those of her elders who regarded 'the dicta of Bradley as having been brought down to the people from Sinai'.[51] The argument about Bradley's Victorianism is not here explicitly discussed but it seems likely that the reason why Miss Campbell, contrary to all the evidence (and her discussion reveals that she in fact had read the relevant

[49] Cf. n. 46 above.
[50] L. B. Campbell, op. cit., p. 193.
[51] Ibid., p. 174.

passages with close attention) thought that Bradley's heroes were morally responsible was because in the recesses of her mind she associated with him her august superiors and their old-fashioned notions of literature, life, and morality.

How far removed Miss Campbell is from understanding Bradley in terms of his actual period and philosophical background is shown by the praise of a part of Bradley's argument which seems to depend very heavily on late Victorian Idealist philosophy:

> the ghost of the late King of Denmark,—majestic, solemn, impersonal—seems to him not only a spirit intent upon serving its own purposes, but also 'the messenger of divine justice set upon the expiation of offences which it appeared impossible for man to discover and avenge, a reminder or a symbol of the connexion of the limited world of ordinary experience with the vaster life of which it is but a partial appearance'. Bradley's intuition here was reaching out toward an Elizabethan commonplace.[52]

If Bradley was reaching out to a conception of Elizabethan drama which seemed to Miss Campbell to resemble common Elizabethan conceptions it was not the work of intuition which brought him to this conclusion but the very Victorian philosophical background of which she takes no account.

The criticisms of Bradley discussed in this chapter have come from varied sources and periods and illustrated widely different aspects of Bradley's criticism and the attitudes of his critics; they all, however, have one thing in common, they do not allow that Bradley reacted to the plays as drama. They all, to a certain extent, rely upon the same conception of Bradley as Kenneth Muir's statement quoted at the beginning of the chapter and Sir Ifor Evans's expressed doubt as to whether Bradley ever visited the theatre. Whatever else is thought about Bradley's criticism in these terms it cannot be allowed to be relevant to the drama. Of the critics discussed in this chapter only Sisson has applied what he said about Bradley's general theory to his criticism of the individual plays; and the very distortion in this one application seems only to emphasize the point that the critics of Bradley's general theory, however generous and sympathetic in their

[52] L. B. Campbell, op. cit., p. 188.

criticism, fail to take into account that his aim was 'dramatic appreciation' of the plays and not merely the formulation of a general theory of tragedy.

In his Preface Bradley suggests that readers 'who may prefer to enter at once on the discussion of the several plays'[53] omit the two general chapters; he nowhere makes the suggestion that readers interested in theory should omit the discussion of the individual plays. But the inclusion of the chapter on the 'Substance of Shakespearean Tragedy' has served to strengthen the idea of an academic criticism remote from the theatrical experience. In 1925 Granville-Barker wrote: 'When Dr. Bradley's masterly *Shakespearean Tragedy* was given us—this was a bright gleam, though it surprised people a little to find an Oxford Professor for whom not only was poetry poetry, but plays were plays.'[54] And as we have seen the surprise for some critics was such that they could not believe it and held to their previous convictions about late Victorian critics. Harold Jenkins offers some explanation of this. He begins by citing the favourite objection: 'Did not Bradley argue the whereabouts of Hamlet at the time of his father's death?' and continues:

> This is an unworthy route by which to arrive at Bradley (*Shakespearean Tragedy* 1904). If the attitude I have spoken of [regarding fiction as history] is particularly associated with his name, it is surely because he is more read than his Victorian predecessors and because no-one can excel him in the careful summing up of evidence which bears on both character and story. But there is always a part of his mind which remembers that *Hamlet* is a drama shaping Shakespeare's imagination.

This leads Professor Jenkins to an interesting estimate of Bradley's position in criticism today:

> Bradley is the bridge which joins the nineteenth century with ours. The greatest of the character critics, he concentrates—how he concentrates—on Hamlet's delay, but he refines on the psychological analysis of his predecessors, attributing Hamlet's inactivity not to his native constitution but to an abnormal state of melancholy arising

[53] *S.T.*, p. vii.

[54] H. Granville-Barker, 'From *Henry V* to *Hamlet*', *B.A.* (1925), p. 26.

from shock. The importance he attaches to Hamlet's distress at his mother's marriage gives a new critical emphasis the effect of which will be seen in a period familiar with Freud. But while apparently absorbed in the analysis of Hamlet's character, Bradley shares the philosophical interests of the nineteenth-century Germans. He is careful to note that 'the psychological point of view is not equivalent to the tragic'. For him of course tragedy is not simply a literary genre; it is a way of interpreting the universe. For all his concern with the matter-of-fact details, the play of *Hamlet* suggests to him, especially but not only through the Ghost, how 'the limited world of ordinary experience' is but a part of some 'vaster life'; and though he does not much develop this, he perceives in the action of the play a meaning greater than itself.[55]

This quotation is interesting not only because it attempts rationally to understand Bradley's relation to the theories of his predecessors and successors but also because in this rational light it acknowledges the source for Bradley's comments on the 'vaster life' beyond in a way of which Miss Campbell was not capable.

The reason for this must be seen partly in the fact that Professor Jenkins was writing an impartial history of *Hamlet* criticism and Miss Campbell a work of criticism to contradict Bradley; she was therefore standing so much nearer to the object. Professor Jenkins is also writing later. The vehemence has gone out of reaction; the classification is complete at last so that the work of objective criticism is no longer impaired.

Here, again, is evidence of the fact that the distorted Bradley found in so much critical writing is only there to fulfil a function which he (and indeed most other critics) could not fulfil in his proper person. Bradley is over-simplified so that he can assume the role of adversary. He is a bookish philosopher so that critics can explore the purely theatrical with greater boldness; he is a theorist rather than a reader so that study of detail can be more fervently carried out; he is a moralist so that the psychological critics can discuss his psychology. All of these labels are to a certain extent true; but none of them serve as a replacement for a reading of Bradley's criticisms.

[55] H. Jenkins, '*Hamlet* Then till Now', in *S.S.*, xviii (1965), pp. 34–45, at p. 40.

6

'BRADLEY THE CHARACTER-CHASER'

THE most famous objection to the Victorian Bradley is that he misread Shakespeare's plays as biographies of the leading characters. The attention which the critical world has accorded to Bradley's unhistorical, philosophical, undramatic attitude to Shakespeare amounts to very little when compared with the widespread acknowledgement that Bradley read Shakespeare because he was interested in the characters.[1] This is the objection to Bradley which has held the attention of the student and critical public longest; partly no doubt this is due to the spectacular nature of Professor L. C. Knights's book, *How Many Children had Lady Macbeth?* published in 1933. There is, however, another reason, which will emerge from this chapter; the so-called Bradleyan over-emphasis on character is in fact an over-emphasis to which every critic and indeed every audience of Shakespeare is prone. The criticism of Bradley in the light of more sophisticated critical attitudes is in part self-castigation. This objection to Bradley has led to others, as Clifford Leech wrote:

> Critics who have parted company with Bradley have accused him of giving a too preponderant attention to the character of the hero, of treating the play like a nineteenth-century novel, of neglecting its poetry, and of being insufficiently versed in Elizabethan thought and stage-conditions.[2]

[1] That these are frequently related in the minds of the critics is most clearly seen in Dame Helen Gardner's summary of Bradley: 'Bradley's main weakness as a critic of tragedy lay in his defective feeling for the stage. He took insufficient account of the distinction between characterization in a novel and characterization in a play . . . Bradley's over-mastering concern with 'why' conflicts with the dramatist's absorption in 'how'. To make discussion of motives our prime concern is to neglect the glory of drama, its power to present before our eyes and ears an image of human life that convinces us of its truth even while it surprises us.' H. Gardner, '*Othello*: A Retrospect, 1900–1967', *S.S.* xxi (1968), pp. 1–11, at p. 8.

[2] C. Leech, 'Studies in *Hamlet*, 1901–1955', *S.S.* ix (1956), p. 3.

The connection between the criticism that Bradley confused character study with drama and the contention that Bradley easily overlooked the difference between art and reality is a natural one; not so natural but no less common is the assumption that the attention Bradley accords the characters in the drama arises from his under-estimating the effects of poetry, and reading the plays like sound Victorian novels.

Such is the fame accorded to Bradley's criticism of the characterization in the four great tragedies, that the process is often renamed after him; 'Character analysis in the Bradley manner'[3] is what one American scholar calls it, as though no other forms of character analysis were possible. Bradley has, however, his confederates in his critical attitude. Professor Hardy classes him with Hazlitt as 'a great character critic' and contrasting him with Coleridge adds: 'Hazlitt and Bradley tell us about human character, taking Macbeth or Othello as a point of departure; Coleridge tells us about the play.'[4] Writing of Falstaff, S. B. Hemingway almost inevitably equates Bradley with Morgann: 'It is the unwritten biography of Falstaff, the Life of Falstaff as it existed in his creator's mind, that is the chief concern of the Morgann–Bradley school.'[5] Oliver Elton classed him with his earlier Victorian predecessor Dowden: 'Edward Dowden and Andrew Bradley spoke with much nicety on Shakespeare's form; but they too were more concerned with penetrating his characters, or his philosophy of life.'[6]

Whatever else has fluctuated in the narrow world of Shakespeare criticism, Bradley the character critic has remained firm. In 1934 T. M. Parrott wrote in an uncontroversial handbook for students:

> Something of the same sort [as is found in Dowden] combined with

[3] F. Bowers, 'Dramatic Structure and Criticism: Plot in Hamlet', *Shakespeare 400: Essays by American Scholars*, ed. J. G. MacManaway (New York, 1964), pp. 207–18), at p. 207.

[4] B. H. Hardy, 'I have a smack of "Hamlet": Coleridge and Shakespeare's Characters', *E. in C.*, viii, pp. 238–55, at p. 242.

[5] S. B. Hemingway, 'On Behalf of that Falstaff', *S.Q.* iii (1952), pp. 307–11, at p. 308.

[6] O. Elton, 'Style in Shakespeare', *B.A.* (1936), p. 5.

a subtler psychological analysis of Shakespeare's characters is found in Bradley's admirable *Shakespearean Tragedy*, 1904. Here after a philosophic aesthetic lecture on the substance of tragedy there follows an illuminating discussion of construction in Shakespeare's tragedies. This might lead one to believe that Bradley meant to deal with Shakespeare primarily as a dramatist but the four lectures which follow on the four great tragedies are in the main character studies, often indeed of the most interesting and suggestive sort but with too little consideration of their prime purpose, that is the presentation on the stage.[7]

This is all the notice this book accords Bradley apart from a summary of titles of his other Shakespeare studies. The tone is sarcastic and superior, some of the content inaccurate (there are eight not four lectures on the individual plays) but the picture of Bradley the character critic emerges clearly. It is a picture which despite varying attitudes remained clear. When George Watson in 1962 wrote a similar handbook, this time on literary criticism in general he summed up *en passant*: 'Bradley's style of criticism was based upon an assumption that Shakespeare's characters are as naturalistic as the characters of nineteenth-century novels.'[8] Even non-specialists are expected to recognize this particular facet of Bradley so that even now when the critical excitement has died down, Irving Wardle could write in *New Society* in the autumn of 1966: 'Bradley and the "objectivistic" school of criticism which tried to resolve the Shakespearian enigma by lifting characters out of context and supplying them with irrelevant "real life" biographies.'[9]

There have been few if any critics to assert that Bradley was not as interested in character as the general opinion seems to think. Oddly, only G. Wilson Knight stands out for a Bradley not immersed in characters, not only in his famous prefatory note to the 1949 edition of *The Wheel of Fire* where he said 'My

[7] T. M. Parrott, *William Shakespeare: a Handbook*, quotation from revised 1955 edn., p. 223.

[8] G. Watson, *The Literary Critics* (1962), quotation from 1964 reprint, p. 24. This comment is only made as part of a defence of Coleridge from the taint of Bradley. In this book Bradley is nowhere mentioned independently.

[9] I. Wardle, 'Arts in Society: Shakespeare as Folklore', *New Society*, 29 Sept. 1966, p. 496.

animadversions as to "character" analysis were never intended to limit the living human reality of Shakespeare's people . . . Nor was I at all concerned to repudiate the work of A. C. Bradley',[10] but also in the prefatory note to the 1951 edition of *The Imperial Theme* where he wrote that Bradley's *Shakespearean Tragedy* 'is too often wrongly supposed to have been limited to the *minutiae* of "characterisation".'[11] But even this counterblast was limited; in *The Wheel of Fire* prefatory note Knight continued: 'Bradley certainly on occasion pushed "character" analysis to an unnecessary extreme.'[12]

Despite the unanimity of critical opinion on this one point there has been a wide diversity of attitudes to Bradley's 'character' criticism. The question has been largely how much this stress on character vitiates Bradley's criticism. There have, however, been a few voices who, aside from this larger issue, question Bradley's ability to carry out the character analysis.

The general attitude to Bradley's character criticism is one of admiration. H. Granville-Barker, discussing Kent in *King Lear*, referred his readers to Bradley 'for a masterly analysis of the whole character'.[13] H. B. Charlton, even in the case of the controversial study of Falstaff, wrote: 'Mr. Bradley's portrait of Sir John impresses one as more like the authentic Falstaff of Shakespeare than any other which the critics have sketched.'[14] In the case, however, of one particular character study and of two critics there has been rigorous criticism not so much of the fact of Bradley's concentration on 'character' but of his inaccuracy in portraying the character. One of the critics concerned explicitly makes the point:

The generally recognised peculiarity of *Othello* among the tragedies may be indicated by saying that it lends itself as no other of them does

[10] G. Wilson Knight, *The Wheel of Fire* (first published London, 1930, prefatory note first published 1949), quotation from 1949 edition, p. v.

[11] G. Wilson Knight, *The Imperial Theme* (first published London, 1931, prefatory note first published 1951), quotation from 1951 edition, p. v.

[12] See n. 10.

[13] H. Granville-Barker, *Prefaces to Shakespeare*, vol. 1 (London, 1958), quotation from 1961 reprint, p. 309 n.

[14] H. B. Charlton, 'Falstaff', *J.R.L.B.*, xix (1935), pp. 46–89, at p. 57.

to the approach classically associated with Bradley's name: even *Othello* (it will be necessary to insist) is poetic drama, a dramatic poem, and not a psychological novel written in dramatic form and draped in poetry, but relevant discussion of its tragic significance will nevertheless be mainly a matter of character-analysis. It would, that is, have lent itself uniquely well to Bradley's approach if Bradley had made his approach consistently and with moderate intelligence. Actually, however, the section on *Othello* in *Shakespearean Tragedy* is more extravagant in misdirected scrupulosity than any of the others; it is, with a concentration of Bradley's comical solemnity, completely wrong-headed—grossly and palpably false to the evidence it offers to weigh.[15]

According to Dr. Leavis, Bradley commits every possible error in his study of the characters of Othello and Iago: 'we must not suppose that Bradley sees what is in front of him'; instead his account is

as extraordinary a history of triumphant sentimental perversity as literary history can show.

At the cost of denaturing Shakespeare's tragedy, he insistently idealises.

Bradley, in the speech he quotes from, misses all the shifts of tone by which Shakespeare renders the shifting confusion of Othello's mind.[16]

Professor E. E. Stoll, whom Leavis calls the 'adversary of the Bradley approach',[17] also extensively criticises Bradley's portrait of Othello; the bulk of this criticism comes in his earliest work *Othello: an Historical and Comparative Study* (1915), but Professor Stoll formulates his objection to Bradley's characterization most clearly in *Art and Artifice in Shakespeare* (1933). 'We have no right, as the critics ever since the days of Romanticism have been doing . . . to interpret the characters by way of the plot, instead of at first hand.' Speaking more specifically of Bradley's mis-interpretation of Banquo, he says: 'this is a case, as with Hamlet,

[15] F. R. Leavis, 'Diabolic Intellect and the Noble Hero: The Sentimentalist's Othello', *Scrutiny*, vi (December 1937), pp. 259–83, at pp. 259–60.

[16] Ibid., pp. 260, 262, 270, 272 respectively.

[17] Ibid., p. 279.

of interpreting the character, indirectly, by the plot, instead of at first hand.'[18] Although Stoll himself, particularly in the earlier work, concentrates on the character of Othello, in the above objection to the Bradleyan approach to character lie the seeds of the objection to the whole character approach to the plays. It is a short step from considering the characters 'at first hand' to considering them as marionettes expressing the dramatist's theme, to seeing them as function, rather than as person; finally, not considering them as entities at all.

Leo Kirschbaum illustrates a position somewhat more advanced than Stoll's in the consideration of character; for Kirschbaum, character is primarily to be considered as function. He talks of 'the folly of automatically adhering willy-nilly to the *a priori* "romantic" notion that every Shakespeare character is as real in unity, depth, and complexity as the reader of this book.' Speaking specifically again of Banquo he says:

> If we consider Banquo as a dramatic function rather than as a character in the usual sense, we shall be able to avoid Bradley's erroneous and confused misreading of him as another whom the witches' influence finally debases. . . . Bradley, with his customary approach, tended to consider Banquo as a whole man, a psychologically valid being; he did not see that the playwright has so depicted the character that he will always be a dramaturgic foil to Macbeth.

Kirschbaum thinks the characters should be regarded 'not so much as people but as morality play figures', and concludes triumphantly: 'Interestingly enough, the non-Bradleyan Banquo emerges as a more dramatically effective figure if only because he is uncomplex, consistent, and trenchant.'[19]

S. L. Bethell takes the argument a stage further in his book *Shakespeare and the Popular Dramatic Tradition*; he firstly criticises the Victorian attitude to character:

[18] E. E. Stoll, *Art and Artifice in Shakespeare* (London, 1933), pp. 101 and 139 respectively.

[19] L. Kirschbaum, *Character and Characterization in Shakespeare* (Detroit/Toronto, 1962), pp. 6, 52, 55–6, 59 respectively. The discussion of Banquo which covers pp. 52–9 is a revised version of an article 'Banquo and Edgar: Character or Function', in *E. in C.* vii, 1. (1957), pp. 1–21.

The study of character is, of course, important, though it is not everything; but the typical Victorian character criticism consisted entirely of psychological speculation, and treated the text as providing scientific data rather than as mediating a poetic experience. By the end of the nineteenth century, Shakespearean criticism was almost limited to the discussion of characters, their motives, their self-consistency and so forth; whilst treatment of the verse was usually confined to eulogies, in passing, of the appropriate anthological passages.

He continues:

the Victorian critics, culminating in Bradley, ignored Shakespeare's conventionalism and falsely simplified their approach by treating him as if he were a purely naturalistic writer

and concludes, undermining all that meant 'character' to the Victorian critic:

Is the naturalistic approach in any way valid for Shakespeare? The naturalistic approach treats characters as if they were real persons, and seeks a psychological explanation for their words and deeds. An audience in the naturalistic theatre is busy with conjecture about the states of mind which would produce certain actions and remarks presented before them. But a Shakespearean audience is even more busy with the subtleties of a highly complex poetry, and it is unlikely that they would have time to spare for any but the most obvious naturalistic indications of character . . . To understand poetry, conscious effort is needed; and to penetrate character from dialogue and action conscious effort is again needed, but of an entirely different type. It is thus *a priori* unlikely that naturalistic criticism should be very fruitful in dealing with Shakespeare.[20]

This last argument triumphantly disregards both logic and reason; it is as rational as saying that one cannot make a friend of someone whose language is other than one's own because the effort of understanding the language makes it impossible to pay any attention to the speaker. The reason why Bethell falls into this attitude is that he is silently adhering to the critical doctrine of the difference between drama and life. This doctrine in many ways received its rigid formulation because of the so-called confusion between the two which is found in Bradley. The first

[20] S. L. Bethell, *Shakespeare and the Popular Dramatic Tradition* (Westminster, 1944), pp. 62, 63, and 66 respectively.

critic of Bradley, A. B. Walkley, printed his essay 'Professor Bradley's Hamlet' in a book appropriately titled *Drama and Life*; and he is substantially concerned with the confusion of the historic and the fictional approach to drama; of this he wrote:

the confusion . . . is natural enough. . . . The confusion gives pleasure, for we seem, by yielding to it, to be witnessing a veritable act of creation and to be enlarging, enriching, vividly colouring our experience of life. But deliberately to import this into criticism is quite another matter.

On this basis he quarrels with Bradley's picture of *Hamlet*. For example when Bradley says 'Hamlet, a popular youth, an actor and a fencer', Walkley comments: 'does it not occur to Professor Bradley that these things are thus merely because Shakespeare wanted (1) a "sympathetic" hero, (2) an amateur of acting (or what would have become of the play-scene?); and (3) a fencer—for the *dénouement*?' Walkley then sums up in an almost prophetic manner the difference in approach between Bradley and himself:

to understand Shakespeare you have to supplement examination of the text by consideration of other matters, and it is here that we hold the Professor to be at fault. What is outside the text? He says (by implication) a set of real lives . . . we say Shakespeare's dramatic needs of the moment, artistic peculiarities, and available theatrical materials.[21]

A. J. A. Waldock expands the objection in his book on '*Hamlet*'. In his discussion of Bradley's theory as to why Hamlet delays, he writes:

Bradley's explanation . . . does not seem satisfactorily to establish 'delay' as the obvious sequel of Hamlet's mental sufferings. Bradley is throughout concerned with showing why Hamlet's special temperament constituted a 'danger' to himself . . . But it seems almost as plausible to imagine his temperament, under the same circumstances, as an asset . . . I do not urge these considerations as dramatically very important but rather as suggesting some failure on the part of Bradley's theory fully to account for the case even as he imagines it. But perhaps more interesting than the theory itself is Bradley's justification of it by

[21] *T.L.S.* 7 Apr. 1905, 'Professor Bradley's *Hamlet*', reprinted in A. B. Walkley, *Drama and Life* (New York, 1907), pp. 148–55.

the plot. Here a certain fallacy in method seems to become apparent, and a principle is raised of the first importance.

'Drama is *not* history' but Bradley on the *basis* of the play . . . reconstructs what *really* happened . . . He is tempted . . . to a super-subtlety that unearths impossible distinctions—impossible, at least, to the theatre.[22]

This quotation is interesting because it illustrates a difficulty which many critics, even including those like Waldock who consciously try to avoid it, meet; that of entering into the argument about Shakespeare's characters as though they were living people. We shall come to other examples of this later.

'Drama is not history'; the obverse of this is that Shakespearian tragedy is 'dramatic poetry'; foremost of the critics who found Bradley wanting on this count was L. C. Knights who in his book *How many Children had Lady Macbeth?* took up the argument about Bradley's character from this particular standpoint. His argument may be summed up: 'A Shakespeare play is a dramatic poem', and his particular aim was to correct 'the assumption that Shakespeare was pre-eminently a great creator of characters'. Of the holders of this assumption he says:

The most illustrious example is, of course, Dr. Bradley's *Shakespearean Tragedy* . . . too well-known to require much descriptive comment, but it should be observed that the Notes, in which the detective interest supersedes the critical, form a logical corollary to the main portions of the book. . . . It is assumed throughout the book that the most profitable discussion of Shakespeare's tragedies is in terms of the characters of which they are composed.[23]

The main argument is here and in the ironical title; unawares, however, in the second part of his book, when he analyses the first scene of the play as poetry to illustrate an alternative method to that of Bradley, he gives the lie to his objections to a specifically Bradleyan approach. In an address to the teachers of Liverpool, 'The Teaching of English Literature', Bradley illustrated a point

[22] A. J. A. Waldock, *Hamlet: a Study in Critical Method* (Cambridge, 1931), pp. 32 ff.

[23] L. C. Knights, *How many Children had Lady Macbeth?* (Cambridge, 1933), pp. 7, 1, and 5 respectively.

about the value of teaching children to read so as to recreate the writer's mind in theirs, by analysing the same scene in a way remarkably similar. Indeed given the fact of the analysis of ten lines of Shakespearian poetry and two critics of the calibre of A. C. Bradley and L. C. Knights, the similarity of analysis is almost inevitable. It is odd that L. C. Knights should have chosen the same scene, as the article is not easily accessible and Knights is unlikely to have seen it. On the other hand, the choice of *Macbeth* seems unfortunate when Bradley himself in *Shakespearean Tragedy* said of this play that the minor characters

> are sketched lightly, and are seldom developed further than the strict purposes of the action required . . . All this makes for simplicity of effect. And, this being so, is it not possible that Shakespeare instinctively felt, or consciously feared, that to give much individuality or attraction to the subordinate figures would diminish this effect, and so, like a good artist, sacrificed a part to the whole? And was he wrong? He has certainly avoided the overloading which distresses us in *King Lear* and has produced a tragedy utterly unlike it, not much less great as a dramatic poem, and as a drama superior.[24]

Not only does Bradley here show an attitude quite contrary to that Knights imputed to him with regard to the characters, but he also uses the very term 'dramatic poem' which L. C. Knights made his watchword. Despite this the view of A. C. Bradley as character critic *par excellence* continues and with it a belief that Knights once and for all exposed Bradley for what he was.

Over thirty years after the appearance of Knights's work, in a critical climate more favourable to Bradley, A. D. Nuttall re-examined Bradley, 'the character-chaser, the motive-hunter', and the L. C. Knights attack. By doing so, he won from the editor of the periodical in which his essay was published the following support:

> In the '30s, '40s and early '50s, there was a tendency to press Shakespeare towards allegory and, at the same time, to avoid discussion of his

[24] *S.T.*, pp. 387–9. Bradley is now getting credit for this view, cf. G. K. Hunter, '*Macbeth* in the Twentieth Century', *S.S.*, xix (1966), p. 5: 'some of the finest statements of the indeterminacy of "character" in a poetic structure appear in the *Macbeth* essays in *Shakespearean Tragedy*.'

'characters' like the plague. Prof. L. C. Knights's *How many Children had Lady Macbeth?* was a notable deterrent. As a student at Cambridge I can still remember thinking it strangely insensitive and superficial, after Bradley; but it was hard to formulate objections at that time.[25]

Nuttall begins his article by summing up the critical situation:

> At the time, everybody used to talk about Shakespeare's characters as if they were real people. To-day, simple folk, like Lord David Cecil and Prof. Dover Wilson, still do; but the critically with-it do not, believing this kind of talk makes no sense.[26]

Leaving aside the jocular style Nuttall examines Knights's charges in detail:

> What exactly is claimed in this charge of Knights?—the charge that Bradley and the rest confound fiction and reality, the charge that it is absurd to ask whether Falstaff is *really* a coward. Is he (for example) claiming that Morgann, Bradley and the rest actually mistook Falstaff, Macbeth and the rest for real people? Obviously not . . . You will not find Bradley burying his head in works of Scottish history which Shakespeare can never have read. Whatever the 'independence' of the dramatic characters means it cannot mean that.
>
> But if Bradley was not actually deluded what are we to say? Does his guilt merely consist in his using the *language* of delusion? . . . the practise of simply naming the persons of a play without always designating them as 'characters' has long been authorised by usage. It has become part of the shorthand of criticism to omit the designation of logical status once the over-all logical context is clear.

Having convincingly discussed these aspects of Knights's criticism Nuttall continues: 'Knights' real objection is to the practice of drawing inferences from the seen to the unseen with respect to persons of the play.' To which he answers: 'It is just not accurate to say that their fictional existence begins and ends with what we actually see',[27] and cites for example the understanding of passage of time and the characters' occupation during that time, which the dramatist expects of his audience.

[25] A. E. Dyson, editorial to C.Q. vii. 2 (1965), pp. 99–101, at p. 99.

[26] A. D. Nuttall, 'The Argument about Shakespeare's Characters', *C.Q.*, vii. 2 (1965), pp. 107–19, at p. 107.

[27] Ibid., pp. 112–13.

It is, however, for doing just what Nuttall says the audience must do that Miss Campbell explicitly objects to Bradley's 'character-analysis':

he failed to distinguish between a dramatic character and a person in real life.

Bradley is forever busy with his paintbrush, filling in what is not there in Shakespeare's portraits, and worse, altering what is there.[28]

Miss Campbell made this point in answer to H. B. Charlton's eulogy of Bradley which included the statement: 'He sees the men who move through them [the plays] as if they were real human beings struggling through a world which seems in moral substance very much like our own.'[29] In the light of these two quotations it seems that Nuttall's answer to Knights's charge is not really adequate to the task; both Charlton and Miss Campbell are describing a non-critical reading of a play and this is really what Knights meant when he said that Bradley laid too much stress on the characters. Both the naturalistic and the thematic approaches to the tragedies are capable of uncritical excesses. The naturalistic view if carried to extremes will ignore the dramatic art, and the thematic will under-estimate the artistic illusion of reality in which the dramatist and the audience both acquiesce.

William Empson states the objection to Bradley's characterization in a much more moderate form than Knights did earlier:

I think it is clearly wrong to talk as if coherence of character is not needed in poetic drama, only coherence of metaphor and so on. The fair point to make against Bradley's approach (as is now generally agreed) is that the character . . . must have been intended to seem coherent to the first-night audience; therefore the solution cannot be reached by learned deductions from hints in the text about his previous biography.[30]

While this statement applies wholly to general critical practice

[28] L. B. Campbell, 'Concerning Bradley's *Shakespearean Tragedy*, *H.L.Q.* xiii (November 1949), pp. 1–18, at p. 2.

[29] H. B. Charlton, *Shakespearian Tragedy* (Cambridge, 1948) (Clark Lectures 1946–7), p. 4.

[30] W. Empson, *The Structure of Complex Words* (London, 1951), p. 231.

it seems not quite true of Bradley, who did not seek to solve the characters' problems, 'by learned deductions from hints in the text'. He did make deductions from the hints in the text but in very few cases were these deductions other than those available to a first-night audience. While it is doubtful that any one member would have been receptive to all the hints which Shakespeare offers and Bradley takes up, the role of the critic must surely be in some measure to supplement the defects of each individual reaction to the play.

Critics write, moreover, as though the theatre audience were by definition insensitive to hints; this seems to deny the excessive economy which a dramatist must practise in order to create a whole world, people it, and depict the course of the action within 'three hours traffic of our stage'. The audience, however, is not so inconsiderate and as the continuity work behind a film suggests, is highly aware of any detail or hint. An interesting example of a critic who thinks that any reading which relies on an exact impression of the work of the text is suitable only for the study and not for the theatre is A. J. A. Waldock. His objection to Bradley's interpretation of the speech beginning 'Now might I do it pat' provides an interesting illustration of a typical critical attitude.

> 'The first five words he utters, "Now might I do it" show he has no effective desire to do it'. Thus Bradley. But surely this is the very ecstasy of sophistication. 'Now *might* I do it': that little *might*! But whoever in an audience could have taken such a hint as that; whoever reading the play with unbiased mind, could possibly check at such a subtlety! How strange that it should have been Professor Bradley who uttered the dictum: 'Shakespeare wrote primarily for the theatre and not for students, and therefore great weight should be attached to the immediate impressions made by his works'![31]

Waldock it seems here is making the confusion of which he considers Bradley to be guilty. He states that neither the audience nor the reader would notice 'one little word' but this is an academic abstraction. It seems likely that a reader, reading with his

[31] A. J. A. Waldock, op. cit., p. 39.

eye rather than his ear might pass over the familiar word, but a theatre audience, or a reader reading so as to recreate a dramatic impression for himself, must hear the word and hearing it can only understand it in its usual context which implies an impossible condition. 'Now might I do it' are not the words of a man about to do something; these words in *Hamlet* moreover have the added emphasis of being the first in a soliloquy. Hearing them the audience could only conclude, it seems to me, that Hamlet was not going to do the deed. The speech and Hamlet's subsequent departure would confirm this. Waldock will not allow this interpretation because he thinks it depends on an academic interpretation of a hint; but if it is a hint in the play then Shakespeare must have intended it for a hint to the audience, they were his sole concern.

Bradley's character criticism constituted not an academic probing into the background of the characters, but an imaginative response to them as appearances of reality. Empson's criticism, although made in a kindly tone, in fact is less accurately just to Bradley than the hostile strictures of L. L. Schücking who, coupling Bradley's approach with that of the German Kuno Fischer, says that it 'must be regarded as quite erroneous, if only for the reason that it always comes perilously near confounding art and reality'.[32] What seems odd about this criticism is that the approach 'must be regarded as quite erroneous'. If the essence of dramatic art was to confound art and reality and, at least, according to Hamlet, this was a dramatist's function, then the nearer a critic comes to the same confusion, always provided he can remain critically aloof from that confusion, the nearer his criticism ought to be to reinterpreting the drama.

If Bradley was guilty of an occasional uncritical confusion, then the other Shakespeare critics of the twentieth century crowd to keep him company. Before enumerating some of these, however, it will perhaps be useful to see what signs Bradley gives of confusing the dramatic characters of Shakespeare with the personalities of real life. The most obviously Victorian

[32] L. L. Schücking, *Character Problems in Shakespeare's Plays* (London, 1922), p. 158 n.

example comes at the end of his characterization of Desdemona when he says:

> Desdemona, confronted with Lear's foolish but pathetic demand for a profession of love, could have done, I think, what Cordelia could not do—could have refused to compete with her sisters, and yet have made her father feel that she loved him well. And I doubt if Cordelia, 'falsely murdered', would have been capable of those last words of Desdemona—her answer to Emilia's 'O who hath done this deed?'[33]

In critical terms there can perhaps be no excuse for this sentimental involvement in the heroine's plight; it must be remembered, however, that Bradley was lecturing when these observations were made; they constitute an informal personal ending to the lecture on *Othello*; under such circumstances a little involvement is excusable. Moreover this lapse of taste, as it may seem now, though it probably did not then, illuminates more economically than long critical debate the essential difference between the characters of the two heroines; it was a difference which stemmed alike from their different functions in the play and the different emotional reactions which Shakespeare wanted from his audience and so, even though Bradley does not explicitly make this excuse for his treating the heroines as though both had life independent from the dramas in which they are set, the comparison is critically valid. By comparing Desdemona and Cordelia in this way, as though they were real persons, he brings into sharp contrast the differing dramatic worlds of *Othello* and *King Lear*.

Perhaps the single character which has most contributed to the idea that Bradley sought to interpret Shakespeare's characters as though they had real lives of their own is Falstaff. The reason for this is partly no doubt Bradley's praise of Morgann's study; praise which has led subsequent critics to make the inference that Bradley read *Henry IV* in exactly the same way as Morgann. This is not in fact so. Morgann's treatise is concerned primarily to free Falstaff from the imputation that he was a coward; to do this Morgann studies all the tiny scraps of evidence as to his life which Shakespeare offers us and pieces together a picture of a

[33] *S.T.*, p. 206.

military Falstaff, wise in strategy and cunning, above all suspicion of cowardice and attendant faults. Bradley's aim is altogether different and more truly critical; his essay is an attempt to understand why the 'Rejection of Falstaff' affects the audience as it does: 'What do we feel, and what are we meant to feel, as we witness this rejection? And what does our feeling imply as to the characters of Falstaff and the new King?'[34] This second sentence is Bradley's undoing and it is not in fact true to the substance of the following lecture. Bradley does examine the character of Falstaff and of Prince Hal but not merely in order to understand them as people, but to see better the operation of Shakespeare's genius in these two plays. The conclusion is Bradley's justification of himself and (if such a word can be true to Bradley's attitude to Shakespeare) of Shakespeare. He calls Falstaff 'the greatest comic character in literature' and adds:

it is in this character, and not in the judgment he brings upon Falstaff's head, that Shakespeare asserts his supremacy. To show that Falstaff's freedom of soul was in part illusory, and that the realities of life refused to be conjured away by his humour—this was what we might expect from Shakespeare's unfailing sanity, but it was surely no achievement beyond the power of lesser men. The achievement was Falstaff himself, and the conception of that freedom of soul, a freedom illusory only in part, and attainable only by a mind which had received from Shakespeare's own the inexplicable touch of infinity which he bestowed on Hamlet and Macbeth and Cleopatra, but denied to Henry the Fifth.[35]

The style is perhaps over-romantic and not as critical as modern professional standards require; but there was not then the same formulated critical style to help (or hinder) the critic. Bradley indeed states that the creation of Falstaff is the sublime element in *Henry IV* but this is not, be it noticed, because we can see in Falstaff a character whom we might any day meet, or a character about whom we know all the intimate details; it is because in Falstaff, Shakespeare was able to embody some of the infinity which to him (and to Bradley) was man's highest achievement. Bradley's last sentence if in its style it implies a rather personal attitude to the characters of the plays also contradicts the idea

[34] *O.L.P.*, p. 249. [35] Ibid., p. 273.

that Bradley considers Shakespeare's characters as real persons: not even Shakespeare could be considered capable of lending infinity to real human beings.

In fact, wherever Bradley seems, because of the general tone of his writing, to be talking of Shakespeare's created characters as living people he is in fact doing something quite different. Either he is illuminating Shakespeare's mind by considering the products of it or he is analysing the audience reaction to the characters. The dangers of using the characters to these ends, however, are apparent in Bradley's later work, where his mind failed in the rigorous intellectual discipline of which there is abundant evidence in *Shakespearean Tragedy* and *Oxford Lectures on Poetry*. In 'Feste the Jester', for example, Feste is considered in what could be called the truly 'Bradleyan' manner. Of Feste's begging he says: 'he is laying up treasures on earth against the day when some freak of his own, or some whim in his mistress, will bring his dismissal', and, 'We are not offended by Feste's eagerness for sixpences and his avoidance of risks. By helping us to realize the hardness of his lot, they add to our sympathy and make us admire the more the serenity and gaiety of his spirit.'[36] Here Bradley is doing little more than conjure up for us something of the reality of Feste; but as it is Bradley's Feste and not Shakespeare's it has little critical value.[37] To this kind of comment the objections of the theatrical illusion, historical research, and comparative literature critics are only too valid. Through Bradley's Feste shines more clearly than anything else a totally different Feste than Bradley imagines, a Feste who is but a dramatist's puppet, a stock type, a commonplace figure, however well done. Shakespeare's accomplishment is diminished, sublime theatrical illusion has become rather maudlin real life.

The contrast between this characterization and even the seemingly biographical remarks about Cordelia and Desdemona illustrate how far in fact the true Bradley was from this type of

[36] *A.M.*, pp. 214–15.

[37] For a somewhat whimsical defence of Bradley's portrait, cf. E. J. West, 'Bradleyan Reprise: on the Fool in *Twelfth Night*', *S.A.B.* xxiv (1949), pp. 264–74.

error. That he should lapse into it in his old age is perhaps not surprising; there have been many other later critics, aware of the dangers, who have erred in the same way and occasionally in the very works in which they talk of the folly of character criticism. There have been other critics who have, in John Holloway's words, been 'inveigled for a moment into a Bradleyan speculation which is not the kind of criticism he takes his stand by',[38] than D. A. Traversi of whose description of Iago's attitude while baiting Othello, Holloway is here speaking. Indeed Holloway seems particularly aware of the fact that critics may, according to fashion, denigrate Bradley's approach and then follow it. Earlier in his book he wrote:

> The current coin of Shakespeare criticism condemns, as is well known, an approach to the plays through Bradleian 'character-analysis' (though the critics of this school are not above ingenious interpretations of character themselves when it suits their purpose).[38]

Holloway does not (as it does not suit his purpose) go on to analyse why a character-study should suit the purpose of a critic who according to his school was preoccupied with some other aspect of Shakespeare. A look at some of the critics concerned may help to make this clear.

H. S. Wilson wrote on p. 66 of his book *On the Design of Shakespearian Tragedy*:

> A. C. Bradley has emphasised the note of accident in *Othello* . . . This is to confuse the events of the play which are critically relevant with possible events in real life, which are not. The unintentional ambiguity in Bradley's statement is concealed in the inclusion of both sorts of happening under the designation of 'accident'.

Thirty pages later discussing *Julius Caesar* he wrote:

> What is most fully tragic about the play is the effect of Brutus's conduct, for it influenced the lives of all his fellow beings, the Roman commonweal . . . Yet we cannot say that the tyranny which followed is wholly Brutus' fault either . . . If Brutus and Cassius had not murdered Caesar others probably would have; for his arrogance in a

[38] John Holloway, *The Story of the Night* (London, 1961), pp. 45 and 21 respectively.

state accustomed to the maximum of liberty for the citizens cried out for such a check.[39]

Which is a stumble, the like of which Bradley never made, into the confused world of drama and life.

Irving Ribner who at the beginning of his book[40] specifically writes of dramatic illusion and the danger in which this involved Bradley as a critic, wrote when discussing *Hamlet*, 'Like Laertes, but unlike Hamlet and Fortinbras she [Ophelia] is incapable of growth.'[41] The objection to this is obvious; their functions did not demand any growth of character, Shakespeare's attention was focused on the growth of the hero's character, the rest were unimportant. This is an objection which Bradley and Ribner himself would both, one feels, make almost involuntarily on seeing the statement; though they might thereafter be perplexed a little at the accuracy of the statement on its own terms (something which is rarely true of Bradley's lapses of this nature). Fluchère, who thought so little of Bradley's criticism that he said 'Shakespeare criticism . . . had made no serious progress since Coleridge before the arrival of Eliot, Leavis &c.', whom he acknowledges as his masters, wrote of *Troilus and Cressida* 'Helen's sovereign beauty, which had once thrown Faustus almost into ecstasy, is a mere illusion', which contains such a complex of mixed drama and life that it renders comical Fluchère's own previous criticism:

> The Nineteenth [century] even more romantic [than the Eighteenth], raising sentiment to the height of the transcendental and poetry to the dignity of an ethic, was prone to take the shadow for the substance, to delude itself with words, and in spite of the fruitful revival which enriched its capacity for wonder, to evade the real problems and be content with illusory realities.[42]

Leo Kirschbaum, who wrote with scorn of 'the "romantic"

[39] H. S. Wilson, *On the Design of Shakespearian Tragedy* (Toronto/London, 1957), pp. 66 and 96 respectively.

[40] I. Ribner, *Patterns in Shakespearian Tragedy* (London, 1960), pp. 2–3.

[41] Ibid., p. 88.

[42] H. Fluchère, *Shakespeare* (London, 1953), pp. 11, 211, and 134 respectively.

notion that every Shakespeare character is as real in unity, depth and complexity as the reader of this book', in the same book wrote more overtly than many critics have, 'Beatrice and Benedick are as real as you and I.'[43]

The prevalence of such outstanding contrasts between avowed theory and lapses in practice illustrates something more than the fact that Bradley was not the only one to treat characters as human beings. That such a number of critics, including those aware of the confusion as a critical heresy, should give signs, either overt or oblique, of making, at least on occasion, the same confusion between art and reality is evidence of the fact that this confusion is stronger than any critical impulse to resist it. The themes, the images, the structure of the plays are important to the thinking critic but when for a moment the critic leaves off his professional guise then it is the characters, and the characters as men and women not ciphers, 'morality play figures', or personifications, which matter.

There has been a wide diversity of critics who have been prepared to state categorically that character is fundamental to Shakespearian drama. C. J. Sisson, for example, wrote, 'Few will doubt . . . that Shakespeare's primary interest lay in men and women, rather than in abstract concepts.'[44] and Jan Kott goes even further: 'Shakespeare not only dramatizes history; he dramatizes psychology, gives us large slices of it and in them we find ourselves'; 'Shakespeare is truer than life.' And of the characters: 'They are living people for Shakespeare was a great writer.'[45] Harley Granville-Barker, seen by many critics as an antidote to Bradley's character criticism, in fact wrote in his study of *Julius Caesar*: 'He (Shakespeare) is more interested, as he always has been, in character than in plot'[46] and as if to bear this out he begins his study of each of the plays with a discussion of each of the leading characters considered under their own sub-titles.

[43] L. Kirschbaum, *Character and Characterisation in Shakespeare* (Detroit/Toronto, 1962), pp. 6 and 129 respectively.

[44] C. J. Sisson, *Shakespeare's Tragic Justice* (London, n.d. [1962]), p. 32.

[45] J. Kott, *Shakespeare our Contemporary* (1964), pp. 14, 221, and 6 respectively. (The Polish original was published in 1961).

[46] H. Granville-Barker, *Prefaces to Shakespeare*, vol. ii (London, 1961), p. 351.

Doing this, he abstracts the characters from their context in a way in which Bradley never did.

In fact, compared with some of the above statements Bradley, as the following quotation will show, seems almost uninterested in character:

> The centre of the tragedy, therefore, may be said with equal truth to lie in action issuing from character, or in character issuing in action.
>
> Shakespeare's main interest lay here. To say that it lay in *mere* character, or was a psychological interest, would be a great mistake, for he was dramatic to the tip of his fingers. It is possible to find places where he has given a certain indulgence to his love of poetry and even to his turn for general reflections; but it would be very difficult, and in his later tragedies perhaps impossible, to detect passages where he has allowed such freedom to the interest in character apart from actions.[47]

Probably none of the above-quoted critics would disagree with this; Granville-Barker himself almost echoes it: 'Drama, as Shakespeare will come to write it, is, first and last, the projection of character in action',[48] though even here he does not allow the same weight to be attached to action as to character.

The principle is widely recognized; Shakespeare wrote drama and not mere character studies, psychological probings better confined to the nineteenth-century novel. Over and over again, though, critics respond to the characterization in Shakespeare's plays in the same primitive way as the now renowned woman who cried out at a performance of *Othello*. The more sophisticated critics having slipped into what they feel to be reprehensible character analysis excuse themselves with a wide variety of critical sophism. D. A. Traversi writes a character of Richard III deduced from his first speech in the play and then adds:

> The creation of recognisable personalities is not to be regarded as the unique end of Shakespeare's dramatic creations . . . but in the delineation of motive beyond the limit of convention his language first attained some sense of its full possibilities.[49]

[47] *S.T.*, p. 12. [48] H. Granville-Barker, op. cit., p. 418.

[49] D. A. Traversi, *An Approach to Shakespeare* (1938), quotation from 1957 edition, p. 16.

A. Clutton Brock wrote:

> I assume that the character of Hamlet has the consistency of a creation, that Shakespeare knew what he would do and made him do it. If I describe his behaviour in psychological terms, it is not with the aim of travelling beyond the play into speculation into a Hamlet who has no existence, but of discovering how his words ought to be supplemented with action and in what mood he ought to speak them.[50]

The American R. B. Heilman almost fell over backwards to avoid any suspicion attached to his discussion of the characters of *King Lear*:

> The extended analyses of individuals in Chapters VIII and IX are only incidentally character sketches: their primary function is to trace, by the person's deeds, and especially their words, those paradoxes of human nature and experience which are the chief structural elements in the drama.[51]

What seems odd about this last remark is that Heilman should feel the necessity to make explicit what he had just done in two full chapters; the reason for this is probably connected with the anti-Bradley fashion current in 1948 when Heilman's book was published. Indeed something like this is probably behind all such protestations that character criticism is something other than biographical inquiry.

The connection between character criticism and the critical position of Bradley seems to be closely related. The 'whirligig of time' has brought criticism to such a pass that themes, images, literary parallels are now as outmoded as character studies were in the late 1920s. In 1960 John Bayley's book *The Characters of Love* was published, defending Bradley and discussing *Othello* in terms of the conflict between Iago and Othello and Desdemona. In the same year the *Critical Quarterly* published two articles by

[50] A. Clutton Brock, *Shakespeare's Hamlet* (London, 1922), p. 36. Gilbert Murray mistook this book for a work by A. C. Bradley and wrote to him praising it. Bradley replied, 'I don't think that even twenty years ago I could have written the best parts of it and now——?' (9 July 1922), but by this time Bradley was in poor health and equally poor spirits.

[51] R. B. Heilman, *This Great Stage. Image and Structure in King Lear* (Baton Rouge, 1948), p. 252.

Barbara Everett, one defending Bradley's balanced view of *King Lear* and the other questioning the value of 'The Figure in Professor Knights's Carpet'—an inquiry into the value of discussing Shakespeare in terms of theme and pattern. This did not of course mean that criticism had suffered a sudden and complete change; Kirschbaum's book *Character and Characterisation in Shakespeare* appeared in 1962 to keep the E. E. Stoll side of the argument alive; on the other hand, it could be argued that such a title for a critical work on Shakespeare would not have been possible in the years when Spurgeon, W. H. Clemen, and Wilson Knight were the height of fashion. From roughly 1960 onwards there appear several articles on Bradley and there is more attention to Bradley in longer critical works. At the same time, there is evidence of a revived interest or, at least, a revived acceptance of interest in Shakespeare's characterization.

The reasons for this connection provide one of the subtlest compliments to the fame and power of Bradley even if they display a lack of knowledge about what he really says. Bradley was not the critic most interested in characters either in his day or afterwards. His predecessors include Mrs. Jameson, author of *Shakespeare's Heroines*, and his followers include John Palmer, author of *The Political Characters of Shakespeare* and *The Comic Characters of Shakespeare*. Bradley nowhere titled a book or even a chapter by using the word 'character'. Nowhere did Bradley make an asseveration like Mark Van Doren's of a Shakespearian character: 'He is first of all a member of the human race',[52] and yet such an attitude is referred back to Bradley. Interesting to notice is R. M. Smith's assertion than Van Doren is 'a worthy successor of the Bradley approach'.[53] In fact Van Doren, although he cites as influences a dozen critics including Dover Wilson and Wilson Knight, H. B. Charlton, and E. E. Stoll, makes no reference to Bradley in the whole of his book, which bears very little resemblance to Bradley's work. The cause for R. M. Smith's remark can only be barely remembered knowledge of Bradley's

[52] M. Van Doren, *Shakespeare* (London, 1941), p. 5.

[53] R. M. Smith, 'Granville-Barker's Shakespeare Criticism', *S.A.B.*, xxiv (1949), pp. 291–3, at p. 293.

criticism of character which in retrospect seems not so different from Van Doren's as represented by the above quotation.

Complimentary as such an attribution of all character criticism to Bradley is, unfortunately it does not further the true influence of the critic. No one is going to trouble to read Bradley if assured by accepted critical writing that his approach is the same as Van Doren's and indeed of any other critic who treated Shakespeare's characters as living beings. Since interest in Bradley himself has become more fashionable, probably in the wake of revived interest in character, a more truly complimentary attitude to Bradley has become apparent; this attitude is more critical and shows evidence not only that the works of Bradley have been recently read, but also that there has been some consideration of the critical attitudes involved. V. Y. Kantak offers a good example of this more recent attitude to Bradley the 'character-chaser'. Characteristically he begins by stating 'the "character" approach, obviously erroneous in the form it took during the nineteenth century, is still a legitimate approach basically related to the dramatic form.'[54] In the wake of this enlightened approach to 'character' criticism comes the following:

> Naturally the attack on this 'character' approach centred upon Bradley, whose monumental work represents the best in that earlier tradition which Coleridge may be said to have initiated . . . It may, of course, readily be admitted that Bradley tends to treat Shakespearian characters as living human beings, seeking to interpret their words, their motives, their activities, in terms we normally assume to be true of the world of living persons, whereas these characters exist only within the carefully determined shadow-world which is the drama in which they make their appearances . . . Bradley himself was aware of the dangers involved . . . but he insisted that the response in the mind of the reader or spectator was fundamentally important.[55]

This is in some measure written as a defence of Bradley against the charges made by L. C. Knights. Kantak also defends Bradley against Ribner's charge that Bradley 'could lead his readers only

[54] V. Y. Kantak, 'An Approach to Shakespearian Tragedy: The "Actor" Image in *Macbeth*', *S.S.* xvi (1963), pp. 42–52, at p. 43.

[55] Ibid., p. 43.

to a Shakespeare without positive belief, to a conception of tragedy merely as the posing of unanswerable questions, and to a moral system in the plays which is on close analysis not a moral system at all'.[56] Kantak replies for Bradley:

> Such an approach, however, seems to ignore the fact that 'the posing of unanswerable questions' is, in the end the very foundation of tragedy . . . The moral order is there, but something has to run counter to it to produce that tension. Bradley found that force centred in the character itself, for instance, in Macbeth as he lives through the ravages of evil.[57]

This seems very suggestive of the true Bradleyan attitude to character—if there is such a thing as a Bradleyan attitude, and not instead only what Bradley thought on the subject. Kantak is one of the few critics to recognize that Bradley is in fact writing in terms of 'response' and not creation; as what he writes is only an article and that concerned with imagery in *Macbeth* he is not at liberty to explore the conclusions to which this observation would lead him. In fact audience response is one of the best justifications for Bradley's using the characters to elucidate the essential experience of the tragedies. No spectator emerging from a performance of *Macbeth* turns homeward pondering the implications of the 'babe' images in the play, or if he did it would not be as a spectator purely but as a student or critic that he thought so. Even he, moreover, in responding to the play is more likely to be moved to thought by the sight of the somnambulant Lady Macbeth than by any abstract consideration which the performance might make plain. Yet *Macbeth* even according to Bradley depends very little for its effect upon the characters.

There are other less sociological and more critical defences of Bradley's approach and there have been other critics to make the defence on Bradley's behalf, Jonas Barish discussing the history of criticism of *Henry IV* wrote:

> The rejection of Falstaff, like much else in Shakespeare, has tended to turn a searchlight on us, and make ourselves reveal ourselves either as moralists or sentimentalists . . . Either of these formulations certainly oversimplifies, but my own instincts lead me to suspect that the latter

[56] I. Ribner, *Patterns in Shakespearian Tragedy* (London, 1960), p. 3.
[57] V. Y. Kantak, op. cit., p. 44.

view is the truer one, and that Bradley's essay still remains the soundest statement of the case . . . I should like to ask whether we do not arrive at much the same view if we take a different route, and consider the incident not so much as a detail in a Bradleyan character analysis as in the light of Shakespearean dramaturgy in general, by measuring it against the pattern of other plays, especially the comedies. I think that when we do, we find Bradley's strictures confirmed.[58]

Barish continues to do what he suggests; this is not the place to follow his argument completely and it will be enough to say that he sees Falstaff as a parallel to the 'dream' in *Midsummer Night's Dream* and the 'holiday' in *Love's Labour's Lost*, neither of which are so harshly rejected when the end comes.

He adds: 'Those who see in the sacrifice of Falstaff a near-tragic reproof of life by the tyrannical demands of state tend also to see in the deaths of Antony and Cleopatra a triumphant escape from the clutches of the same tyranny.'[59] This latter remark throws light on Bradley, who, in fact, is one of those who react as Barish says; Barish, however, makes no acknowledgement in the light of this parallel that Bradley like himself might have come to his conclusions by means of a comprehensive study of Shakespeare's plays and not merely by the pursuit of 'Bradleyan character'. Such a failure to shift his attitude to Bradley in the light of his findings may not seem very worthy on Barish's part but for the purpose of this argument it is useful because it illustrates the possibility of coming to Bradley's conclusions by different (or at least independent) means.

Another defence of Bradley's method comes curiously enough from F. R. Leavis who wrote:

That it should be possible to argue so solemnly and pertinaciously on the assumption that Iago, his intellect and good fortune belong, like Napoleon and his, to history, may be taken as showing that Shakespeare succeeded in making him plausible enough for the purposes of the drama.[60]

[58] J. A. Barish, 'The Turning away of Prince Hal', *Sh.S.* i (1965), pp. 9–17, at p. 9.

[59] Ibid., p. 15.

[60] F. R. Leavis, op. cit., p. 277.

Leavis is writing with what J. Holloway called 'exasperated sarcasm'[61] but the fact remains that Bradley's treatment of the characters offers a silent and persuasive tribute to Shakespeare's powers as a dramatist of creating a convincing illusion. H. S. Wilson made a similar point:

> The vitality of Cleopatra is so great—like that of Hamlet and Falstaff as Bradley finely remarks in his essay on *Antony and Cleopatra* that we may be in some danger with Antony of simply submitting to her spell, which might conceivably be the greater part of critical wisdom.[62]

Wilson is far from being an oversentimental critic totally involved in the fates of heroes and heroines; the above quotation comes from his book *On the Design of Shakespearian Tragedy* and his concern is with the characters only when they are considered as essential to the design of the plays. Moreover, he is speaking of 'critical wisdom' not the wisdom of a right aesthetic response. Wilson here seems to be making a case for the critical validity of a seemingly uncritical response to the characters in the play; he is saying in a more extreme form something like what Dr. Leavis wrote concerning Iago; that to succumb to the illusion is to testify to its power.

In the twentieth-century boom of critical specialization this may seem a rather amateurish approach, but Bradley, one of the first professional students of literature, was, at least at Oxford, lecturing mostly to amateurs. He was not trying to impart information or critical concepts which would put students through examinations successfully, nor was he publishing his critical findings as a justification for the years of labour he had spent on them. He was talking about Shakespeare and more especially the response to Shakespeare in such a way as to communicate that response. His aim was to increase 'dramatic appreciation' of the tragedies; in furthering this aim some uncritical submission to the dramatic illusion could only be a help.

This may seem to remove the debate from the legitimate field

[61] J. Holloway, *The Story of the Night* (London, 1961), p. 156.

[62] H. S. Wilson, *On the Design of Shakespearian Tragedy* (Toronto/London, 1957), p. 172.

of critical accuracy to the somewhat dubious areas of a critic's effectiveness in communicating his reading. At least in the case of Bradley, however, there seems to be some point in considering the critic in this particular light. Firstly, because Bradley was obliged to attract his hearers; there was no compulsion to listen or even attend; secondly, because Bradley is almost without doubt one of the most 'effective' critics this century has ever known.[63] Unquestionably Bradley owes something of the renown with which his name is repeated throughout critical works to the very effectiveness of his presentation. In many ways this consists in using what Nuttall called 'the shorthand of criticism':[64] talking about Shakespeare's dramas without always limiting his expression by calling to the hearer's mind that what he is talking about is only really illusion. But if we read Bradley carefully we find that he never, or seldom, uses the words 'human beings' when talking of Shakespeare's characters, that he seldom considers (even in the notes) what might have happened if the action had not proceeded as it did. Seldom does he take the play for anything except what it is, a dramatic experience, capable of an infinity of meanings, but complete and perfect in itself. It is unusual to find within the body of the discussions of the individual plays Bradley making this point explicitly, though his discussion of aesthetic principles in general make his position abundantly clear.[65] There is, however, a footnote in *Shakespearean Tragedy* which illustrates how far removed from the 'character critics' with whom he is often associated Bradley in fact was. It displays not only Bradley's truly critical attitude to dramatic character but also the follies of which his period was capable.

The tendency to sentimentalise Lady Macbeth is partly due to Mrs Siddons's fancy that she was a small, fair, blue-eyed woman, 'perhaps even fragile'. Dr. Bucknill, who was unacquainted with this fancy, independently determined that she was 'beautiful and delicate', 'unoppressed by weight of flesh', 'probably small', but 'a tawny or

[63] Macmillan's printing figures for *Oxford Lectures on Poetry* and *Shakespearean Tragedy* are 13,320 and 56,100 cloth, 50,000 paper respectively. In 1957 Noonday of New York also issued a paperback edition of *Shakespearean Tragedy*.

[64] Cf. above n. 27.

[65] Cf. Chap. 3.

brown blonde', with grey eyes: and Brandes affirms that she was lean, slight, and hard. They know much more than Shakespeare, who tells us absolutely nothing on these subjects. That Lady Macbeth, after taking part in a murder, was so exhausted as to faint, will hardly demonstrate her fragility. That she must have been blue-eyed, fair, or red-haired, because she was a Celt, is a bold inference, and it is an idle dream that Shakespeare had any idea of making her or her husband characteristically Celtic. The only evidence ever proffered to prove that she was small is the sentence, 'All the perfumes of Arabia will not sweeten this little hand', and Goliath might have called his hand 'little' in contrast with all the perfumes of Arabia . . . The reader is at liberty to imagine Lady Macbeth's person in the way that pleases him best, or to leave it, as Shakespeare very likely did, unimagined.[66]

In relation to excesses like this Bradley seems drily academic and in fact he was; his style may occasionally remind the reader of the wilder Victorian excesses, and he indubitably approaches the tragedies by means of the characters; but he is not an amateur of the 'belles-lettres' tradition, writing suitable Sunday-afternoon reading for vicars. His work shows everywhere the rigorous discipline of the truly academic approach to literature, but shows it only to the careful scrutineer, for the reader there is no sign that what he is reading was not written purely for enlightenment and entertainment.

It is only as the attitude to Bradley has become more truly critical and less conditioned by response to fashion that Bradley has been understood for what he was. This is true in the case of his character criticism as well as of his philosophic preoccupations. In 1956 Nagarajan wrote:

The emphasis that the study of Shakespearian characterization once used to receive has almost disappeared. Indeed, anyone who now talks of Shakespearian characterization draws the suspicion of being little more than a mere surviving Bradleyite, and Bradleyism, till recently, was the very essence of reaction. But of late there have not been lacking a few independent voices bravely harking back, though, of course, with a difference, to Bradley's approach. Such for instance are Prof. Charlton and Mr. J. I. M. Stewart. Prof. Knights, who was one of the

[66] *S.T.*, p. 379 n.

'rebels' against Bradley has himself freely acknowledged that if he were writing *How many Children had Lady Macbeth?* to-day he would make far more allowance for the extraordinary variety of Shakespeare's tragedies and that he would not write as though there were only one 'right' approach to each and all of them. Knights' admission indicates, I believe, the end of the reaction against Bradley. To deplore the reaction entirely, as 'a devout Bradleyite' is tempted to do, is to be ungrateful to the solid contribution to our reading of Shakespeare that the 'new critics' made. One type of interpretative excess, at least, has disappeared, and there is a greater awareness of Shakespeare's use of the arts of language. We are now insured against Bradley's tendency to lift Shakespearian characters out of the dramatic context where they realize their being and meaning. Having said this, we are free to acknowledge the essential soundness of Bradley's approach. We can now declare without danger of misinterpretation that a Shakespearian play is more a poetic drama than a dramatic poem, letting the emphasis fall on the final product, the drama of the play, and treating the poetry as a means to an end. The end of a Shakespearian play often escapes the simplifying process of verbal definition . . . Anyway, Bradley's study of Shakespeare's characters included an attention to the poetry of his plays; that is obvious from his penetrating discussion of the characters. Bradley was able to win such an insight into the motivation of the characters surely because he responded fully to the language of Shakespeare. His approach was partial; of course, it was bound to be, since in a study of Shakespearian tragedy, it is not possible to give equal attention to all the aspects of Shakespearian tragedy. Are we sure, even now, that we have discovered all the facets? The question, therefore, is rather whether a particular critic, whatever aspect of Shakespeare he has selected, has succeeded in communicating the richness of his subject. The aspect studied must be, naturally, of some fundamental importance. To deny this kind of importance to Shakespearian characterization in order to exalt language or imagery is frivolous today when the objective of the Great Rebellion Against Bradley has been gained.[67]

As early as 1949 J. F. Danby felt that 'Shakespeare criticism has had enough experience of the "symbol" and "image" and "theme" approach to be warned of the danger invited by too naïve a

[67] S. Nagarajan, 'A note on Banquo', *S.Q.* vii (1956), pp. 371–6, at p. 371.

reaction against Bradley and common sense'.[68] Yet more than ten years later J. Bayley was paying lip service to the fashion of denigrating Bradley while at the same time expressing confidence in his method of criticism. Critical change is slow to establish itself as a historical fact. The mark left by the anti-Bradley school has proved stronger than that of most reactions. If Bradley was and is still a widely influential critic, F. R. Leavis and the L. C. Knights of *How many Children had Lady Macbeth?* were equally, or maybe more, startlingly effective. Danby's hint in 1949, Nagarajan's article in 1956, are indications of the way fashions were changing, but perhaps not until John Bayley wrote his book *The Characters of Love: A Study in the Literature of Personality* did character criticism claim for itself once more a right to be considered as one of the most valid approaches to literature. Bayley's work deals with a Chaucerian poem, a Shakespeare play, and an early twentieth-century novel; and to all three his approach is by means of the characters, which throws odd light on those who like George Watson[69] think that characters naturalistically considered belong only in the nineteenth-century novels. Almost inevitably for a critic discussing characters in such a way and in particular dealing with one of the four tragedies with which Bradley dealt, Bayley devotes some careful attention to Bradley's position in the critical theories of the day. He wrote:

the whole idea of discussing the tragedies and their characters in terms of fiction is now very much frowned upon. It is an approach associated with Bradley's classic on Shakespearean Tragedy, and though Bradley's perceptions are still respected his critical premises are not. They are held to lead to the kind of query which Maurice Morgann had raised a hundred years before in his essay suggesting that Falstaff was not *really* a coward at all—the kind of query which L. C. Knights satirized as *How many Children had Lady Macbeth?* But perhaps the time has come to ask ourselves whether this sort of query is really quite so absurd as it sounds. Its great virtue . . . is that it takes for granted the scope and completeness of Shakespeare's tragic setting, and also his success in conveying the wider consciousness of his major figures as

[68] J. F. Danby, *Shakespeare's Doctrine of Nature: A Study of King Lear* (London, 1949), p. 17.

[69] Cf. above, n. 8.

well as their dramatic and functional personality. There is a sense in which the highest compliment we can pay to Shakespeare is to discuss his great plays as if they were also great novels. Can one, in fact, ask an irrelevant question about the completely successful 'inside and outside' character? Of either the Ancients or Moderns, observed Dryden, Shakespeare had the largest and most *comprehensive* mind, and one can be sure that somewhere in that mind the problem of Lady Macbeth's children would find its appropriate resolution.[70]

The publication of this work did not see the end of the anti-Bradleyan attitude to character study which will last, no doubt, as long as Bradley is read; but it sees the beginning of a period in which it will be possible to discuss character in terms very similar to those used by Bradley without being subject to the sort of criticism which would previously have attached to that approach. While it is still possible for chairmen at public lectures to make jokes at Bradley's expense, the more cautious world of literary periodicals is treating Bradley with more respect, as an approach to literature which accepts the illusion of character as a legitimate vehicle for the author's meaning is becoming more and more accepted.

In the case of Bradley the Victorian, Bradley the philosopher and moralist, it was seen that the work of reaction was necessary so that the twentieth century could justify, in an air free from excessive reverence to the past, its own peculiar approach to Shakespeare. This is not true in the same way of the reaction to Bradley's character criticism, where another element creeps in. Bradley's character-studies of the four great tragedies, *Antony and Cleopatra*, and to a lesser extent *Coriolanus* and *Henry IV*, were so thorough that for following generations Bradley's characters came to be accepted as Shakespeare's. This, as Bradley himself would readily have admitted, was neither accurate nor helpful and a rejection of the validity of Bradley's characters and at the same time of Shakespeare's followed quickly. By his very success Bradley had exhausted the approach which he followed. If that was the way to discuss Shakespeare, then Bradley did it to perfection. The answer to this was that, of course, this was not the

[70] J. Bayley, *The Characters of Love* (London, 1960), p. 41.

way to discuss Shakespeare and alternatives abounded. Of the alternatives few if any found as competent and winning a practitioner as Bradley. A guide to Shakespeare studies written in 1962, thought that Bradley, H. Granville-Barker, and Wilson Knight were the three outstanding critics of this century;[71] the expounders of the comparative literature, and the historico-sociological research schools, the imagery-seeking, theme-hunting critics are all omitted. It is a picture which would probably gain common assent. *Shakespearean Tragedy* whatever its shortcomings is a comprehensive survey. *How many Children had Lady Macbeth?* is merely a sketch; the one was a serious attempt to increase 'dramatic appreciation' of Shakespeare by the means considered most appropriate to the subject matter, the consideration of 'action issuing from character or . . . character issuing in action': the other a piece of polemical writing concerned only to indicate an alternative and not concerned with testing that alternative by thorough application to the subject. What was true of one scene need not necessarily be true of one play let alone a whole corpus.

Right or wrong Bradley was of such a critical stature that for over fifty years critics were afraid to enter the same field for fear of being overshadowed. The foolishness of this critical cowardice is demonstrated by Dr. Leavis's successful attempt to beat Bradley on his own ground. Leavis's tone has annoyed many of his potential following, but there is now always the Leavis *Othello* to be placed in juxtaposition to the Bradley *Othello* and from these alternatives a more accurate picture of *Othello* (Shakespeare's *Othello*) must emerge. Reverence for Bradley in this particular field of his criticism has displayed itself largely by a harsh and unremitting refusal to accept the validity or in some cases the existence of that critical approach. It is a reverence which has been harmful not only to the reputation of Bradley but to the development of a truer criticism of Shakespeare. Bradley was seen as only a biographically-minded critic (which he was not) and conversely a critical approach which includes

[71] D. J. Palmer, 'A Short Guide to Shakespeare Studies', *C.S.* i (1962), pp. 34–8 at p. 38.

consideration of the characters has been thought to be therefore only an exploration of biography; both are rejected totally. Only when this state of affairs had reached its extreme did a natural reversal set in; character was again seen as an integral part of drama and Bradley was again consulted and found not to be so narrowly concerned with character as was previously the general opinion.

7

BRADLEY AS AUTHORITY

NOT only a critic's general ideas and theories but also his observations of detail make his reputation live. In some ways the one is a test of the other; obviously a critic's general position is to a large extent justified in the eyes of the reader in proportion as the reader approves the perspicacity of the critic's remarks on hitherto unnoticed aspects of the drama. Succeeding generations, moreover, often cling to the judgements of particulars while discarding the general assumptions behind a critic's writing; then as time erases even the memory of the general assumptions it is in part perhaps due to the lasting influence of the particular criticism that interest is revived in the critical attitudes of the critic in question. On the other hand, a critic is likely to be reduced to an obscure name much referred to in editorial footnotes, and elsewhere ignored, unless there is enough weight in his general criticism to support the occasional insights.

In criticism more value is placed on method than results; the much decried attitude 'I know what I like' still receives the final reverence; no one person's interpretation of the play can be allowed to be true, or even necessarily more true than another. If criticism is part of an equipment for reading then obviously the methods of the critic must be of more interest than his results —which are his and his alone, applicable only to the particular works he writes of and of no further use. On the other hand, the need is felt to test the critical method against the original; the way to do this is to scrutinize his judgement on particular issues. Often without effort the reader does this; if the critic makes an observation of which he approves, and which he thinks supported by the text but unnoticed by other critics and himself, then he is going to feel more kindly towards the critical methods which produced those results. Moreover a critic who concentrates on method to the exclusion of producing a reading is not going to impress a reader with the validity of his method.

In more sophisticated critical times writers are apt to defend themselves against the unspoken accusation that they are merely adding to the already excessive quantity of Shakespeare criticism by saying that they have evolved a modified method of looking at the plays and that this produces a new reading, more likely to be accurate to the original and relevant to the present generation. In Bradley's time it was not necessary to begin one's exposition 'it is hoped that the account which follows will do something to justify the choice of method'.[1] Criticism was not then so scientific a process, but even so the assessment of Bradley's influence in twentieth-century Shakespeare criticism would not be complete without some reference to Bradley's judgements on particular issues, as Bradley in the famous Notes was responsible for many such observations of detail. The more so because it was at least at one time true as John Bayley wrote: 'though Bradley's perceptions are still respected his critical premises are not.'[2]

An examination of the extent of reference to a critic's particular judgements will illuminate his position and also the ways in which critical influence works. Casually expressed ideas are seized upon, major theories wrongly attributed and time builds endless ramifications on one man's foundation. This can best be seen by examining one such example at length and in the course of this chapter a close look will be taken at the permeation of two of Bradley's judgements on *King Lear*.

In fact, Bradley's influence in matters of detail is widespread. Understandably enough in some respects; the more renowned the name, the more worthwhile it is to quote it. Consequently Bradley's opinion is cited in matters to which he only referred briefly and *en passant*. Thus C. J. Sisson writes: 'Much has been made, as by A. C. Bradley, of the certainty that Aaron in *Titus Andronicus* is a negro, and is a Moor.'[3] A reader of that remark

[1] D. A. Traversi, *An Approach to Shakespeare* (London/Glasgow, 1938), quotation from 1957 edn., p. 5.

[2] J. Bayley, *The Characters of Love* (London, 1960), p. 41.

[3] C. J. Sisson, *Shakespeare's Tragic Justice* (London, n.d. [? 1962]), p. 39.

might justifiably expect a paragraph devoted to the subject. In fact all that can be found is the following:

> No-one who reads *Titus Andronicus* with an open mind can doubt that Aaron was, in our sense, black; and he appears to have been a Negro. To mention nothing else, he is twice called 'coal-black'; his colour is compared with that of a raven and a swan's legs; his child is coal-black and thick-lipped; he himself has a 'fleece of woolly hair'. Yet he is 'Aaron the Moor', just as Othello is 'Othello the Moor'.[4]

And this as the final sentence reveals is merely a buttress to the main argument about Othello's colour. Yet according to C. J. Sisson, A. C. Bradley is 'making much of the issue'; what Sisson's remark in fact reveals is the weight which Bradley's opinion carries even in a matter with which he only deals parenthetically. It is testimony to the reliability of Bradley's judgement that he should be cited thus, but it is perhaps even more evidence of the power of his name. This is an instance that could be repeated. H. S. Wilson refers to Bradley's judgement on the dramatic function of the quarrel scene in *Julius Caesar*: a judgement made in less than half a page in order to sustain Bradley's argument about the lower tension which follows the central scenes of the play.[5] R. W. Chambers in a lecture on *Measure for Measure* quotes what is virtually an aside of Bradley's: 'Even the sober A. C. Bradley thought that here Shakespeare lent himself to a "scandalous proceeding" ',[6] that is in making Isabella marry the Duke. In fact at his least sober, Bradley throws out at the end of his lecture on 'Construction in Shakespeare's Tragedies':

> We know well enough what Shakespeare is doing when at the end of *Measure for Measure* he marries Isabella to the Duke—and a scandalous proceeding it is; but who can ever feel sure that the doubts which vex him as to some not unimportant points in *Hamlet* are due to his own want of eyesight or to Shakespeare's want of care?[7]

[4] *S.T.*, p. 200. The index reveals no other source of information on this subject.

[5] H. S. Wilson, *On the Design of Shakespearian Tragedy* (Toronto/London 1957), p. 242, n. 20 (reference p. 97); *S.T.*, p. 58.

[6] R. W. Chambers, 'The Jacobean Shakespeare and *Measure for Measure*', *B.A.* (1937), p. 57.

[7] *S.T.*, p. 78.

Such is Bradley's stature as a critic that his name is valid in an argument whether or not he is in fact an authority on the subject in hand. It seems almost as though critics feel that their work is not complete without some reference to Bradley. In the case of the last reference by Chambers, for example, there are two explanations as to why Bradley's opinion on the question should be quoted. Either Chambers knows the Bradley comment so well that he can make a casual reference to it, or he scoured Bradley's work for a reference to *Measure for Measure*. The former seems more likely; there are other references to Bradley in the article and Chambers was one of the original reviewers of *Shakespearean Tragedy*. In either case, however, the quotation is highly flattering; though possibly not so flattering as the following sentence of A. P. Rossiter's comment on *King Lear*: 'Bradley is uninterested in such comic effects.'[8] Rossiter is not here talking about Bradley but about the play and yet Bradley's failure to show any interest in this aspect is considered significant enough to be worthy of mention. Rossiter it seems expects critics, or at least Bradley, to cover all aspects of the work discussed and so in the case of Bradley here finds significance in the omission of any reference. What Rossiter in fact seems to be saying is that despite the attention paid to the comic in *King Lear* Bradley, who studied the plays so thoroughly, omitted any reference to it, so that in fact the comic cannot be so important. Either that or Rossiter is making a slight sneer at Bradley which in its way offers equal testimony to his power as a critic.

Of more critical significance perhaps is the eagerness of critics to refer to Bradley as authority for their own particular approach. Perhaps the most outstanding case of this is J. M. Murry's *Keats and Shakespeare* which seems to use A. C. Bradley as evidence for the feasibility of its main idea. Murry wrote:

it seems only an accident that Prof. Bradley did not treat of Keats' letters and poetry together as a kind of preamble to his famous lectures on Shakespeare. . . . Time and again in his lecture and his essay, Professor Bradley seems to me on the brink of formulating the view and the doctrine I have been driven to expound in the book. Time and

[8] A. P. Rossiter, *Angel with Horns* (London, 1961), p. 270.

again he marshals the evidence, in his masterly fashion, so that the conclusion to which I have been forced appears inevitable: yet for some reason he does not draw it.[9]

In fact to any reader of both works it does not seem like an accident at all and the reason why Bradley does not draw Murry's conclusion is only too apparent. If Bradley teetered on the edge of the mystical, Murry worked almost exclusively in it; if there are dangers in Bradley that he should descend to the merely whimsical, Murry falls into those dangers. The methods of the two critics may have been in some ways similar but in this case, for instance, Bradley was making a critical point about the nature of Keats's mind and the possibility that it resembled in quality the mind of the young Shakespeare; Murry is exploring the chance of continuity between the two poets which amounts to something like the transmigration of souls. That Murry should make so much of his claim that, at least according to Murry, Bradley had had similar ideas before him but not actually stated them illustrates the nature of Murry's mind but also shows a real and influential respect for the intuitions of Bradley.

Though there are wide differences between the approach of these two critics there is a much wider difference not only in approach and period but also in sympathy between Miss L. B. Campbell and A. C. Bradley and yet even she seems to see Bradley as hovering on the brink of making the discoveries which she herself made later. In her article 'Bradley Revisited: Forty Years After', she has some particularly harsh things to say about Bradley's attitude to Shakespeare but nevertheless we find:

That Bradley was feeling for some truth beyond his inadequate explanations of the supernatural is apparent from passing remarks.

Bradley's intuition here was reaching out towards an Elizabethan commonplace.

Bradley seems to be reaching toward a more integrated philosophy in the tragedies than that which he expounds in fragments.[10]

[9] J. M. Murry, *Keats and Shakespeare* (London, 1925), p. 8.

[10] L. B. Campbell, 'Bradley Revisited: Forty Years After', *S.Ph.* xliv (1947), pp. 174–94, at pp. 187, 188, and 189.

This amounts either to a grudging admission that there is more in Bradley than at first appeared to Miss Campbell's critical eye or to a quite uncritical reluctance to believe that Bradley's results could have totally differed from her own. What in fact seems likely is that both Bradley and Miss Campbell are aware of some aspects of Shakespearean tragedy in exactly the same way; Miss Campbell, however, began her article as a refutation of the validity of Bradley's approach and seeing these similarities can only account for them as vague probings by the Victorian Bradley after a more modern, more Elizabethan approach. Reluctant to admit that her approach and Bradley's are not so essentially dissimilar, she cannot fail to recognize the similarities between his and her own findings; these she then can only explain by a picture of Bradley unconsciously striving to be a historical critic.

It is an odd testimony to Bradley's comprehensiveness as a critic that other critics should father the vague beginnings of their method on Bradley; but the above are not the only cases. Wilson Knight's claim[11] to be the mere continuer of a line of criticism begun by Bradley is the most obvious example and perhaps the most obviously justifiable. These two critics have much in common. W. Empson and Bradley, however, would be expected to have nothing at all similar to say. The contrary is in fact true and Empson generously and fully acknowledges Bradley.[12] This general acknowledgement, however, would be of little interest in the present discussion if it were not for the favourable reference Empson makes to Bradley's interpretation of the lines:

> The knave turns Fool that runs away;
> The Fool no knave, perdy.[13]

Empson seems to be acknowledging Bradley as a comparable master in his own peculiar field of word-play and verbal interpretation.

[11] G. Wilson Knight, Prefatory Notes to 1947 edn., *The Wheel of Fire*, and 1951 edn., *The Imperial Theme*.

[12] W. Empson, *The Structure of Complex Words* (London, 1951), p. 125, quoted Chap. 1, p. 9.

[13] Ibid., p. 132.

Empson only returned to Bradley having drafted his piece; he is acknowledging not so much the use of a particular reading and study of *Shakespearean Tragedy* but the power of the general influence of Bradley on his thought. This is perhaps one of the highest compliments which a critic can receive, especially if, as is the case here, the writer produces work quite different from that of the first critic. Empson was not the only critic to read Bradley after he had written his own findings on the subject. D. G. James read Bradley on Wordsworth for the first time after he had written his section on Wordsworth in *Scepticism and Poetry* and says in a footnote: 'The reader who feels that in the above section I have over-emphasized one aspect of Wordsworth's imaginative life may be advised to read Bradley's remarkable lecture.'[14] Obviously the fact that one other person, however obscure, has produced similar findings is going to add substance to what is felt to be an unusual or extreme reading. Equally obviously, though, the more authority the other person has the more substance there is in the support. It is evidence of James's respect for Bradley that he should cite him as an authority in this matter.

A critic, however, is not only cited by his followers and disciples, he is as likely, if his criticism has attracted enough serious attention to be quoted by those who consider his criticism mere folly. John Dover Wilson in his book *The Fortunes of Falstaff* quotes or refers to Bradley in order to disagree with him at least seven times.[15] In cases where the critic has, like Bradley, attempted a comprehensive survey of controversial matters and where he has attracted sufficient attention from readers and other critics, he is likely to be quoted as summing up one side of the argument. Thus Granville-Barker takes Bradley for his opponent in his discussion of whether *King Lear* is fitted for the stage. This is not because he is unaware of the fact that it was Charles Lamb who first started the argument but because, as he says, Bradley's is 'a profounder and a more searching indictment of the play's

[14] D. G. James, *Scepticism and Poetry* (London, 1937), p. 164.

[15] J. D. Wilson, *The Fortunes of Falstaff* (Cambridge, 1943), pp. 85, 88, 95, 104, 118, 122, and 123 respectively.

stage-worthiness'.[16] For other critics Bradley's view represents the whole argument against the stageworthiness of *King Lear*—this involves some inaccuracy in the representation of Bradley's case but inaccuracy in such matters is the natural result of popularity. It becomes known that Bradley thought *King Lear* unfit for the stage; people who have not read his argument refer to it and in so doing embroider upon the bare facts.

In the same way as Bradley represents one extreme about *King Lear*'s fitness for the stage so he does the argument about *Othello*. At least, since F. R. Leavis's article, he is taken to represent the Romantic Othello, the incarnately evil Iago, although this is a gross oversimplification of Bradley's view. But to several critics since, the criticism of *Othello* seems to have developed into a debate between the Leavis interpretation and the Bradley response.

John Holloway has an appendix on the subject; he makes plain that, in fact, the difficulty of choosing between Leavis and Bradley can be avoided by choosing *Othello* but none the less the general impression left by the whole is that the reader must affiliate himself to one or the other. He writes:

> If the reader had to choose between this [Leavis's] error, (for error it is) and Bradley's steady under-rating of the strength and evil of Othello's jealousy once he does become jealous; if that is to say, he did not have Othello's own simple 'One not easily jealous, but being wrought Perplex'd in the extreme'; he would be in difficulty. If we have to choose between errors we might prefer Dr. Leavis's to Bradley's. Bradley's account is not only wrong, it is irritatingly so, and one cannot accuse Dr. Leavis of blindness to this source of irritation. His responsiveness to it does not show, indeed, merely in asserting that Bradley tried to 'sentimentalize Shakespeare's tragedy and displace its centre'. That comment is a just one. But it seems almost like praise of Bradley by comparison with the abuse which runs, distractingly in my own experience, through the opening pages of Dr. Leavis's essay. . . .—thanks to the dash and momentum of Dr. Leavis's essay—

[16] H. Granville-Barker, *Preface to Shakespeare*, vol. i (London, 1958), quotation from 1961 edition, p. 262. Cf. Chap. 5 for other comments on Bradley's views in this matter.

we can now afford to consider whether Dr. Leavis, in his exasperation, replaced Bradley's errors by errors of his own.[17]

This seems to sum up the situation accurately enough and Holloway goes on to replace Leavis's overhastily jealous Othello with an Othello more fitted to the role of hero. Before this appendix closes though, Holloway cannot but return to the original debate; it is as though he feels that he must make it plain on whose side he stands:

Whether this recurrent hastiness and distortion are the products of Dr. Leavis's not unnatural exasperation with Bradley, and eager desire to refute Bradley's findings, it is impossible to say. But this seems a not unlikely account of the note of vexation which runs throughout his piece. . . . The whole brilliant piece is geared to the destruction of Bradley's case. The genius which it displays is a forensic genius; none the less so for being (I assume) forensic without intention. 'Diabolic Intellect' does not display Dr. Leavis's powers at their best; but for a display of his powers at their highest 'Diabolic Intellect' is perfect. It is no wonder that one may justly say of Dr. Leavis what he said of Bradley and assert that what he wrote 'is still a very potent and mischievous influence'. Probably it will survive this, and abler, examinations of it. That will not be for its merits as criticism.[18]

The implication is that it will be for its success in the forensic art directed against Bradley's interpretation of *Othello*. It is a compliment to Bradley no less than to Leavis.

If Holloway is a partisan of the Leavis attack on Bradley's *Othello*, Bradley's *Othello* is not quite without supporters. John Dover Wilson in the introduction to the New Cambridge edition, like Holloway, feels that the reader must choose one or the other:

Readers and speculators may take their choice of these Othellos. Bradley's, with minor qualifications, is unhesitatingly mine. For I agree with him that human integrity is still possible and that Shakespeare, whether he knew his Aristotle or not, wrote this final scene as he wrote those of most of his other tragedies, with the double purpose

[17] J. Holloway, *The Story of the Night* (London, 1961), Appendix A: 'Dr. Leavis and Diabolic Intellect', pp. 155–6.

[18] Ibid., p. 165.

of first harrowing his audience with the terror and pity of the catastrophe and then sending them home with the feeling of redemption, reconciliation and even exultation which the great tragedians of all ages have aroused.[19]

Neither Holloway for Leavis nor Wilson for Bradley is noticeably critical in their approach. It is as though they thought that judgement had been taken out of their hands. Bradley and Leavis had summed up the arguments for their respective opinions; all that is left for successive readers and critics, they seem to say, is to choose between them. The same is to a certain extent true of criticism of the Falstaff history plays. It is unstated but widely shown that critics feel they must choose between Bradley's view of the 'Rejection of Falstaff' or J. Dover Wilson's of 'The Restoration of Law and Order'. Jonas A. Barish labelled the two camps sentimentalists and moralists. He, as was seen in Chapter 6, chose the former.[20] J. I. M. Stewart reviews both Bradley's view and J. Dover Wilson's at length; not for their own sakes specifically but as a help towards understanding the role of Falstaff in the history plays. Nevertheless, and despite a critical acuity which prevents any simple demarcation of criticism on this point, Stewart's position is made quite clear.

Bradley's is still, perhaps, the best explanation: our having this sense results from Shakespeare's failing of his intention to manoeuvre Falstaff into an unsympathetic light. But is there anything more to be said?

Obviously, one possibility remains. Shakespeare *succeeded* in manoeuvring Falstaff into an unsympathetic light. If, with Bradley, we feel otherwise, we are being sentimental, un-Elizabethan, and disregardful of the fortunes of Falstaff as the drama develops. This is the contention of Professor Dover Wilson.[21]

And after paying due respect to Bradley's view which as he notices also provided us with Charlton's explanation, Stewart chooses, with his own modifications, Dover Wilson's view.

[19] A. Walker and J. D. Wilson (eds.), *Othello*, New Cambridge Edition (Cambridge, 1957), p. liii.

[20] Cf. Chap. 6, p. 140.

[21] J. I. M. Stewart, *Character and Motive in Shakespeare* (London, 1949), pp. 132–3.

In the paperback edition of *Oxford Lectures on Poetry* M. R. Ridley wrote of Bradley's essay on Falstaff: 'its reading of the problem is by now, I believe, generally accepted.'[22] This seems to oversimplify the state of studies in Falstaff in a way which is not necessarily any kinder to Bradley's reputation than the truth. The fact is that criticism still hovers between the sentimentalist's and the moralist's view; some critics choose one and some the other but none makes his choice without paying respect to the opposing view. Bradley's service to criticism in this sphere is that he has summed up the 'sentimentalist' case with all the perspicacity and eloquence possible. His name has become a symbol for his criticism; and his criticism itself has become a milestone, from which progress forward can be measured. It is no longer necessary to cover again the ground covered by Bradley (and before him by Morgann and Lamb); Charlton's essay,[23] for example, offers little of permanent value to criticism on the subject.

Bradley's criticism of particular instances has not only served as a summing up of the past, in certain cases he has provided the starting point for critical ideas which are still developing. In these cases it is possible to over-estimate the importance of Bradley's contribution, to imply, if not to say, that without Bradley, criticism on this subject would not be the same. This seems highly unlikely. What Bradley does provide in such instances is a germ of an idea which quite often only much later received any critical attention. It is not on account of Bradley's comment that *Hamlet* is in the widest possible sense a religious drama that modern criticism has laid so much stress on this aspect of the play. What seems to be true is that Bradley's hint is taken to give substance to the argument. Critics like Ribner for example, are apt to cite Bradley in a footnote;[24] in fact all that Bradley says on the subject is:

> It will be agreed that, while *Hamlet* certainly cannot be called in the specific sense a 'religious drama', there is in it nevertheless both a

[22] M. R. Ridley, Introduction to paperback edn. *Oxford Lectures on Poetry* (London, 1965), p. xiv.

[23] H. B. Charlton, 'Falstaff', in *J.R.L.B.*, xix (1935), pp. 44–89.

[24] I. Ribner, *Patterns in Shakespearian Tragedy* (London, 1960), p. 66.

freer use of popular religious ideas, and a more decided, though always imaginative, intimation of a supreme power concerned in human evil and good, than can be found in any other of Shakespeare's tragedies.[25]

This hardly warrants even a footnote; it is testimony to the range of Bradley's fame that he should be cited in a peculiarly modern critical argument, on the strength of such an almost apologetic remark.

The modern criticism of *King Lear* provides another example of the effect of one remark of Bradley's on subsequent criticism. In effect modern criticism of *King Lear* concentrates on one minor point, to which it gives seemingly unnecessary stress, and depending on this minor point makes its general judgement of the whole play. Bradley wrote of Lear's last words:

He is sure, at last, that she *lives*: . . . To us, perhaps, the knowledge that he is deceived may bring a culmination of pain: but if it brings *only* that, I believe we are false to Shakespeare, and it seems almost beyond question that any actor is false to the text who does not attempt to express, in Lear's last accents and gestures and look, an unbearable *joy*.[26]

The other point to which in later criticism, at least, the first seems to be related is that instead of dwelling on the pain the reader should remember 'The Redemption of King Lear'. Stress has been laid, as will be seen, largely on this 'redemption' but in fact Bradley's whole statement was much more complex; it seems worthwhile to summarize his argument here, before proceeding to discussion of the fortunes of these two ideas in subsequent criticism. Bradley in discussing Lear's character emphasizes how his fate, at least in part, is a direct result of his action:

The perception of this connection, if it is not lost as the play advances, does not at all diminish our pity for Lear, but it makes it impossible for us permanently to regard the world displayed in this tragedy as subject to a mere arbitrary or malicious power . . . But there is another aspect of Lear's story, the influence of which modifies, in a way quite different and more peculiar to this tragedy, the impressions called pessimistic and even this impression of law. . . . The

[25] *S.T.*, p. 174. [26] Ibid., p. 291.

old King who in pleading with his daughters feels so intensely his own humiliation and their horrible ingratitude, and who yet, at fourscore and upward, constrains himself to practise a self-control and patience so many years disused; who out of old affection for his fool and in repentance for his injustice to the Fool's beloved mistress, tolerates incessant and cutting reminders of his own folly and wrong; in whom the rage of the storm awakes a power and a poetic grandeur surpassing even that of Othello's anguish; who comes in his affliction to think of others first, and to seek, in tender solicitude for his poor boy, the shelter he scorns for his own bare head; who learns to feel and to pray for the miserable and houseless poor, to discern the falseness of flattery and the brutality of authority, and to pierce below the differences of rank and raiment to the common humanity beneath; whose sight is so purged by scalding tears that it sees at last how power and place and all things in the world are vanity except love; who tastes in his last hours the extremes both of love's rapture and of agony, but could never, if he lived on or lived again, care a jot for aught beside—there is no figure, surely, in the world of poetry at once so grand, so pathetic, and so beautiful as his. Well, but Lear owes the whole of this to those sufferings which made us doubt whether life were not simply evil and men like the flies which wanton boys torture for their sport. Should we not be at least as near the truth if we called this poem *The Redemption of King Lear* and declared that the business of 'the gods' with him was neither to torment him nor to teach him a 'noble anger', but to lead him to attain through apparently hopeless failure the very end and aim of life?[27]

This has been quoted at length because the assumption that it makes has become one of the critical facts of modern Shakespeare criticism. This assumption was not new with Bradley; Dowden as Bradley himself points out[28] talked of the 'purification' of Lear. Nevertheless, it is in the words 'The Redemption of King Lear' that the idea has permeated subsequent criticism. Before discussing the critical history of this conception of the whole play, however, it will be interesting to investigate the fate of Bradley's interpretation of the final speech. Bradley was the first critic to suggest that Lear died in joy because he believed Cordelia lived; the fate of this easily isolated critical perception

[27] Ibid., pp. 284–5. [28] Ibid., p. 285.

will illustrate perhaps, the waywardness of critical development and the erratic progress of seminal ideas.

As a corrective to any suggestion that all critics recognize the sources for their ideas or are even conscious that their ideas have sources except in their own minds, there exists a remarkable number of critics who refer to this interpretation of Lear's death without making any reference either to Bradley's original thesis or to the fact that the idea is a controversial one. P. N. Siegel, a critic who gives plenty of evidence of having studied Bradley, expresses his opinion that Lear thinks Cordelia lives and makes no reference to A. C. Bradley.[29] H. S. Wilson likewise is of the opinion that 'he dies in the belief that Cordelia lives'[30] and makes no reference to Bradley although three pages before he wrote 'what Bradley missed we may think is the symbolic appropriateness of this final scene. It is worth examining carefully'.[31] In the course of this examination he produces Bradley's own idea, quite unrecognized. Fluchère further refers to Bradley's own quoted lines 'Look there' to demonstrate that Lear thought Cordelia lived; but he makes no reference to Bradley.[32] M. D. H. Parker similarly shows no knowledge of the source for her statement: 'He dies believing that, after all, she does live.'[33]

John Holloway, however, goes further than this and rejects what he refers to as 'R. W. Chambers' opinion that both Gloucester and Lear die of joy'.[34] This seems a little perverse. A. C. Bradley propounds the idea, using almost exactly these words in a well-known work of Shakespeare criticism, published in 1904, available and well known ever since; yet Holloway accredits this idea to a lecture delivered in Glasgow by a man not noted for his Shakespeare criticism thirty-five years after the idea was first made known. What would be interesting if it were possible

[29] P. N. Siegel, *Shakespearean Tragedy and the Elizabethan Compromise* (New York), pp. 183–5.

[30] H. S. Wilson, *On the Design of Shakespearian Tragedy* (Toronto/London, 1957), p. 204.

[31] Ibid., p. 201.

[32] H. Fluchère, *Shakespeare* (Toulouse, 1948), quotation from London edn., 1953, p. 248.

[33] M. D. H. Parker, *The Slave of Life: A Study of Shakespeare and the Idea of Justice* (London, 1955), p. 143.

[34] J. Holloway, *The Story of the Night* (London, 1961), p. 90.

would be to know how knowledge of the idea's true source would have affected Holloway's attitude towards it. Bradley because he is a conscious innovator expends some time over proving his point within the body of the lecture and also for the benefit of the readers in a footnote. Chambers was relying on an already proven idea and accompanies his statement only by reference to his sources. This in itself makes Holloway's confusion even more illuminating of the ways of critics because Chambers recognizes and acknowledges the source of the idea. Chambers wrote of the 'unbearable joy' theory: 'That Bradley's interpretation is *not* fantastic but a true perception of Shakespeare's meaning, can be proved I think when we examine Shakespeare's sources.'[35]

The American critic Heilman, on the other hand, recognizes the source and the supporters of the idea: 'Bradley, Granville-Barker, and Chambers agree that Lear dies in the ecstasy of thinking that Cordelia is alive.' Heilman, however, is not sure that Bradley and the others are right. Lear, he says, is 'possibly convinced that he does see life'.[36] This dissent from Bradley's interpretation of the fact is not uncommon among people who recognize the idea as Bradley's, though there are those among mid-century critics who like Ribner approve the interpretation and acknowledge its not altogether fashionable source.[37]

On this point there is a surprising number of critics who are prepared to let the issue rest on an 'if'. It seems almost as though they are unwilling to agree with Bradley overtly and yet need to use his basic idea. There is an almost awed reluctance to enter into the debate, combined perhaps with a resigned feeling that the rightness or otherwise of Bradley is a matter not to be decided by man. It is a regrettable effect of the extent and nature of the Bradley controversy that this has come about; for if critics' opinions are to be allowed to stand prefaced by the writer's 'if' almost any opinion will come to serve its turn.

Helen Gardner, it must be allowed, was lecturing when she

[35] R. W. Chambers, *King Lear*. The First W. P. Ker Memorial Lecture delivered in the University of Glasgow, 1939 (published Glasgow, 1940), p. 44.

[36] R. B. Heilman, *This Great Stage* (Baton Rouge, 1948), pp. 305 and 55 respectively.

[37] I. Ribner, op. cit., p. 122.

said, 'If Bradley was right in thinking Lear dies in joy—he dies in typical hope',[38] and so could urge shortage of time as an excuse for passing over the debate in her remark. On the other hand, the second part of her comment ceases to have validity as a comment upon the play if the first half of the sentence is not true, and surely whether or not the hero of a Shakespearean tragedy dies in illusion (Dame Helen Gardner went on to point out that the other characters knew Cordelia to be dead) is of crucial importance in any criticism of the play. She seems here to be content to throw out a conjectural idea based on the original perception of another critic to whom she is not prepared to give her unconditional support. It seems an odd way to conduct a critical argument, especially as this is not an isolated example. Early in the lecture Dame Helen said: 'It is possible and is done very finely by Bradley to display this progress of Lear.' This seems a method of criticism verging on the ridiculous; the conception would hardly be worth repeating if it did not have at least enough critical validity for another critic to build upon it. If it has such critical validity then it seems a tortuous way of presenting the argument to hedge it with 'it is possible' and 'if'. All criticism must to a certain extent be conjectural, but all critics must also make up their minds which conjectures they are going to accept. To deny an audience the help of knowing whether or not the speaker agrees with the ideas he relies upon for his argument, is sophistication at its worst.

In view of the uncritical nature of the Bradley controversy it is perhaps in many ways not surprising that critics are unwilling to enter into a debate to which, at least at one time, there seemed no answer and which was possibly going to brand them for their critical life. Certainly Miss Gardner is not alone in her 'if'. G. L. Bickersteth in a British Academy Shakespeare Lecture wrote: 'If Bradley be right, it is not the chance, but the certainty that she does indeed so live which causes even Lear's hitherto indomitable heart to break, and the great sufferer dies at last, not of sorrow, but in an ecstasy of joy.'[39] Here the 'if' in the light

[38] H. Gardner, *King Lear*. John Coffin Memorial Lecture, 1966.

[39] G. L. Bickersteth, 'The Golden World of *King Lear*', *B.A.* (1946), p. 27.

of the rest of the sentence seems only rhetorical; the hesitation of a 'modern' critic who had earlier moreover dealt with Bradley with the disdain more fashionable in 1946, to accept one of that critic's most typical utterances. To have agreed downright would no doubt have been an uncomfortable admission for a critic who wrote sternly:

> The effect of *King Lear* . . . has never been denied even by critics like Charles Lamb and Andrew Bradley who were persuaded . . . that by no mere stage-representation of the play could it ever be more than dimly suggested, if indeed by this means it could be communicated at all.[40]

Geoffrey Bush, however, is prepared to leave the whole issue in question: 'Lear dies in happiness, if Bradley is right'[41] he says and this seems to be his total contribution to the debate. The question is settled as simply as that; all that is needed, it seems, is for some arbiter of criticism to decide whether Bradley is right or not. The question cannot, according to this highly flattering (if somewhat bewildering) reference to Bradley, be settled any other way; reference to the text, the structure, the characters and the source of the play, all these are omitted—Bradley offers the only answer.

Other critics have, however, been prepared to quarrel with Bradley. Narayana Menon felt: 'It befits tragedy that Lear should die of a paroxysm of anguish (Dowden . . .) rather than of the ecstatic joy (*Shakespearean Tragedy*, 291) born of delusion';[42] which presents and accepts the alternative reading. Two later critics in articles in *Shakespeare Survey* discussed the matter at length. J. K. Walton devoted an article wholly to the last speech of *King Lear*; that this article should have been written is probably owing primarily to Bradley's original interpretation. Perhaps the highest award which criticism can make is to devote a whole article to the discussion of one idea first propagated by one critic.

[40] Ibid., p. 7.

[41] G. Bush, *Shakespeare and the Natural Condition* (Cambridge, Mass., 1956), p. 128.

[42] C. Narayana Menon, *Shakespeare Criticism an Essay in Synthesis* (London, 1938), p. 225 (note to p. 121).

Walton, of course, acknowledges the source of the 'joy' interpretation, but he cannot agree with it as he finds no support for it in the text. Walton, unlike several other critics, not only recognizes Bradley's original reading of the speech but also pays some attention to the argument with which Bradley supported his reading—such notice, as is often the case, only arises because of disagreement. It is a disagreement which at least allows the reader to see that there are alternatives. Walton wrote:

> Bradley thought that there was a cry 'represented in the oldest text by a four times repeated "O" ', but since it occurs only in the Quarto it is presumably an actor's interpolation, a fact of which Bradley in the then existing state of textual studies could not be expected to be aware.[43]

J. Stampfer agrees with Walton's judgement and rejects the theory: 'that Lear's death is a transfiguration of joy . . . because the textual evidence points to the opposite interpretation',[44] though he sees fit to quote Bradley's view at the beginning of his article. This is because he, like Walton, connects the interpretation of the whole play with the interpretation of this one speech. Stampfer wrote: 'It is only by giving Lear's death a fleeting, ecstatic joy that Bradley can read some sort of reconciliation into the ending, some renewed synthesis of cosmic goodness to follow an antithesis of pure evil.'[45] This seems to simplify and distort Bradley's reading of the play; it makes a connection between the two points which Bradley himself does not make. Walton provides an even more original comment:

> We should remember that Bradley's interpretation of Lear's last speech finds its logical development in the view proposed by William Empson, who regards Lear in the last scene as mad again, and, as, finally, the eternal fool and scapegoat who has experienced everything and learned nothing.[46]

Whether this is just to Empson's interpretation or not, is not of

[43] J. K. Walton, 'Lear's Last Speech', *S.S.*, xxiii (1960), pp. 11–19, at p. 17.
[44] J. Stampfer, 'The Catharsis of *King Lear*', *S.S.*, xxiii (1960), pp. 1–10, at p. 5.
[45] Ibid., p. 4.
[46] J. K. Walton, op. cit., p. 17.

importance here; what is of interest is that both these critics read into Bradley's interpretation of the last speech a psychological connection with the rest of the play. Bradley himself here was indulging in a piece of interpretation of which Stoll himself would have approved. He was considering the emotional effect of the one scene without considering its coherence to the general theme of the play or its plausibility in terms of character. The Bradley tendency to cohere all the facts of the drama into a living whole appears in far more critics than would like to admit to it.

To Bradley's conception of the tragedy as a poem, 'The Redemption of King Lear', even more critical attention has been accorded; and in this matter Bradley has generally, though not always, received due acknowledgement.

C. J. Sisson, whose remark:

> We have long ago learned to recognise in its action and development a theme which might justify the title *The Redemption of King Lear* in place of *The Tragedy of King Lear*, pointing to a happy ending of deeper truth than Tate's or that desired by Bradley,[47]

seems to imply an ignorance of Bradley's argument about the nature of Lear's redemption even if it does not display ignorance of the source of the new title. This, however, is an isolated case: though D. G. James repeats Bradley's argument about Cordelia's death but makes no reference to Bradley. James wrote:

> to give her (Cordelia) some thirty years of life in his world would have been as silly as to give us some assurance of temporal immortality for her in another. She, and through her Shakespeare, had come to a sense of life, and therefore of death, in which the soul makes no demand either of life or death.[48]

There is an obvious connection between this view, which Bradley expressed:

> What happens to such a being does not matter; all that matters is that she is. How this can be when, for anything the tragedy tells us, she has ceased to exist, we do not ask; but the tragedy itself makes us feel that somehow it is so[49]

[47] C. J. Sisson, *Shakespeare's Tragic Justice* (London, n.d. [? 1962]), p. 88.

[48] D. G. James, *The Dream of Learning* (Oxford, 1951), p. 119.

[49] *S.T.*, p. 325.

and Bradley's general view of the progress of Lear in the tragedy, which James fails to notice.

In general though, critics have been ready to acknowledge and to use Bradley's interpretation of the play: 'It was Bradley who suggested that the play might be called "The Redemption of King Lear"; and the account given above of the development of his character is partly based on his analysis.'[50] Kenneth Muir wrote this in his introduction to the 'Arden' edition of *King Lear*. There have been dissenters from this view of *King Lear* but in general it has suited the new religious criticism of Shakespeare to see this play, as O. J. Campbell put it in an article fashionably titled 'The Salvation of Lear': '*King Lear* is in my opinion, a sublime morality play, the action of which is set against a backdrop of eternity.'[51] This is reflected in James's remark, above, and in Sisson's, which he saw as a contrast to the view held by Bradley and his followers:

> Bradley's dissatisfaction [he wrote] finds itself reflected in the not uncommon estimate of the play as a tragedy of pessimistic outlook upon the world of men, and undue stress is still frequently laid upon Gloucester's words: 'As flies to wanton boys, are we to the gods; they kill us for their sport.'[52]

It is shown in titles of articles: 'The Catharsis of King Lear', 'The Salvation of Lear', 'The Golden World of King Lear'.[53]

As usual it is those who dissent from Bradley's view who have provided the most thorough critical commentary on Bradley's interpretation. One of the earliest of these was W. Empson, who counters Bradley's optimistic if not religious view of *King Lear* with a commentary on the necessary conclusion to which Bradley's argument tends. Having summarized Bradley on the work of the gods and the end of *King Lear* he says:

> Nothing matters except to build up a good character, and once

[50] K. Muir, ed. *King Lear*, Arden Edition (London/New York, 1952), p. lix.

[51] O. J. Campbell, 'The Salvation of Lear', *E.L.H.*, xv (1948), pp. 93–109, at p. 94.

[52] C. J. Sisson, op. cit., p. 78.

[53] J. Stampfer, 'The Catharsis of *King Lear*', *S.S.*, xxiii (1960), pp. 1–10; O. J. Campbell, 'The Salvation of Lear', *ELH*, xv (June 1948), pp. 93–109; G. L. Bickersteth, 'The Golden World of *King Lear*', *B.A.* (1946).

that is done the sooner you die the better. Bradley does not put it so brutally . . . but it is what his argument requires . . . I do not see what else he can have meant except that Cordelia would have become corrupted after a happy ending, so that the gods defended her in the only possible way. We can call this pessimism if we like, he remarks, it is in the play, but cannot be prominent in it or the play would no longer be tragic. The main thing about this argument, no doubt, is that it succeeds in turning the blasphemies against the gods into the orthodox view held by Mrs. Gamp that the world is a Wale. I do not know how seriously he took his last little twist of piety, the view that Cordelia was sure to become corrupt. It is curious how often this puritan high-mindedness can be found interlocked with an almost farcical cynicism. But even if involuntary it seems to be a *reductio ad absurdum* of his line of argument . . . This is not to deny, of course, that pious members of an audience might adopt Bradley's point of view at any date.[54]

This deliberately cynical attitude to Bradley's criticism is salutory as it provides one of the few antidotes to the emotional Bradley approach which seduces most readers by its very emotionalism. On the other hand, as Empson warms to his point he becomes less accurate; Bradley did not say that Cordelia would be corrupted by the world; moreover he explicitly warned the reader against taking too extreme a position with regard to Cordelia's death. He wrote:

The extremity of the disproportion between prosperity and goodness first shocks us, and then flashes on us the conviction that our whole attitude in asking or expecting that goodness should be prosperous is wrong; that, if only we could see things as they are, we should see that the outward is nothing, and the inward is all. And some such thought as this (which, to bring it clearly out, I have stated, and still state, in a form both exaggerated and much too explicit) is really present through the whole play.[55]

Empson, in criticizing Bradley, adopts the other extreme; one of the dangers of criticism is that in order to achieve clarity the critic is obliged to embrace extremes which he knows are not really tenable. Almost ten years after Empson published his antidote to Bradley's interpretation of *King Lear* Barbara Everett

[54] W. Empson, *The Structure of Complex Words* (London, 1951), p. 153.
[55] *S.T.*, p. 326.

wrote an article tracing the history of this particular criticism of *King Lear*. It is a summary worth quoting at length for the light it throws on modern critical adaptations of Bradley. Miss Everett wrote:

> Though these critics [Lamb, Hazlitt, and Coleridge] stress 'feeling' in *King Lear*, their treatment of the play could scarcely be called transcendental. The first critic of whom the word might be used is, of course, Bradley; though he himself acknowledges his debt to Dowden, who stresses the sovereignty of the 'moral world' in the play. Bradley's profound study of the play is remarkable, both for the way in which he feels a Romantic sympathy for, or participation in, the central character, to an extreme degree, and also for the way in which he soberly refuses to take it any further. If he directs the reader to a more 'transcendental' interpretation of the play, he does so hesitantly, hedging his observations round with careful reservations. . . . Thus, though Bradley is the first to make an impressive appeal for a more 'mystical' interpretation of *King Lear* he insists again and again that it is 'a mystery we cannot fathom' and that no explicitly religious interpretation will serve . . . His feeling for the intense actuality of Shakespearian characterisation (and the ability to see a dramatic character as a cluster of images is not, perhaps, one that comes without some peculiar habituation) makes him resist any theoretical design overriding such characterisation . . . For him the plays stand rather at the point where intensity of experience becomes religious potentiality: but that potentiality finds no fit expression in the world that is a necessary stage for tragedy and becomes rather aspiration, suffering, moral responsibility. It might perhaps be said that this sense of unfulfilled potentiality is a part of his vision of Shakespearian tragedy. To turn from Bradley to the criticism of *King Lear* that has appeared over the last twenty or thirty years is to realise to what a startling extent it is indebted to him—startling, in that he has hardly been popular among critics for a very long time. Obviously the 'new' approach to *King Lear* cannot wholly be explained by Bradley's influence. . . . But it is interesting to see so many of Bradley's cautious hints and suggestions purified of their accompanying reservations and now as dominating the play.

Miss Everett here gives as example the vogue of Bradley's theory about Lear's death with Empson, Wilson Knight, and Muir.

What is most remarkable is the predominance of the idea of 'reconciliation' at the end of the tragedy, which is Bradley's attempt to answer the question of 'tragic pleasure': since one finds this quite as strong in those who would probably deny keenly any affiliation to Bradley, or even any desire to see the play as a Christian allegory; the sense of a 'happy ending' takes the form of what is called variously the Restoration of Order, or of the Family Bond, or of Reason. In reading such studies, one is impressed by their inner coherence or their cogent force; yet one remembers, perhaps, Bradley's own introduction of such a thesis of moral order and his doubtful conclusions . . . Bradley's 'Redemption of King Lear' is tempered by such considerations. The modern *King Lear* is certainly redeemed: what has disappeared is Bradley's 'honest doubt'.[56]

Five years later the extreme position of Lear criticism is still attracting attention. John Rosenberg is a little less sympathetic to Bradley and his review of the position varies accordingly:

The movement away from the Tragedy of *King Lear* to the modern revision—'The Redemption of King Lear'—began with A. C. Bradley's *Shakespearean Tragedy* (1904). The most persuasive Shakespeare critic since Coleridge, Bradley suggested that the play is primarily about Lear's situation rather than his fate and this suggestion, fruitful enough in his own hands has since proved fatal. 'Adversity to the blessed in spirit' Bradley writes 'is blessed . . . Let us renounce the world, hate it, lose it gladly.' This is the language of religion not of dramatic criticism.[57]

Here, however, Rosenberg is creating his own extreme view of Bradley, using Bradley's text to suit his own purpose. The paragraph following the one from which Rosenberg's carefully chosen quotations are taken represents the true corrective:

As we have seen, it is not by any means the whole Spirit of the tragedy, which presents the world as a place where heavenly good grows side by side with evil, where extreme evil cannot long endure, and where all that survives the storm is good, if not great. But still this strain of thought, to which the world appears as the kingdom of evil and therefore worthless, is in the tragedy . . . Pursued further and

[56] B. Everett, 'The New King Lear', *C.Q.*, ii (1960), pp. 324–39, at pp. 328–30.

[57] John D. Rosenberg, 'King Lear and his Comforters', *E. in C.*, xvi (1966), pp. 135–46, at pp. 135–6.

allowed to dominate, it would destroy the tragedy; for it is necessary to tragedy that we should feel great suffering and death to matter greatly, and yet happiness and life are not to be renounced as worthless. Pursued further, again, it leads to the idea that the world, in that obvious appearance of it which tragedy cannot dissolve without dissolving itself, is illusive.[58]

This as Bradley says leads to *The Tempest*. Seen in context Bradley's remarks become once more 'dramatic criticism', but Rosenberg needed the extreme to further his argument and it is flattering to Bradley that Rosenberg should prefer to use him as that extreme (even at the expense of a partial view of his criticism) rather than take as his chief example one of the many others who, following Bradley, 'overwhelmed by the impact of *King Lear* . . . [resort] to the only idiom adequate to such intensities—the language of religious experience'. As Rosenberg points out: 'If Bradley goes soft at the end of his second essay on Lear, G. Wilson Knight all but gibbers at the end of his.' One may in fact wonder if it is not something of Wilson Knight's extreme view which in Rosenberg's mind has rubbed off on Bradley's. There is nothing in Bradley to touch:

> The naturalism of the play travails to produce out of its earthly womb a thing of imaginative and miraculous splendour, high-pitched in bizarre, grotesque, vivid mental conflict and agony: which in turn pursues its rocket flight of whirling madness, explosive, to the transcendent mystic awakening into love, dropping bright balls of silent fire, then extinguished, as the last tragic sacrifice claims its own, and the darkness closes.[59]

Here in fact is Rosenberg's perfect extreme; but it is Bradley whom he quotes and Bradley on whom he places his emphasis. Rosenberg is trying to capture a star for his argument and Bradley is a greater star than Wilson Knight; this is one of the implications of Rosenberg's article.

To conclude this somewhat tortuous survey of the history of an idea there can be nothing more suitable than the above dis-

[58] *S.T.*, pp. 327–8.

[59] G. Wilson Knight, *The Wheel of Fire* (London, 1930), quotation from 1949 edn., pp. 204–8.

cussion of Rosenberg's article, for which he himself said at the conclusion of the debate:

> This essay is in a sense an epitaph on the last half century of criticism of *King Lear*—the period that began with Bradley's *Shakespearean Tragedy* and has ended in the publication in English of Jan Kott's widely praised *Shakespeare our Contemporary* (1964). . . . If the older Lear was too celestial the 'contemporary' one is merely squalid, an anti-Lear who is the inverted image of his predecessor. Bradley's King was part tragic hero, part Christian saint. Kott's hero is a clown King in a refuse can. . . . Idealisation has been replaced by caricature.[60]

It is doubtful if the mere writing of the epitaph will serve to put to death a whole structure of critical ideas. Rosenberg's conclusions about the play, that it is 'A savage and beautiful confrontation of the ambiguities of human experience',[61] in some way undermine his epitaph. There is little in that summary which is not also found in Bradley's:

> Its final and total result is one in which the pity and terror, carried perhaps to the extreme limits of art are so blended with a sense of law and beauty that we feel at last, not depression and much less despair, but a consciousness of greatness in pain, and of solemnity in the mystery we cannot fathom.[62]

Out of two ideas which could be summed up in the two short quotations 'unbearable joy' and 'The Redemption of King Lear' has sprung the whole critical complex discussed above. It would be folly to attribute the birth of such ideas to Bradley, it is merely that he first stated them in the form which has penetrated to modern criticism. Neither can the subsequent prevalence of such ideas be attributed wholly to the originator. Many if not all of the critics involved in the debate would have no doubt come to similar conclusions without the influence of Bradley, had Bradley never put his ideas on paper.

The fact remains that Bradley did publish those ideas and that, whatever critical fashion has to say of Bradley every critic worth the name must have, at some stage in his career, read about those

[60] J. D. Rosenberg, op. cit., p. 145. [61] Ibid., p. 146.
[62] *S.T.*, p. 279.

ideas in Bradley's own words. As M. R. Ridley wrote of *Shakespearean Tragedy* as a whole:

> Whatever else that book was, whether it was just or mistaken in its conception, skilful or unskilful in its execution, it was a landmark in the history of Shakespearian criticism. No criticism which followed it could, unless its author was negligent, be the same as it would have been had that book not been written; no reader who had taken the trouble to study the book could either read or see any of the four great tragedies of Shakespeare in the same frame of mind as that in which he had read or seen them before.[63]

If Bradley's observations on *King Lear* have done little else they have helped to give shape to critical ideas on the subject. His criticism has become a support or a whipping-boy, a touchstone or at very least a peg for the arguments of subsequent criticism. Such is Bradley's stature, that to ignore Bradley on such a topic is to make a comment in itself; to discuss one's criticism in terms of Bradley's criticism (even if this means some distortion of Bradley) seems to be what more and more critics desire. It is as though they wish to pit their minds against that of one of the most widely and read most perceptive of Shakespeare critics.

This example has been taken and followed through in detail,[64] but it is not possible to do this in the case of every one of Bradley's critical ideas. On the other hand, it would not be right to leave the impression that the processes remarked in the above summary only occur in the case of criticism of *King Lear*. Other and more mechanical ideas of Bradley's have been of similar influence. One such was his observation of the animal imagery in *King Lear*. Miss Spurgeon in her first published work on Shakespeare's imagery remarked on her predecessor in this aspect: 'The large number of animal images and their effect in the play has been noticed (notably by Bradley, *Shakespearean Tragedy* pp. 266 and

[63] M. R. Ridley, *Shakespeare's Plays. A Commentary*, pp. 4–5.

[64] An article, which I have not seen, came to my notice after this was written. It is possible, of course that it might contradict my conclusions, but the very fact of its having been written bears witness to the importance of Bradley in this aspect of criticism. The article is J. T. Spikes, 'Bradleyism at Mid-Century: The Death of King Lear', *Southern Quarterly* v (1967), pp. 223–36.

following).'[65] If she relied on the established position of Bradley to add authority to her then highly original method of reading Shakespeare, the same could not be said of either the editors of the New Cambridge *King Lear* who quote Bradley on this subject,[66] or Barbara de Mendonça who writing of the relationship between *Gorboduc* and *King Lear* referred to 'Animal imagery, examined by Bradley in his *Shakespearean Tragedy* and by Caroline Spurgeon in her *Shakespeare's Imagery*'.[67] This it would seem is a perception which Shakespeare criticism is unreservedly aware that it owes to Bradley.

The same is true of his comment on Macbeth's killing of Duncan. This has been noticed by several critics. Wilson Knight went so far as to say: 'One of the finest interpretative remarks ever made on Macbeth is A. C. Bradley's to the effect that Macbeth sets about the murder as "an appalling duty". This is profoundly true.'[68] If it is true to Wilson Knight it is not to A. P. Rossiter who says:

> I know what he is pointing to, but cannot accommodate the word 'duty' either to my own philosophy or to what I take to be Shakespeare's. Hence my use of the term 'compulsion'. It does prevent one's delving back into Macbeth's past biography after this fashion. 'But when Macbeth heard them [the witches' prophecies] he was not an innocent man. . . .' Later on (as he so often does) Bradley says the right thing: 'The temptation was already within him'. No man is, or ever can be, 'innocent' where his advantage is concerned.[69]

The debate is on again.

Even if it were possible to count how many debates in Shakespearian criticism Bradley started by his chance remarks or tersely phrased perceptions, it would not be possible to set them down

[65] C. F. E. Spurgeon, *Leading Motives in the Imagery of Shakespeare's Tragedies* (1930), p. 35.

[66] G. I. Duthie and J. D. Wilson, eds. *King Lear*, New Cambridge Edition (Cambridge, 1960), G. I. Duthie was responsible for the introduction. The reference occurs on p. xlvii.

[67] B. H. C. de Mendonça, 'The Influence of *Gorboduc* on *King Lear*', *S.S.*, xiii (1960), pp. 41–8, at p. 45.

[68] G. Wilson Knight, op. cit. Quotation from 1965 edn., p. 125.

[69] A. P. Rossiter, *Angel with Horns* (London, 1961), p. 214.

here. Moreover, it would give a distorted view of Bradley's influence. Other critics have provided ideas which have started debates; Bradley's utterances seem insignificant when compared with the fate of Coleridge's 'motiveless malignity'. There are critics who write books of Shakespeare criticism and never make reference to Bradley.[70] The nature of this book is to give perhaps excessive emphasis to the importance of Bradley in Shakespeare criticism; but he wrote little on the histories and comedies and omitted discussion of large areas of criticism within his chosen field. No critic can cover all aspects of his subject or even exhaust his chosen aspect.

The influence of Bradley has been and still is considerable. But while A. Clutton Brock admitted 'It may be that I owe more to [*Shakespearean Tragedy*] than I know',[71] W. K. Wimsatt and C. Brooks in their history of literary criticism discuss Bradley only in terms of his Hegelianism. He is for them only an example of the 'great and lasting influence of Hegel'; the only quotation that they make from Bradley is from his lecture 'Hegel's View of Tragedy' and the only critical comment on Bradley is a mild complaint that he diverged from the true Hegelian spirit.

> In rejecting as a ground for tragedy, Hegel's austere idealism in favour of a milder humanism, Bradley certainly acted in the spirit of the age. He praised tragedy for bringing home to us the spiritual qualities of the hero—his self-assertion, his noble endurance, his magnificent vitality—and nearly all recent writers on the subject have joined Bradley in this emphasis.[72]

One has the feeling that were it not for his lecture on Hegel, Bradley would not have been worth including in the history. Other historians of literary criticism have felt the same as was noticed above. G. Watson in his book *The Literary Critics* only

[70] Among such are: P. Cruttwell, *The Shakespearean Moment* (London, 1954); B. Stirling, *Unity in Shakespearean Tragedy* (New York, 1956); H. Granville-Barker, *Prefaces to Shakespeare: Hamlet* (London, 1936).

[71] A. Clutton Brock, *Shakespeare's Hamlet* (London, 1922), p. vi.

[72] W. K. Wimsatt and C. Brooks, *Literary Criticism: A Short History* (New York, 1957), p. 559.

includes Bradley as an example of a latter-day Morgann and a faded Coleridge.[73]

Nevertheless, in the narrower world of Shakespeare criticism, Bradley has been received as an accepted standard. Over sixty years have passed since *Shakespearean Tragedy* was first published and there are still works which accord him considerable interest. As critics have been quick to point out he belongs to a past age and was once termed old-fashioned. To be old-fashioned and to survive when 'no day is so dead as the day before yesterday' is to survive as a classic even if only as a minor classic in a specialist field. The thousands of footnoted references to Bradley, the use of his phrases, his ideas, and sometimes of his research, in works of contemporary criticism, testify to his position as an accredited authority (even if in the nature of the work, that credit sometimes involves disagreement).

[73] G. Watson, *The Literary Critics* (London, 1962), reference from 1964 edn. pp. 108 and 124.

8

BRADLEY'S CRITICS

BESIDES the large number of Shakespeare critics who have turned aside from their main study to attack or defend Bradley, there have been some critics who have written expressly about him. Usually, but not always, they have been admirers of Bradley's work and more often than not they have been Shakespeare critics. But in this chapter it is for their criticism of Bradley that they are included. This has meant, since only those works which consider Bradley as a whole, and not one aspect of his work in relation to Shakespeare and the writer's own criticism, the omission of many of the most influential works which have dictated the fashionable attitude to Bradley. What emerges is a parallel course of more sober and considered judgements. In general this book has avoided a historical approach, as it was felt that this would complicate rather than clarify, and at the same time suggest an inevitable process of amelioration, instead of a long chain of critics each worthy consideration in his own right.

Nevertheless, criticism cannot be totally divorced from history and in the foregoing chapters it has sometimes been thought useful to suggest the part which the passage of time has played in the establishment of Bradley's reputation. It is for this reason that in discussing criticism of Bradley in this chapter chronology will be taken into consideration. As compared with the mass of Shakespeare criticism, there is very little Bradley criticism; and what there is falls into three convenient groups. The review of his works, the notices of his death, and the critical notices which have become prominent in the nineteen sixties—although the first of them appeared in 1948.[1] It is hoped that these articles considered in this historical framework will act as landmarks in the history of Bradley's reputation as a critic.

[1] P. N. Siegel, 'In Defense of Bradley', *C.E.*, ix (Feb. 1948), pp. 250–6.

In 1904, when *Shakespearean Tragedy* was first published, Bradley had received some critical attention on account of his *Commentary on Tennyson's 'In Memoriam'*. As the quotations from reviews, displayed in the advertisements for its second edition appended to the first edition of *Shakespearean Tragedy*, show, however, he was not then the literary figure that he was to become shortly after the publication of *Shakespearean Tragedy*. The nature of Bradley's reputation is suggested, however, even by those early reviews. The first quotation from *The Pilot* praises the section of the commentary

> entitled 'The Way of the Soul', reviewing the spiritual experience which 'In Memoriam' records. This is quite admirable throughout, and proves conclusively that Dr. Bradley's keen desire to fathom the exact meaning of every phrase has only quickened his appreciation of the poem as a whole.[2]

The Saturday Review concentrates on Bradley's thoroughness:

> Here we find a model of what a commentary on a great work should be, every page instinct with thoughtfulness; complete sympathy and appreciation; the most reverent care shown in the attempted interpretation of passages whose meaning to a large degree evades, and will always evade, readers of 'In Memoriam'. It is clear to us that Mr. Bradley has devoted long time and thought to his work, and that he has published the result of his labours simply to help those who, like himself, have been and are in difficulties as to the drift of various passages.[2]

These quotations illustrate clearly that Bradley's reputation was not made by the publication of this commentary; but this was known already. More important perhaps, they display the distrust of commentary and precise criticism, especially perhaps in the case of quasi-religious works like *In Memoriam* and, as is shown more clearly in the second than the first, a refusal on the part of the critic to be won over to any of Bradley's interpretations. The individual readers ought to come first, he seems to say, and Bradley is only one individual reader. Bradley himself was aware

[2] Cf. *S.T.*, first edn., end-page.

of this attitude revealed in the reviews and wrote to Murray of reviewing:

> *What* a trade that is! I would rather be an honest publican. Some of the reviews with other things have made me think that perhaps most people who are more or less fond of poetry do not *want* to do what I should call reading or understanding the poem—i.e. making the same process occur in themselves as occurred in the poet's head—but rather want what may be called the effect of the poem—i.e. something vaguer which is produced in them by reading the words. And if this is so I understand why commentaries annoy them so much.[3]

In 1904, then, the world was not particularly receptive to academic criticism or commentary, and in part Bradley made his reputation rather as a popular preacher of Shakespeare than as a modern critic and university don. This is evident to varying degrees in all the reviews, even if none of them goes so far as R. Y. Tyrrell writing in *Academy*:

> Professor Bradley's book is popular in aim. He desires to propagate a familiarity with Shakespeare's work. . . . That which chiefly tends to render Professor Bradley's book an essentially popular one is the method of criticism employed. Every question, every controversy, theory, view or supposition which arises, he subjects to the same test. His divining rod is in every case guided solely by an appeal to the written words.[4]

This view leads the writer to some unexpected conclusions:

> The first lecture, perhaps the least good in the book, is suspiciously like a sop thrown to the 'Dons'. It consists in a generalisation with regard to the *substance* of Shakespearean Tragedy in the abstract, a subject which would never occupy the attention of anyone except a professional academic critic. And indeed it is not a matter of great importance, even for such an one, that the 'tragic fact' should be accurately defined.

In contrast to this condemnation there is praise of the other general lecture: 'The second lecture is an interesting and illuminating disquisition on dramatic construction.'[5] Moreover, he speaks

[3] Letter to G. Murray, 22 Sept. 1901.
[4] R. Y. Tyrrell, 'Tragedy', *Academy* lxviii (11 Mar. 1905), pp. 229–31, at p. 230.
[5] Ibid., p. 230.

favourably of the appendices and unfavourably of the characterization of the minor characters in *Hamlet*. Of Claudius he says, Bradley 'recognises the nobility of his bearing but he construes his character in the ugliest light, which interpretation, in the opinion of most people, would subtract somewhat from the interest of the play'.[6] Oddly enough in adopting the 'opinion of most people' as his criterion for judging Bradley's criticism Tyrrell has gone quite against the general body of later criticism.

While Tyrrell has little but praise for the popular nature of *Shakespearean Tragedy*, John Churton Collins writing in the *Westminster Gazette* was rather stern in his disappointment:

We very much regret that we have not been able to speak more favourably of these lectures. Possibly knowing Professor Bradley's deservedly high reputation as a critic and scholar, we have expected too much from them and have measured them by a standard to which they were not intended to conform. No doubt like Aristotle, he has his exoteric as well as his esoteric side as a teacher and lecturer; we certainly wish that he had given in a work which must necessarily appeal to Shakespearian scholars a little less of the exoteric and a little more of the esoteric.[7]

Churton Collins seems to have had the same idea as R. Y. Tyrrell as to what appealed to popular taste and what to the academic:

The real points of interest and importance in the drama are not so much as touched on and the particularity with which what is touched on is dealt with is almost invariably in an inverse ratio to its interest and importance. . . . Every lecture teems with . . . irritating superfluities, aggravated it may be added by the unnecessary diffuseness with which they are discussed. . . . Thus Professor Bradley treats us to special dissertations on such subjects as; 'Did Lady Macbeth really faint?' 'Did Emilia suspect Iago?' 'Had Macbeth any children?'[7]

Gilbert Murray wrote in defence of Bradley to the *Westminster Gazette*[8] but Bradley regarded the outburst with more detachment;

[6] Ibid., p. 230.

[7] *Westminster Gazette*, 28 Jan. 1905, signed J. C. C., who, according to a letter from A. C. Bradley to G. Murray (undated [1905]), was John Churton Collins.

[8] Cf. Chap. 1, p. 4.

he wrote that the article goes 'so much too far that I don't think his review will damage the book with sensible readers'.[9]

The Times Literary Supplement also and for different reasons is critical of the details of Bradley's criticism. The Literary Supplement then newly established as part of *The Times* perhaps represents best the general attitude to critical work prevalent at that time. Certainly the comments made in its review of *Shakespearean Tragedy* are reminiscent of the above-quoted review of Tennyson's *In Memoriam*. The only general fault found is that 'he is at his best in the large questions and at his weakest in the details. He is apt to consider words too curiously and find too much in them.' The praise, however, is more indicative of the reviewer's attitude to criticism:

> Mr. Bradley keeps his finger on the heart of the poet and deals with that part of his achievement which is of all, the most essential, the most universal, the most immortal.
>
> Shakespeare is a large subject and not a little of Mr. Bradley's wisdom is seen in the part of it he has chosen to deal with.

that is not language, versification, relation to contemporary society or sources. This constitutes an interesting comment on later objections that Bradley, like the Victorian he was, omitted these modern aspects of study because he was unaware of them. Most telling of all, however, is the conclusion with its hinted reproach and heavy hyperbole: 'Even to attempt to put in to prose the impression left by the tragedy, as Mr. Bradley does, though right and inevitable, ought only to be done, as he does it, with a consciousness that one is measuring the heavens and translating the voice of the winds.'[10] The critical process is regarded

[9] Letter to G. Murray, n.d. [1905].

[10] *T.L.S.* 10 Feb. 1905. This review is, of course, unsigned, but F. W. Bateson in an article 'Organs of Literary Opinion. IV: *The Times Lit. Supp.*', *E. in C.*, vii (1957), pp. 351–62, wrote that the most frequent reviewers before 1914 were Clutton-Brock and J. C. Bailey, Thomas Seccombe, E. V. Lucas, Mme Duclaux (*née* Robinson), H. C. Beeching, Quiller-Couch, De la Mare, G. S. Gordon. 'It is only necessary to recite these names to show the low critical level at which the pre-1914 *T.L.S.* functioned. . . . The period between the death of Arnold and Eliot's beginnings was a nadir of English criticism. A. C. Bradley and Arthur Symons must be excepted though neither of them, I think contributed to *T.L.S.*'

with suspicion. Criticism according to this view quickly becomes sacrilege.

The review in *Revue des deux mondes* reveals further the amateurish approach to criticism. Bradley's book was reviewed in the same article as J. W. Gray's *Shakespeare's Marriage and Departure from Stratford*. The two books, to the critic, belong to the same class, and moreover Gray's work occupies half the space and was the first reviewed of the two. Bradley's work was regarded as that of a devoted amateur, one among many: 'c'est . . . essentiellement, un professeur, consciencieux et volontiers pesant, procédant à son exposition par les voies les plus banales, avec force divisions et subdivisions scolastiques.' The reviewer notes the fashionable reception of the work in England but considers: 'Que demain un autre critique nous définisse d'une autre façon le caractère des héros de Shakspeare, nous le suivrons à son tour, oubliant les définitions de M. Bradley.'[11] The greater part of this review comprises a eulogy of Shakespeare and a summary of Bradley's characterization of Cordelia, Desdemona, and Ophelia. This critic is clearly finding in Bradley what he wants to find—praise of the miraculous nature of Shakespeare's characterization.

With the exception of Churton Collins all the above reviewers have been more interested in communicating their appreciation of Shakespeare's genius than in estimating the usefulness of Bradley's criticism. In the light of such reviews some of the excesses of Bradley's style are more easily understood. To say that he was pandering to public taste would be to distort the facts; there is nothing to suggest that Bradley's taste was essentially much different from that of, for example, the reviewer in *The Times Literary Supplement*. The fact is that when Bradley was writing the fashionable term was 'appreciation' not 'criticism'; Bradley himself says his aim is 'dramatic appreciation'. Anything which approached analysis, dissection of speeches, or collection of relevant background facts was suspected of depreciating the almost religious importance of the original. This attitude to criticism was not likely to do justice to Bradley's criticism, as an

[11] T. de Wyzewa, review of *Shakespearean Tragedy* in *Revue des deux mondes*, xxvi (May–April 1905), pp. 935–45, quotations from pp. 941 and 942 respectively.

appreciator he ranks no higher than Swinburne, or even Frank Harris. What in Bradley's criticism fits him to be considered as a Shakespeare prophet is that which has had least relevance in the growing profession of Shakespeare criticism, that which, in the long run, has marred his reputation.

This was not, however, the only attitude to criticism at that time. Churton Collins, as was noticed, reproached Bradley for his too popular approach to Shakespeare and Collins was, like Bradley, a university man. C. H. Herford, writing in the newly established *Modern Language Review*, also represents the more professional attitude. He, moreover, seems to be conscious that criticism as such needs to analyse its purpose and methods. The praise of Bradley is perhaps the highest in any contemporary review, but Herford strives always to avoid the merely eulogistic and to analyse in what Bradley's peculiar success consists.

> The interpretation of Shakespere has been proverbially a touchstone for men and methods. The giants of criticism have exposed their limitations there as clearly as their strength . . . Shakespere is full of pitfalls alike for the poet who uses nothing but his imaginative intuition, for the 'realist' who uses nothing but his practical sagacity, and for the philosophic interpreter who uses only his synthetic and constructive intellect. What makes the problem so fascinating and so difficult is that each of these methods is up to a certain point so legitimate and so successful. . . . To say that Prof. Bradley's criticism seems to combine in a rare degree all these three types of faculty and method may sound like journalistic hyperbole but it is merely an attempt to define and explain the impression which it will we think produce upon any open mind at all inured to the Shakespearean controversies of the past. And the combination has proved singularly fruitful. In several quite distinct domains he has either clarified old discussions or made traditional dogmas insecure, or at least, driven home ideas, not in themselves unfamiliar, with fresh cogency and insight.[12]

Herford alone of the reviewers of *Shakespearean Tragedy* seems prepared to recognize that it is the work of a man who is at once scholar and amateur; to make this observation at a time when the

[12] C. H. Herford, 'Review of *Shakespearean Tragedy*', *M.L.R.*, i (1905–6), pp. 128–33, at pp. 128–9.

amateur was supported by all the traditional poetry readers and the scholar only just carving himself a niche among the more respectable classical scholars shows considerable foresight, but it must be apparent to any open-minded reader of Bradley that it is true to his criticism. Herford has perhaps one of the truest comments to make upon Bradley's character studies:

> Critics preoccupied with the study of Shakespere's art are apt to estimate his characters only in terms of their rank as artistic creations. Prof. Bradley's criticism in reality owes much of its technical mastery to his quick human sympathy with them. He treats them as men and women, with as lively a feeling for personal values as for plot-functions.[13]

Herford was able not only to see both the 'technical mastery' and the 'human sympathy' in Bradley's character studies, he recognized in a way which few later critics have, Bradley's comprehension of the paradox of tragedy.

> What gives Prof. Bradley's discussion [of 'The Substance of Shakespearean Tragedy'] its chief value and interest is his peculiarly vital grasp of the contradiction latent in all properly tragic emotion, where the sense that suffering and death are both real and greatly matter, and the sense that they are somehow transcended and sublimated, are equally involved . . . No-one has analysed this exaltation more keenly than Professor Bradley, or distinguished more subtly its varying sources and complexions, in the several tragedies.[14]

This review might be seen as the first mark of approval which the academic world offered to Bradley; it is more wholly favourable than many later criticisms but its value lies in the seriousness with which it sets out to discover Bradley's means and results.

The amateur of Shakespeare has hardly ever withdrawn his approval; Bradley perhaps offers more obvious food for Bardolatry than any later critic (with the possible exception of G. Wilson Knight). It was, perhaps, in Bardolatry that Bradley worship had its roots and inevitably reaction came to both. In the review quoted above there has been some lavish praise of Bradley. *The Times Literary Supplement*, for example, said: 'One

[13] Ibid., p. 131. [14] Ibid., pp. 130–1.

may well doubt whether in the whole field of English Literary Criticism anything has been written in the last twenty years more luminous, more masterly, more penetrating to the very centre of its subject.'[15] The best example, however, of that adulation of Bradley of which Miss L. B. Campbell later spoke[16] with such scorn comes from the review in *The Spectator*. This is unsigned and Bradley commenting upon it to Gilbert Murray thought it might be Lucas or Graves but in fact the author was John Buchan.[17] The note of eulogy is sustained throughout: 'From the beginning to the end the level of sustained, exact criticism never sinks, and at times there is in the interpretation an imagination and a poetry which make the book in the truest sense a work of creation.' The writer disagrees with Bradley's views on the Porter and the blackness of Othello, but hastily prevents any suspicion of sacrilege:

> But these are merely personal preferences on details; and on the greater matters we should feel it heresy to question his conclusions. Certainly the Oxford Chair of Poetry has never produced a finer fruit, and we do not forget the Younger Warton. Many have had their say on Shakespeare, in this country and elsewhere, and among his critics have been many sound scholars and excellent writers. But we have no hesitation in putting Professor Bradley's book far above any modern Shakespearean criticism that we know, worthy to rank very near the immortal work of Lamb and Coleridge. It is, indeed, difficult to praise it in language which shall do it justice and yet seem free from exaggeration. For it is more than a study of Shakespeare: it is a unique piece of constructive criticism, which from its freshness of method and distinction of form deserves to rank as the most important exercise in the craft since Matthew Arnold's *Essays in Criticism*.

This review in fact seems almost wilfully to stress those aspects of Bradley which were to make him anathema to following generations. It continues:

> it is in his treatment of the story and *personnel* of each play that Professor Bradley's critical power is at its highest . . . The axiom he starts from

[15] *T.L.S.*, 10 Feb. 1905.

[16] L. B. Campbell, 'Bradley Revisited: Forty Years After', *S.Ph.*, xliv (1947), p. 174.

[17] Letter to G. Murray, n.d. [1905].

is that every character is psychologically intelligible, if only we labour sedulously to understand it. Shakespeare was far too great an artist and profound a thinker to attempt to give the effect of the mystery of life by psychological confusion.

Towards the end of the review there is praise of an aspect of Bradley which when it has met with critical attention has always been approved, although the expression of the praise gives more credit to Bradley's dramatic sense than was later fashionable. 'He has also a full understanding of the dramatic value of the *mise-en-scene* in each case and when as in *Lear* and *Macbeth* the background becomes as terrific as the action, it is interpreted with an imaginative power that it would be impertinence to praise.'[18] The review closes with a lengthy quotation of Bradley's interpretation of Lear's last speech, an odd foretaste of later critical stress on this one piece of criticism.

This adulation is apparent elsewhere, if not to such a great extent. R. Y. Tyrrell wrote a second article on *Shakespearean Tragedy*, largely to answer criticism made by Aldis Wright in the Clarendon Press edition of Shakespeare, which he ended: 'In our opinion a book like that which is before us is not much less essential for the complete comprehension of Shakespeare's tragedies than an atlas is for the fruitful study of geography.'[19] *The Times Literary Supplement* thought Bradley almost equally indispensable: 'If there is anyone who after reading the four tragedies and what Mr. Bradley has to say about them, is still in the dark as to the essential lines of Shakespeare's achievement as a tragic poet, he will never come into the light.'[20] *The Times* does stipulate for a reading of the tragedies as well as use of Bradley but the attitude which induced the following squib is apparent:

> I dreamt last night that Shakespeare's ghost
> Sat for a Civil Service post;
> The English paper for the year
> Had several questions on *King Lear*

18 *The Spectator*, 28 Jan. 1905, pp. 140–1.

19 R. Y. Tyrrell, *Academy* lxviii (18 Mar. 1905), pp. 266–7, at p. 267.

20 *T.L.S.*, 10 Feb. 1905.

Which Shakespeare answered very badly
Because he hadn't read his Bradley![21]

There was, however, another dissident voice, one which received more attention; A. B. Walkley's criticism in *The Times Literary Supplement* of April 1905.[22] This article is not wholly unfavourable to Bradley, but it contains amid its conventional praise a casual expression of a criticism of Bradley which later became critical law:

Now I have seen it stated, and I quite agree, that Coleridge has had no such worthy successor as Professor Bradley, author of *Shakespearean Tragedy*. Certainly this is a notable book, always sane and accurate, sometimes profound, a credit to our academic scholarship. It is the last book wherein one would expect to find so unsound a critical method as that which Morgann first indicated and the 'Romantic' critics so zealously adopted. Nevertheless the method is there, not overt, but unconsciously.

To understand Shakespeare you have to supplement examination of the text by consideration of other matters, and it is here that I hold the Professor to be at fault. What is outside the text? He says (by implication) a set of real lives, . . . I say Shakespeare's dramatic needs of the moment, artistic peculiarities, and available theatrical materials.[23]

Like later critics also Walkley cannot maintain this austere attitude. Having answered Bradley's characterization of *Hamlet* with the question: 'does it not occur to Professor Bradley that these things are thus merely because Shakespeare wanted (1) a "sympathetic" hero; (2) an amateur of acting (or what would have

[21] This verse was referred to in a review of C. S. Lewis's 'Hamlet, The Prince and the Poem', *Notes and Queries*, clxxxiv (4 Apr. 1943), pp. 269–70. The quotation oddly enough seems to take the verse at face value: 'We are not surprised when in the delightful dream of Shakespeare standing for a Civil Service post he was confronted with a question which "he answered badly Because he hadn't studied Bradley".' Correspondence ensued and on 3 July 'Ignoto' wrote that the verse which was quoted in full in *Notes and Queries*, clxxxiv, p. 445, was by Guy Boas who wrote it for *Punch* and published it later in *Lays of Learning* (1926). 'Ignoto' favours 'studied' for the last line. (*Notes and Queries*) clxxxv (3 July 1943), p. 25: 'Prof. Bradley's Hamlet'.)

[22] *T.L.S.*, 7 Apr. 1905. This is unsigned of course but was collected in A. B. Walkley's *Drama and Life* (New York, 1907).

[23] Ibid., quotations from *Drama and Life*, pp. 151 and 153 respectively.

become of the play scene?); and (3) a fencer—for the *denouement*?' Walkley later agrees with Bradley's equation of Hamlet with Shakespeare (which in Bradley goes no further than a paragraph or two at the end of the lecture 'Shakespeare the Man', delivered in 1904 but not published until 1909 in *Oxford Lectures on Poetry*), and expostulates: 'Why does he not perceive that Shakespeare "the man" is speaking again and again in the form of Hamlet, whose busy, curious, hedonistic, characteristically Renaissance temperament is the outcome of the dramatist's need for self-expression and of nothing else?'[24] This seems an odd idea if Hamlet only had a character to fit the exigencies of the plot: even Walkley could not have meant that Shakespeare was as devoid of character as the Hamlet he originally depicted; in fact he is reversing, however unconsciously, his former criticism.[25]

There is very little criticism of Bradley after this, apart from reviews of *Oxford Lectures on Poetry* and *A Miscellany* (1929) which are not our concern here, although there is a note of scepticism in *The Times Literary Supplement* review of *Oxford Lectures on Poetry* which is worth noting. Bradley is criticized for having 'Sometimes too much the mind of the philosopher'.[26] The praise of *Shakespearean Tragedy* has been modified. Whereas then the critic said: 'Mr. Bradley keeps his finger on the very heart of the poet';[27] the critic of *Oxford Lectures on Poetry* has reservations: 'He scarcely ever takes his finger off the pulse of human feeling and character. And he is wise, for that is where his peculiar strength lies.' He is compared unfavourably with W. Raleigh, then Oxford Professor of Poetry, and even the praise of 'Poetry for Poetry's Sake' is a little patronizing: 'this lecture shows that he can if he chooses employ this method of detailed criticism in

[24] Ibid., p. 152 and 155 respectively.

[25] R. W. Chambers's review in *The Hibbert Journal* is interesting chiefly for the lukewarm nature of its comments. There is no sign here that the work was to become a classic, or a bugbear in later years: 'Professor Bradley's lectures will be as necessary to every student of Shakspere's tragedies as his commentary on "In Memoriam" has become to students of Tennyson.' *The Hibbert Journal*, iv (1906), pp. 213–17, at p. 213.

[26] *T.L.S.*, 10 June 1909, p. 209.

[27] Ibid., 10 Feb. 1905.

his own way and for his own purposes with consummate skill and effect.'[28]

In *A Sketch of Recent Shakespeare Investigation 1893–1923*, C. H. Herford not unnaturally included a criticism of *Shakespearean Tragedy* which he praised as 'an essay in purely critical interpretation' ignoring current trends of research. This seems a dangerous simplification; 'purely critical' is a phrase which would need pages of justification. Later Herford makes his point more explicitly: 'No critic of comparable aesthetic power had interpreted Shakespeare on the basis of so rigorous a scrutiny into the dramatic data of the text.' While this is a questionable judgement (the name of Coleridge, for one, leaps to mind) it at least attempts to describe the peculiar nature of Bradley's criticism. Herford also from his twenty years distance attempts for the first time to assess the historical importance of Bradley's work.

> *Shakespearean Tragedy* gave a new impulse to the literary and aesthetic way of approaching Shakespeare. Its appearance synchronized . . . with the beginning of the more intensive study of the Elizabethan stage conditions; but Bradley's book created a countercurrent of, for the time, comparable force.[29]

The second volume of Augustus Ralli's *History of Shakespeare Criticism* appeared in 1932, it is the last assessment of Bradley made while he was alive and the most adulatory of the uncritical eulogies. Unaware of the changing patterns in Shakespearian criticism, Ralli pours out his praise of Bradley:

> . . . acknowledged to be the greatest living Shakespearian critic, and one of the very greatest in the history of Shakespearian criticism.
>
> . . . never merely philosophical, . . . there are occasions when imagination partly retires and yields place to a more purely and scientific method, and in these, as we shall see, he is less successful.[30]

This sets Ralli with those earlier reviewers who worshipped Bradley as he helped them to worship Shakespeare. Ralli leans

[28] Ibid., 10 June 1909.

[29] C. H. Herford, *A Sketch of Recent Shakespearean Investigation 1893–1923* (n.d.), pp. 32 and 37 respectively.

[30] A. Ralli, *A History of Shakespeare Criticism*, ii (London, 1932), pp. 200–11, at p. 200.

to the criticism which F. R. Leavis later called 'sentimental'; that is the criticism of Othello, for that of Hamlet and Iago (notice that Ralli subdivides the criticism according to character and not to play) he has less sympathy. His reasons for this are interesting. Of his criticism of Iago he says: 'Here again, as with Hamlet, the analysis is colder and more informed by knowledge of life outside Shakespeare than inspired by direct communion with his mind.'[31] The words 'colder' and 'communion' are telling, they destroy what would otherwise be a valid critical point. What Ralli is talking about is not insight into, or sympathy with, the author's mind but a quasi-mystical cosiness which is totally enveloped in a fictional world. The same is displayed in the following:

> Professor Bradley has carried on the thought of Coleridge and rightly summarised Macbeth's soliloquies as the protest of his deepest self. These two points exemplify his power—his steady poetic vision which brings him nearest of critics to Shakespeare's mind, his meditation on this vision which does not fade, and his analytic power. He also has the seriousness of one with whom the great things unveiled by the reading of Shakespeare have been no external show, but a strange and wonderful experience.

This is a distortion of criticism, in fact it is almost a denial that criticism has any useful function to perform; this attitude of reverence could only have harmed Bradley's reputation and such remarks as 'one might almost say that, by means of Shakespeare, Professor Bradley has advanced one of the most practical existing arguments in favour of the moral government of the universe'[32] bring Bradley down from his prophetic heights only to turn him into some ultra-Victorian Sunday School teacher. This appeared, moreover, after works by H. Granville-Barker, Wilson Knight, Dover Wilson, Miss Spurgeon, and Miss Campbell had been published.

Of the few obituaries which his death attracted the two by J. W. Mackail[33] are concerned primarily with the facts of his life.

[31] Ibid., p. 203.

[32] Ibid., pp. 209, 201 respectively.

[33] J. W. Mackail, 'A. C. Bradley 1851–1935', *Proceedings of the British Academy*, xxi (London, 1935), and 'Andrew Bradley', *The Oxford Magazine*, 17 Oct. 1935.

Criticism of Bradley by this time had reached conclusions not fitted for obituaries. Mackail was a close friend of Bradley's and yet his only criticism of Bradley's Shakespeare criticism (the sole reason why Bradley was worthy extended obituary) is reluctant and defensive:

it may be said that it tended to be supersubtle and that the psychology of dramatic art, rather than the art itself, was sometimes what interested him most. But it may be confidently added that it was, and is, in the highest degree awakening, stimulating, and vivifying.[34]

The word 'confidently' is belied by what follows, a most timid estimate of Bradley's contribution to Shakespeare studies. *The Times* obituary is more overtly critical:

Bradley approached the poets as thinkers and philosophers rather than as what they are first of all, creative artists, and had an imperfect apprehension of the practical and technical considerations to which the dramatist, and even the lyrist, must have regard. He tended, too, to treat Shakespeare's theatrical and imaginative figures as those of Dickens are treated—as if they were living men and women, subject to the law of the real world and not of an artificial world; and his theory that the substance, in the style and the soul is the body of poetry can be pushed too hard. But Bradley displayed a singularly attractive, vivacious, swift, and keen intellect . . . was an effective and winning lecturer, with the natural charm, lightness, and thrilling note of a delightful bird.[35]

Apart from the last concession this comment, considering its place in an obituary, is harsh and uncompromising.

It is tempting to say that this period represents the blackest in all Bradley criticism. Critical works published about this time would amply support this view, but little more than six months after the appearance of *The Times* obituary *The Times Literary Supplement* published an article on Bradley whose very title, 'The Surrender to Poetry', contradicted the criticism of the obituary. This is the first lengthy estimate of Bradley's contribution to criticism as such and appearing when it did it is worth close scrutiny. The writer described Bradley as a critic with whose

[34] J. W. Mackail: 'Andrew Bradley', *The Oxford Magazine*, 17 Oct. 1935.
[35] *The Times*, 4 Sept. 1935.

judgements other critics aspire to agree;[36] and then to preserve a balanced view adds:

> It may be that this is not the highest praise than can be given to a critic. Possibly that critic serves the cause no less effectively who stimulates the eager mind to explorations from which it must draw back, and to judgments which it must finally relinquish. Nor does the praise necessarily imply that the critic to whom it is given is the greatest of his kind; for comprehensiveness in range may well be reckoned more important than intensity of appreciation; a fair (though not a strong) case could be made for judging that Bradley's scope was too narrow, and his output too small.

It seems worth while to quote this sober and not highly favourable comment in order to see the following high praise in a proper light; whether or not it is accurate, it is not the result of blind adulation. Bradley's pre-eminent quality is seen by the critic to be

> the capacity for a total experience of the work criticized, and for retaining that experience throughout the subsequent work of analysis and comparison. In this respect, all other English critics appear in comparison with Bradley fragmentary, or partial or casual or capricious. . . . Other critics may have experienced poetry as intensely as he, but none surely was so richly endowed with the faculty of retaining the experience in its pristine integrity throughout the arduous process of intellectual analysis, so that he seems never to have even felt the temptation, to which so many of our great critics have succumbed to substitute the concept for the experience. . . . Bradley might have said, the critic is the most uncritical of anything in existence, except that the poetic achievement is the condition of this surrender and transmigration. It is the poetic fact which makes possible the experience of poetry. So that the recognition of this fact is at once the preliminary and the fundamental critical act. From this aspect it might almost be said that other critics left off where Bradley began. That would be extravagant; it would commit the critical solecism against which Bradley was always on his guard—that of exaggerating distinctions into antithesis. But it is certainly true that Bradley was more fully

[36] *T.L.S.*, 'A. C. Bradley: The Surrender to Poetry', 23 May 1936, pp. 425–6. Cf. Chap. 1, p. 6.

conscious of the nature of his own activity than any critic before or since.

This is high praise but it is also meticulous criticism; it is accurate at least to the best of Bradley if not to all, and it is true of his intentions, if not of all his achievement. The analysis of the peculiar nature of Bradley's criticism leads the reviewer to place Bradley very high in the order of critics. *Shakespearean Tragedy* is described:

> It is an account of an experience of Shakespeare which was found finally satisfying by a man of unusual capacity for profound thought and deep feeling. Bradley's passionate enthusiasm is tempered throughout, sometimes tempered almost to the point of apparent suppression, but it is there, thrilling and unmistakable from beginning to end.[37]

The writer quotes the end of *Oxford Lectures on Poetry*, 'wherever the imagination is satisfied, there, if we had a knowledge we have not, we should discover no idle fancy but the image of a truth',[38] and resists, as many critics do not, the temptation to oversimplify. He added: 'Because he believed in the imagination after this fashion he was the most genuinely imaginative critic our country has produced. Not even Coleridge, for all his flashes, can compare with Bradley in this regard.' This is praise indeed and praise repeated: 'no critic of Wordsworth before Bradley had done anything other than "take the road round" Wordsworth's mind—not even Coleridge.'[39]

Finally, two other quotations the only excuse for the length of which is that they seem to say something helpful about Bradley's criticism, and his critical attitudes, in a way which is not found anywhere else. Of criticism the article says:

> it was, as he practised it, one of the severest conceivable exercises of the soul. First to separate the pure imaginative experience from the subtle usurpations of the intellect and the emotions—that is a work demanding a rare combination of intellectual subtlety and spiritual serenity; then to maintain that unique experience, undiminished, uncoarsened, unchanged throughout the delicate work of analysing it and comparing it with other unique experiences, which must also

[37] *T.L.S.*, 23 May 1936.

[38] *O.L.P.*, p. 395. [39] *T.L.S.*, 23 May 1936.

remain undiminished, uncoarsened, unchanged—this required the steadiness of a master indeed. And no critic with whose work we are acquainted whether in England or abroad, has displayed an equal power of control of his own processes. At his best, and his best is fully three quarters of the work he published, Bradley is in the middle of the note all the time. He leaves nothing out, and he allows nothing in that is not essential.

Bradley made no parade of the sheer work of scholarship he had done; and it may be said that it was done in order to be forgotten; in the sense that it was to him only a necessary means to the perfecting of his own capacity for the imaginative experience. But those who have carefully followed his criticism are aware how many separate paths of knowledge he had travelled in order to reach the point where the imaginative synthesis was possible, and how unerring was his discrimination between the intellectual and the imaginative. Such a discrimination is difficult to imitate. That is the reason why Bradley's influence on the actual practice of criticism has been so small. He offered no short cuts to the acquisition of a method; he demanded of those who would follow him not only the primary endowment of the creative artist—the 'experiencing nature' of which Bagehot speaks—but also the intellectual capacity to discriminate an experience to its elements, and the moral will to be satisfied with nothing less than a complete interpretation of it. The return must always be to the imaginative experience, and the task of the critic is to complete his analysis so faithfully and to order it so harmoniously that the imaginative experience naturally supervenes in a new fulness.[40]

This article seems to have had little influence on the falling fortunes of Bradley;[41] perhaps because it speaks generally of Bradley's criticism and does not descend to particulars, answering the recent attacks on Bradley. At all events, the attacks did not cease. In the late 1940s L. B. Campbell published her two closely argued criticisms of Bradley's theory of tragedy and all through the forties works appeared which undermined Bradley's judgement. It is not therefore surprising that the next article on Bradley's criticism should be called 'In Defense of Bradley'. In this article P. N. Siegel attempts to answer some of the recent criticism of

[40] Ibid.

[41] Cf. Chap. 1, p. 5, for an example of the critic who was influenced by it.

Bradley; because he discusses details first and foremost his 'defence' in fact does not convince in the same way as the earlier less defensive *Times Literary Supplement* article did: 'This essay is a defense of Bradley's work and a reaffirmation of the immensity of his contribution to the interpretation of Shakespeare.'[42]

First of all Siegel summarizes Knights's attack and then sets out to show how totally irrelevant it is to Bradley's work:

> Knights' central thesis has a degree of validity. Certainly, the lowest level of criticism is of the sort which treats the characters of a work of art as if they were human beings . . . To detach a character from this atmosphere [within the play], analyzing him without reference to the universe in which he lives, is fatal to an understanding of the play. But this is precisely what Bradley does *not* do. . . . Knights sees a drama of Shakespeare's simply as a poem which he reads 'as we should read any other poem'. He does not seem to understand that the drama is an art form with requirements of its own. All the 'dramatic patterns' and 'poetic symbols' in the world would not make *Macbeth* what it is if it did not present us with . . . characters with whose fate we felt vitally concerned. Knights is quite correct in insisting that Shakespeare was not primarily intent on creating characters—and Bradley agrees with him on this; he was intent, however, on exciting our emotions by the imitating of tragic events—and events are only tragic as Aristotle pointed out, when they proceed from the actions of characters with whom we can identify ourselves. Nothing can be truer than the sentence of Bradley, which Knights introduces as Exhibit A, that the center of Shakespearean tragedy lies 'in action issuing from character, or in character issuing in action'.[43]

When Siegel transfers his defence into more general ground, he agrees in substance with *The Times Literary Supplement* article:

> What Knights and Bradley's other critics are in reality demanding from him is adherence to their own highly technical critical methods, whether they be the study of Shakespeare's language or of his plays in the light of the historical development of the drama. Bradley's method seems to them plain and old-fashioned. It is indeed a very simple one. All that a book such as *Shakespearean Tragedy* demands is

[42] P. N. Siegel, 'In Defense of Bradley', *C.E.*, ix (Feb. 1948), pp. 250–6, at p. 250.

[43] Ibid., pp. 251–2.

an intense imagination, a fine sensibility, a highly developed power of analysis and of generalization, and a close familiarity with Shakespeare's works. We are mistaken—*Shakespearean Tragedy* is also the product of its author's knowledge of literary history and of stage history . . . one reason why it is not readily apparent is that Bradley's scholarship rests lightly on his shoulders. He uses it as a means to a keener understanding of the plays and not as an end itself. He points out, for instance that *Hamlet* has great nervous instability of temperament and that disposition to be totally absorbed in the mood of the moment which the Elizabethans called 'melancholic'; he does not write a scholarly paper, however, proving that *Hamlet* is a study of the melancholic temperament, for he knows that it is a study of Hamlet.

With this equipment Bradley produced a remarkable book the fruit of prolonged study of the text of Shakespeare's dramas and of sustained thought about its problems. Perhaps the most remarkable lecture is the opening one, on the nature of Shakespearean tragedy. There is nothing in Shakespearean criticism which can be compared to these thirty-four pages. All other writers must in some measure base themselves on it. For what Bradley has done is from an intimate knowledge of Shakespeare's tragedies to extract their salient features. It is a task requiring a great ability for generalization, such as Aristotle displayed.[44]

Siegel boldly transfers all the typical criticism of Bradley into praise.

Bradley not only keeps his eye fixed on the text; he keeps the entire dramatic universe in which Hamlet has his being in his mind's eye.

Bradley's perceptions illuminate not only Shakespeare's tragedies: they illuminate the thought and emotion of the Elizabethan age from which those tragedies arose. Such students of that thought and emotion as Theodore Spencer and W. C. Curry have found Bradley useful for their purposes.

If the study of social history, intellectual history, and literary history serves to illuminate the work of a great artist like Shakespeare, the close and imaginative study of the works themselves also serves to illuminate such history.[45]

In this article Siegel is seeking more than anything else to redress

[44] Ibid., pp. 253–4. [45] Ibid., p. 255.

the balance of criticism to poise the predominant research of the time with Bradley's aesthetic criticism. He thus illustrates that the work of Miss Campbell, Willard Farnham, Theodore Spencer, and W. C. Curry[46] come to conclusions not dissimilar from Bradley's and he ends his article: 'The Shakespearean critic of the future will profit by the labor of all his predecessors. One of the most rewarding of these he will find to be A. C. Bradley.'[47]

The article by M. R. Ridley in the *Dictionary of National Biography* (1949) understandably enough concentrates mostly on Bradley's life and a catalogue of his works. However, Ridley observed: 'Even those who disapprove alike of his aims and of his methods reluctantly admit his stature, and his position is secure above the shifting currents of critical fashion.'

This stature Ridley saw only in terms of Shakespeare criticism. Bradley he thought 'one of the greatest of English critics of Shakespeare; possibly the greatest',[48] but he had little praise for his other criticism. Also in 1949 appeared an article defending Bradley's essay on Feste reprinted in *A Miscellany*. The essay itself is not very considerable and the article is even less so; it is best summed up by the judgement, 'I am enchanted with Bradley's impressionism'.[49] The fact, however, of its having been written at all is indicative of some revived respect for Bradley.

In 1951 Kenneth Muir wrote for *Shakespeare Survey* a history of the last fifty years of Shakespeare criticism. Under a sub-heading 'Bradley and the Bradleyites' Muir summarized the contribution of *Shakespearean Tragedy*. As this appeared just when Bradley's fortunes were reviving it will be worth while to consider this summary closely:

> Bradley's *Shakespearean Tragedy* (1904) was at once the culmination of the kind of criticism which had started a hundred years before—that of Morgann and the great Romantics—and it was also to be for a whole generation the truest and most profound book ever written on

[46] Cf. Chap. 4, p. 74.

[47] P. N. Siegel, op. cit., p. 256.

[48] M. R. Ridley, 'A. C. Bradley', *D.N.B. 1931–1940* (London, 1949), pp. 98–100, at p. 99.

[49] E. J. West, 'Bradleyan Reprise': On the Fool in *Twelfth Night*, *S.A.B.*, xxiv (1949), pp. 264–74.

Shakespeare. Indeed, when all deductions have been made, it probably retains that high position to-day with the majority of readers. Bradley is not without weaknesses, though they are mostly those of his age and not peculiar to himself. The catalogue he gives of Shakespeare's faults, for example, seems now as presumptuous as Johnson's similar list in his great Preface. . . . There is not one of these accusations which would be supported by a competent modern critic, at least without many qualifications. And this fact is not, of course, due to the superiority of modern critics, but rather to the fact that the conventions of the Elizabethan stage are now better understood and appreciated.

Bradley was very conscious of the imperfections of even the best stage performance compared with the ideal performance in the critic's mind; and unfortunately the actors of his day never gave him the opportunity of seeing a play uncut and unhampered by the elaborate scenery which was supposed to be indispensable to success . . . Bradley's avowed object was to examine each play more or less as if he were an actor who had to study all the parts. This—and the example of Coleridge and Hazlitt—led him to devote two thirds of his space to a consideration of the characters of the plays. It is not quite fair to say that he substituted an interest in psychological for a dramatic interest, for he was well aware that 'the psychological point of view is not the equivalent of the tragic'; but it may be said fairly enough that he was sometimes led to consider the characters as real people rather than as imaginary characters in a drama.

In accordance with this view Muir considers that the side of Bradley represented by the discussion of what Cordelia would have done in Desdemona's place as the weaker: 'On the other hand, his Hegelianism is comparatively harmless, and the frequent accusation that is made against him that he reads into the plays subtleties that would have astonished their author is seldom true.' Moreover, he considers that despite disagreement

the main characters of the great tragedies have never before or since been analysed so brilliantly or so convincingly; we diverge from him, as we often must, at our peril. His other Shakespearian essays in *Oxford Lectures* and *A Miscellany* possess the same qualities, though he perhaps sentimentalizes the rejection of Falstaff or fails to appreciate the wonderful constructive power displayed in *Antony and Cleopatra*.[50]

[50] K. Muir, '50 years of Shakespearian Criticism 1900–1950', *S.S.*, iv (1951), pp. 1–25, at pp. 3–4.

What is interesting about this summary is the way Muir adheres to some of Bradley's judgements and rejects others; this more than anything else is a sign that Bradley has now become an accepted classic; a basis for progress, an authority and a whipping-boy, an Aunt Sally and a grand old man. Muir's article is the first evidence of this in criticism of Bradley, although ever since reaction first set in Bradley's survival of repeated attacks in the wide field of Shakespeare criticism made it clear that, whatever its shortcomings, *Shakespearean Tragedy* was not the work of an inconsiderable and totally misguided mind but that it was an exposition of Shakespeare's tragedies which would survive the passing of time and become a true classic.

It is evidence of Bradley's status that *The Times Literary Supplement* should publish a centre page article on the centenary of his birth. The article itself, though, is no trumpeting of Bradley's virtue, no miniature *festschrift*. The tone of the opening seems to indicate odd surprise that the man should be worth a centenary notice and a desire to explain to the readers who this remote figure long forgotten actually was.

> For a large part of the nineteenth and twentieth centuries Andrew Cecil Bradley, the centenary of whose birth falls this week, was like a fixed star. The light was fading before his death in 1933, and it seemed an act of tremendous courage in PROFESSOR H. B. CHARLTON a few years ago to descend upon Cambridge with the Clark lectures proclaiming 'I am a devout Bradleyite'. The new realists, the plotters of the Cantabrigian laboratory, seem to have been little affected by his unabashed weaving of Bradley's strands of ethics and romanticism into the pattern. All the signs indicate that the day of these weavings is over—or awaits the return of a more propitious season. There were times when students took notice; they were compelled under the fresh impact of A. C. B.'s eloquence and learning. He brought the tradition of philosophical and subjective criticism to a climax in *Shakespearean Tragedy* and *Oxford Lectures on Poetry*. Change must follow a climax, so there is nothing to surprise in the coming of a new fashion, the exploration of new ways of approach.[51]

This seems to be about nearly twenty years out of date except

[51] *T.L.S.* 'A. C. Bradley', 30 Mar. 1951.

perhaps for the lack of vehemence. The inaccuracy over the date of Bradley's death, the seeming unawareness of the 'Surrender to Poetry' article and of recent works treating of Bradley in an altogether more respectful way, indicate that this article represents that sort of criticism which is always ready to associate itself with what it considers to be fashionable trends. Like all who seek to follow fashion it follows at too great a distance; a closer reading of Bradley or even more attention to what critics were actually saying about Bradley would prevent the casual and inaccurate picture painted above. The praise of Bradley such as it is (this is supposed to be a centenary article and would presumably not be worth writing if there were not something to praise) studiously avoids any praise of his Shakespeare criticisms:

> Bradley had a poetic mind, a fine appreciation of the romantic poets and since he could write and talk on his subject with ease, colour and dignity, inevitably his generation was impressed, and the surprising thing would be if it were not impressed. What has happened is less a change in our view of Shakespeare than a change in notions of the function of criticism. Years before the death of Bradley the realism of Sir Walter Raleigh in his Shakespeare book and other writings, was preparing the way for the critics, led by shock-trooper Professor E. E. Stoll, who urge upon our consideration the poet and dramatist known to the Elizabethan audiences, in place of Bradley's philosopher, the cloud-topping thinker and the creator of heroes, and especially of heroines whose virtue and bright eyes led to affairs with so many Victorian sentimentalists.

It seems a little odd that after this cruel and inaccurate portrait of Bradley that the article should conclude by crediting Bradley almost nonchalantly with a most rare achievement: 'What Bradley can be honoured for chiefly now is the awareness he showed of the nature of Shakespeare's work in relation to the nature of poetry itself.' and: 'Allowing for all chance and change, Bradley can still offer us a wide comprehension of the meaning of poetry and the imagination.'[52] If this is true then the remark about 'the cloud-topping thinker' and 'Victorian sentimentalists' are curiously out of place. It seems almost as if the writer cannot

[52] Ibid.

disentangle himself from the paradoxes of fashion; he seems perplexed by the choice of Bradleys which accepted criticism has to offer. The Bradley of *How Many Children*, and the Bradley of 'The Surrender to Poetry' article, are confused within the writer's mind; desirous of illustrating at least that he is abreast of the current trends he seems unable to locate exactly where the trend is moving.

This perplexity shows also in Bertram Joseph's article, in fact it shows even in the title 'The Problem of Bradley' under which Joseph wrote. Unable to deny the value of Bradley's criticism Joseph is unwilling to relinquish what he considered to be the prevalent attitude of his time, distrust for Bradley's Victorianism.[53] The beginning and the end of this article perhaps best illustrate the confusion in Joseph's mind. He begins:

> Even now, half a century after its publication, Bradley's *Shakespearean Tragedy* still influences the teaching of Shakespeare, despite all efforts to oust it; for however misleading he may well be in the assessment and appreciation of the art and intention of a renaissance dramatic poet, Bradley happens to be an extraordinarily good critic, and not the least of his virtues is his unusual gift of being able to write consistently from a viewpoint which never changes. He can be praised, as he can be attacked, for refusing to consider Shakespeare's characters except in relation to what the later nineteenth century felt to be the truth about human character in motive and action: and, similarly, in the presentation of Shakespeare the dramatist, Bradley bases himself on the naturalistic assumption that his author had contrived to write what was for the most part something near consistently naturalistic drama, miraculously embodied in verse.[54]

He concludes:

> Bradley, after all, gives a Shakespeare which is coherent and satisfying to the mind attuned to the late nineteenth century view of human nature and of art: and it seems very likely that the mind of the adolescent of today does not find that view fundamentally untenable. Certainly undergraduates in their first year have told me that even when they can see that in the renaissance a Bradleian interpretation was obviously

[53] Cf. Chap. 4, pp. 68–70, for a discussion of B. Joseph's theories about Bradley's Victorianism.

[54] B. Joseph, 'The Problem of Bradley', *U.E.* v (1953–4), pp. 87–91 at p. 87.

impossible, they nevertheless find it more satisfying in that it gives them human beings behaving in a way which they have always thought of human beings behaving. If it should be the case that boys and girls at school find it impossible to imagine a consistent recreation of an Elizabethan play with the same intensity as they imagine Bradley's interpretation, then perhaps they should be given Bradley.[55]

This last seems almost unbelievably muddleheaded; it cries out for some reconsideration of Bradley's criticism in the light of the facts which Joseph reproduces. If Bradley's view of Shakespeare is coherent, it would seem worth while to consider whether, after all, this coherence is not Bradley's but Shakespeare's; if young and presumably not wholly unintelligent readers of Bradley find his view of Shakespeare more satisfactory even though they know it is not true to modern concepts of renaissance practice, Joseph's reaction should surely be then, not resignation but an inquiry into whether Bradley's exposition of Shakespeare is not in fact truer to the experience of the plays than any academic inquiry into its sources and parallels.

It is hardly surprising that an answer should soon emerge. In the same periodical Macdonald Emslie wrote: ' "Perhaps they should be given Bradley" says Mr. Joseph (*The Use of English*, v. 2, p. 91). I don't see why: I find that the better way of teaching Shakespeare can also be the easier', and proposes his alternative:

to view the plays as poetic wholes, to examine the themes they contain and the patterns made by those themes, to give attention to the relationships between the *personæ* and the shifts and readjustments of such relationships—this is an approach to replace Bradley's that can be consistently applied to all Shakespearean drama, in an elementary form, by G.C.E. candidates.[56]

The alternative to Bradley must seem to anyone acquainted with Bradley's work strangely like Bradley himself; this is an inaccuracy which Joseph's confusion has forced on the more straightforward Mr. Emslie. It illustrates how persistent was the

[55] Ibid., p. 91.
[56] M. Emslie, 'Shakespeare: Another Approach', *U.E.*, v (1954), pp. 174–6, at p. 176.

view of Bradley as a 'character' critic unconcerned with the dramas.

In 1955 Herbert Weisinger published an article called 'The Study of Shakespearian Tragedy since Bradley'. This is a sane attempt to see all later criticism against the background of Bradley. The nature of the attempt makes it seem rather a partisan affair; he says, for example, 'for all the strictures he heaped on Bradley's discussions of *Macbeth*, Mr. L. C. Knights finally manages to say pretty much the same thing about the play that Bradley does, and in words not very different from Bradley's'.[57] He defends Bradley similarly against the imagery and historical schools; the balance of the article is preserved, however, by such comments as:

> just as Bradley's learning and critical depth put an end to nineteenth-century didactic, impressionistic, and romantic interpretations of Shakespeare's tragedies, so now a number of developments in modern criticism and scholarship have tended in turn to undermine his labors . . . brought about a general disparagement of Bradley's point of view and a corresponding lack of interest in the idea of tragedy and its applications[58]

and:

> Despite the trends which I have briefly characterized here, the kind of approach which Bradley represents still seems to me the most fruitful for the understanding of tragedy. However, I do not at all mean to suggest that we must forthwith return to him in his entirety for there is, after all, a lack in his work which must be supplied, a necessary correction which must be made, before this criticism can be employed in its proper perspective.[59]

After this criticism of Bradley became quiescent, though Nagarajan devoted some attention to Bradley in his 'Note on Banquo' as did Kirschbaum in his essay 'Banquo and Edgar Character or Function'. L. C. Knights reversed some of his former strictures in 'Some Shakespearian Themes' and at the beginning of the 1960s considerable critical attention was accorded to

[57] H. Weisinger, 'The Study of Shakespearian Tragedy since Bradley', *S.Q.*, vi (1955), pp. 387–96, at p. 388.

[58] Ibid., p. 387.

[59] Ibid., p. 396.

Bradley in diverse works of Shakespeare criticism.[60] Not until 1963, however, was there another attempt to estimate Bradley's criticism for its own sake, as opposed to use of it as a stepping-stone to further a certain critical method.

In a *Times* series of articles called 'Critics who have Influenced Taste', Peter Alexander wrote an article on A. C. Bradley published on 11 July 1963. Alexander's treatment of Bradley is unusual in that he considers in detail Bradley's historical background. He notices, for example:

> In 1880, the year in which Bradley contributed his early essay 'Aristotle's Conception of the State' to the collection edited by Evelyn Abbot[t] called *Hellenica*, Matthew Arnold introduced *Ward's English Poets* with his essay 'The Study of Poetry', which begins:
>
> 'The future of poetry is immense, because in poetry, where it is worthy of its high destinies, our race as time goes on will find an ever surer and surer stay. . . .'[61]

Also writing of the superseding of F. H. Bradley's philosophy by Cambridge philosophers he observed:

> With the coming of the logical positivists who felt that metaphysics as expounded by Hegel and his school was meaningless and should be replaced by a rigorous analysis of language, there also appeared on the literary rostra those who pronounced Bradley's attitude to characters in drama and his interest in their cosmic significance as irrelevant, and prescribed instead a study of the dramatist's imagery and symbols and search for what was called the tentacular roots of every word. A. C. Bradley's criticism shared the fortune of his brother's philosophy.[61]

While this seems to imply a general association in the minds of other philosophers and critics of the two brothers for which there is little evidence, at the same time it does proffer an original explanation of Bradley's loss of favour, which probably comes near the truth. It was undoubtedly the same spirit in philosophy

[60] e.g. J. Bayley, *The Characters of Love*; I. Ribner, *Patterns in Shakespearian Tragedy*; J. Lawlor, *The Tragic Sense in Shakespeare.*

[61] P. Alexander, 'Critics who have Influenced Taste. xv: A. C. Bradley', *The Times*, 11 July 1963. The collection of these articles was published in 1965, edited by A. P. Ryan.

and criticism which promoted the birth of scrutiny of linguistic detail rather than the visions of the Absolute.

Alexander quotes as examples of Victorian writers who made the largest claims for poetry, Myers the classical scholar and Huxley the famous scientist. With regard to the latter writer's feeling that in dramatic poetry 'the cosmos might well seem to stand condemned', Alexander feels: 'It was part of Bradley's mission to give a different answer and to offer a vindication of the cosmos; and here many of his listeners found the satisfaction in such re-assurance that they had looked for and missed elsewhere.'[62] Whether or not this was what Bradley consciously intended in writing *Shakespearean Tragedy* it seems unlikely that by 1904 there were many readers still looking for this kind of consolation from works of criticism. As has been seen at the beginning of this chapter, none of the early reviewers made any special reference to this aspect of Bradley's criticism.

In his conclusion Alexander seems almost deliberately to become more Victorian in this way than Bradley ever appears. He concluded, Bradley

> regarded the tragic characters as embodiments of the qualities that will always command the respect and admiration of men; yet at the same time he seemed to find a formula that justified the scheme of things and absolved the cosmos from the charges that Huxley and others were bringing against it. In addition to the careful, learned, and sympathetic analysis he gave to every author he discussed there was the additional attraction, for those generations that were disturbed by the implications of biblical and scientific criticism, of finding in Bradley what seemed, in Arnold's words a stay in an age of religious doubts and questionings.[62]

Alexander's whole article studiously avoids the more modern literary critical approach to Bradley and concentrates on what he presumably feels to be a more Bradleian approach to Bradley; the value of this exercise seems doubtful, even if it could have been done successfully at a distance of over half a century; on the other hand, the historical parallels are interesting and deserve

[62] P. Alexander, op. cit.

the attention which Alexander alone of Bradley's critics draws to them.

The following year there appeared an article on Bradley written more in the true vein of twentieth-century academic literary criticism; the result, not surprisingly, is a more interesting study in the terms of this book. D. J. Palmer, who wrote this criticism, had spoken of Bradley before in his *Short Guide to Shakespeare Studies*. This impartial guide gives no indication of particular interest in Bradley, although he includes him among, if not at the head of, the three leading modern Shakespeare critics: 'excluding Bradley, he [Granville-Barker] and Wilson Knight are the two most important critics of Shakespeare produced in this century.'[63] Also his *Rise of English Studies* published in 1965 accords no undue credit to Bradley. He is in fact referred to as Walter Raleigh's predecessor at Liverpool and Glasgow without there being any mention of his professorship for its own sake. Of Raleigh's book on Shakespeare moreover Palmer wrote: 'As a piece of criticism it avoids that occasionally oppressive thoroughness of Bradley's method by maintaining a balanced and flexible point of view; the brevity lends itself to the aperçu rather than to close analysis and speculative interpretation.'[64]

However, before the publication of this book Palmer printed an article devoted entirely to A. C. Bradley which he begins almost defiantly:

> Bradley's *Shakespearean Tragedy* belongs with Dr. Johnson's *Preface*, Morgann's *Essay on Sir John Falstaff*, the *Prefaces* of Harley Granville-Barker, and G. Wilson Knight's *Wheel of Fire* in that surprisingly small collection of Shakespeare criticism which however diverse in its assumptions is by general agreement authoritative. Bradley joins the immortals on the strength of this one book for his other writings are fragments beside the massive structure and substance of *Shakespearean Tragedy*.[65]

[63] D. J. Palmer, 'A Short Guide to Shakespeare Studies', *C.S.*, i (1962), pp. 34–8, at p. 38.

[64] D. J. Palmer, *The Rise of English Studies: An Account of the Study of English Language and Literature from its Origins to the Making of the Oxford English School* (1965), pp. 120–2.

[65] D. J. Palmer, 'A. C. Bradley', *C.S.* ii (1964), pp. 18–25, at p. 18.

Palmer's article is the first to display almost historical interest in the fluctuations of Bradley's reputation. That Palmer probably could not read before the great anti-Bradley works were published probably accounts for this; also the passage of time has helped to clarify the movements of fashion. Palmer writes:

> The history of his critical reputation is curious and instructive. While no other book on Shakespeare has been reissued as often,[66] indicating that Bradley's immense prestige and following among the general reading public has continued undiminished, his name in academic circles has only recently begun to emerge from the scorn or embarrassment which it has provoked for over thirty years. Even now it is almost impossible to assess his work sympathetically without adopting a defensive posture. This duality of Bradley's reputation is a measure of the gulf which has opened between academic criticism and the common reader since Bradley's own lifetime.[67]

This historical approach enables Palmer to make points about Bradley's criticism which had earlier gone unnoticed:

> The number of individual judgments and perceptions which originate in *Shakespearean Tragedy* and have since passed into common currency is remarkable in view of all that has been written in refutation of Bradley.
>
> *Shakespearean Tragedy* is a kind of watershed in the history of Shakespeare criticism; if many of the minor points which Bradley takes up for discussion seem futile or irrelevant to-day it is often because he himself has made them seem so. . . . Bradley's work includes a great deal of tidying up (much of it done in the despised notes) in the process of clarifying and defining what are now taken for granted by his successors as some of the crucial facts bearing upon interpretation.
>
> It is worth remembering that Bradley's theory of tragedy was the first alternative account to appear since the neo-classical preconceptions of eighteenth century criticism.[68]

It is possible that Bradley owed something to the metaphysics of his elder brother F. H. Bradley.

[66] In 1966, for example, it was issued in Italian translation and cf. figures, Chap. 6, n. 64.

[67] D. J. Palmer, op. cit., p. 18.

[68] Ibid., pp. 19–20.

Not only does Palmer see Bradley historically in perspective he also defends Bradley's right to be considered for what he did say and not condemned for what he did not say.

The travesties which have passed current for Bradley's views deny him even a modicum of critical intelligence. Of course he never supposed that the characters of a play are real people; but he did believe that we respond to them as if they were human beings, that they are sufficiently credible for our interest to be caught by their actions and relationships. And he shared his belief not only with his critical predecessors but with almost every reader and spectator of Shakespeare at all times. . . . If then Bradley not infrequently writes as though the characters did have an existence off the stage, or as though they were capable of an unconscious level of thought and motive like real people, he is employing a stratagem, a kind of critical shorthand which assumes for the purposes of dramatic conviction that behind the rest there is an identity, a coherence of individuality which it is possible to investigate and articulate.

Like *The Times Literary Supplement* and Paul N. Siegel earlier, Palmer considers that Bradley's peculiar ability was to render a coherent account of the dramatic experience:

It is a task requiring infinite patience, detailed reference to the text and a philosophical consistency to draw everything together into an integrated and convincing experience. 'The experience is the matter to be interpreted': this is a key to Bradley's method. It reveals his great debt to the Romantic critics and explains why he adopts the stratagem of writing about characters as though they are living beings. . . . Bradley's fidelity to this experience of the tragedy is scrupulous and almost never deserts him, despite his awareness of the extreme difficulty of the undertaking.[69]

Palmer, however, tempers his praise. He feels that the criticism of *Hamlet* fails of Bradley's aim and that in general Bradley does not go far enough:

Sufficient for him is the belief that Shakespeare's characters are lifelike and this belief after all has the authority of tradition behind it. Nevertheless the critic's task is not merely to render our responses more articulate but to explain what in the work of art produces and

[69] Ibid., pp. 21–3.

controls those responses. And here Bradley stops short: he does not really tell us why we feel this illusion of extraordinary lifelikeness in Shakespeare's characterisation, he only shows us how lifelike the illusion is.

This seems an odd criticism to make since it makes a totally inaccurate assumption about what Bradley says in a way which Palmer previously had avoided. If Bradley's idea of Shakespearian tragedy were that it presented us with life-like characters, then his failure to show how and why would be a grave shortcoming: any reading of *Shakespearean Tragedy*, however, will show that Bradley nowhere says that the aim of tragedy is to show seemingly real people, the aim of tragedy in so far as Bradley presumes to define it is a much deeper thing—the presentation of a conflict of two good forces, which involves tragic waste but the resolution of which brings a sense of reconciliation to the audience. This experience Bradley repeatedly attempts to define and account for.

Palmer's conclusion similarly attempts to reduce the stature of Bradley in a way which disagrees oddly with his opening remarks. He ends the article:

The great debate in modern Shakespeare criticism has been about dramatic form, about the kind of structure and unity to be sought in a Shakespearian work whether in the poetic imagery of the 'themes' or the framework of inherited literary or stage conventions, or in the rhythmic patterns of tensions and contrasts. In this respect we cannot go back to Bradley as though nothing had happened since; though no criticism is ever to be swallowed whole but rather swallowed and digested. Apart from his exemplary manner of conducting the critical argument what above all Bradley still offers is that sensitive response to the amplitude and detail of Shakespearian criticism which later criticism has tended to underestimate or neglect. The challenge he leaves us with and in the spirit which pervades his own work:

'that close familiarity with the plays, that native strength and justice of perception and that habit of reading with an eager mind which make many an unscholarly lover of Shakespeare a far better critic than many a Shakespeare scholar.'[70]

[70] D. J. Palmer, op. cit., pp. 24–5.

This omits any mention first of all, of Bradley's attempt to find a synthesis behind the varied responses to tragedy and his attempt to account for those responses and finally forgets that Bradley was scholar and academic. All of these things had been mentioned before by Palmer; why there is this final reversal is difficult to say but it is tempting to see the dictates of fashion intimidating the writer.

When M. R. Ridley wrote an introductory essay for the paperback edition of *Oxford Lectures on Poetry* fashion was clearly on Bradley's side. To be reprinted in paperback is an accolade in itself, but to merit the addition of an introduction is a sign of a reverent acceptance surpassing any previously accorded Bradley. Ridley's introduction is vitiated to a certain extent by his biased attitude: 'Much of the adverse criticism of Bradley has sprung, I believe from no more creditable or better considered a feeling than a jealous exasperation at the extreme difficulty of disproving his conclusions.' This overlooks many serious objections to Bradley's criticism, and the more balanced comment carries more conviction:

> The final justification of Bradley's method is surely the plain fact that it *works*, as with an inferior dramatist it would not work. I am not saying that Bradley's is the only method which is worth while, but it is certainly one such method; and he brought to his chosen method a knowledge, a sensitivity, and an acuity of perception which put him in the very top rank of all our critics of Shakespeare.[71]

Most of the introduction is taken up with specific criticism of the lectures which are not of first importance here but there are some illuminating comments:

> He is inviting his readers to a joint exploration, not to a docile reception of doctrines promulgated *ex cathedra*. I do not know whether it has been observed how much of his criticism proceeds by the method of questioning; in this he is singularly like Longinus, and Socrates.[72]

[71] M. R. Ridley, Introduction to Papermac edition of *O.L.P.* (1965), pp. vi.

[72] Ibid., p. viii. Palmer also said: 'His manner of progress is almost Socratic leading us gradually from stage to stage by qualifications and elaborations of increasing subtlety always referring back to the text at each point' (op. cit., p. 21).

Ridley closes his introduction with almost Bradleian bombast, this is his praise of the lecture on *Antony and Cleopatra* which he thought 'the crowning of his critical achievement'.

> It is extremely close-knit, never wandering for a moment from the main road; the analysis, alike of the structure and general temper of the play, and of the characters in it, is as acute and intimately perceptive as any that had preceded it. But there is something more than that, a new kind of excitement. It is not just that kind of excitement which must have attended the progress of the earlier analyses to a slower emergent and satisfyingly rounded conclusion. It is, however strictly controlled, a warmth of emotional excitement, unique in his work, which is extraordinarily compelling.[73]

This comment is worth while quoting for what it says about the *Shakespearean Tragedy* lectures as well as about *Antony and Cleopatra.*

Also in 1965 there appeared in England, a year after its American publication, Morris Weitz's *Hamlet and the Philosophy of Literary Criticism.* The aim of this work is as the title suggests to use *Hamlet* criticism to arrive at some idea of the whys and wherefores of literary criticism in general. The book's first chapter is devoted to A. C. Bradley. Many of the judgements passed are peculiar to A. C. Bradley on *Hamlet* and others are coloured by Weitz's scheme. There are, however, some interesting general criticisms of A. C. Bradley which are the more interesting because they take no notice of the general criticism of Bradley or the controversy surrounding his name:

> Bradley is certainly one of many critics who include as integral parts of their critical essays fundamental excursions into poetics and aesthetics. More particularly, Bradley, as a critic of *Hamlet*, engages in poetics when, as we have just seen, he offers a definition of tragedy. He also practises poetics in his attempt to answer the question, How can criticism best analyse *Hamlet* as a drama? *Hamlet*, he claims, can be best analyzed as substance, i.e. characters and plot, and form, i.e. construction and versification. Of course, he insists that the substance and form are organically related; the aesthetic implications of which he develops fully in his classic, 'Poetry for Poetry's Sake'. But he also

[73] M. R. Ridley, op. cit., p. xiv.

claims that what is most important in *Hamlet* is its substance, especially the character of the hero, around which everything else revolves.

> Bradley raises the very important problem of the relation between criticism and poetic-aesthetic theory. For many critics, including Bradley, state or imply that no criticism is possible without a theory of art, or at least of the particular genre of art in question.
>
> In Bradley, there is a remarkable paucity of evaluation.[74]

Later in the book where Weitz is writing more generally there are other remarks which help to define Bradley's particular criticism: 'We know a great deal about Hamlet. One reason we do, I am suggesting, is that Bradley tells us about him.' Bradley's *Hamlet* criticism

> is an intelligible utterance because it employs certain criteria of 'tragedy' that derive from the Greek tragedies, which after all, constitute the home base of the concept and from Bradley's own recommendations and arguments for other, new criteria that were suggested to him by Hegel.[75]

Weitz in this book accords Bradley a factual treatment which in itself testifies to the writer's sense of the value of the subject; also he treats Bradley, as well as Ernest Jones, G. Wilson Knight, J. Dover Wilson, and others, as an established figure in twentieth-century *Hamlet* criticism. Furthermore, the study of Bradley is, next to that of John Dover Wilson, editor as well as critic, the longest in the book. These things as well as what Weitz actually says about Bradley's work are of considerable critical significance.

In spring 1966 J. M. Newton published in the *Cambridge Quarterly* an article in which he set out to defend Bradley from the effects of just one school of the opposition, the *Scrutiny* writers. The attack from these quarters persisted throughout the lifetime of the magazine, and is found to a greater or lesser degree in many of its articles of Shakespeare criticism (F. R. Leavis's 'The Diabolic Intellect and the Noble Hero' is, perhaps, the best-known example.) Two quotations may perhaps be taken

[74] M. Weitz, *Hamlet and the Philosophy of Literary Criticism* (1965) (first published in America, 1964), pp. 15, 16, 17 respectively.

[75] Ibid., pp. 230, 311 respectively.

here to summarize the *Scrutiny* position. The first comes from the opening article, and the second from the introduction to the Retrospect, or final volume. Both are by Leavis himself.

> It will not, for instance, do to refer as matter of commonplace to the almost complete absence of profitable Shakespeare criticism after two centuries of what must, for want of another word, be called critical activity. It may be said, that as a rule, the more respectable the critic the more deplorable the result: if, of the academics, Bradley is the best, he is the worst. How long has Hamlet been down from Wittenberg? How many children had Lady Macbeth? Those *Appendices* of Bradley's are, perhaps, now commonly thought odd, and if they don't bring home the preposterousness of his approach (which is the orthodox), argument hardly will. There may sometimes be uses for the detective, psychological, moral, philosophical or acrostical approaches, but they are not literary criticism, and unless controlled by literary criticism they are vicious. . . . The critical approach to a Shakespeare play will not consider it as, primarily, a pattern of characters (or persons), with their 'psychologies', in action and interaction, but will remember that *we* form these by abstration from Shakespeare's words—that he didn't create persons, but put words together—and it will apply this principle or truism in a strenuous critical method. This does not mean that the critic will not have to consider character, action, and moral questions, but that his concern with these will be a relevant one and so profitable. Bradley's is, as a rule, more or less subtly irrelevant, and has little to do with the appreciation of Shakespeare. His method is not intelligent enough and . . . the defect of intelligence is a default on the part of sensibility; a failure to keep closely enough in touch with responses to particular arrangements of words.[76]

Scrutiny's Shakespeare criticism, contributed to by a good many hands, shared the ethos and the impulsion of its criticism in general. It did indeed effect the relegation of Bradley, and did it by bringing home to the academic world, in the course of exemplifying positively a number of more subtle and intelligent approaches to Shakespeare, how inadequate and wrong the Bradley approach was. Eight or nine different critics, writing critiques of particular plays or reviewing books on Shakespeare, demonstrated, implicitly or explicitly, that it would not do to discuss a Shakespeare play as if it were a character-

[76] F. R. Leavis, 'The Literary Mind', *Scrutiny*, I. i, May 1932, pp. 20–32, at p. 25.

novel answering to the established Victorian (and post-Victorian) convention. . . . The relegation of Bradley has been so complete that the intensity of resentment aroused by *Scrutiny's* work needs some insisting on. A rising young Cambridge Shakespearean . . . took the opportunity, when doing a review for *The New Statesman and Nation*, to make his soundness superabundantly plain with a fervent 'Thank God for Bradley!'[77]

The main thing that strikes a reader of Bradley as he reads the first passage is how similar the *Scrutiny* approach is to Bradley's. The second passage verges on the ridiculous with its too easy assumption that Bradley has been killed off, despite plenty of evidence to the contrary, and its nostalgic memory of old battles fought in the good cause of relegating Bradley. Not without interest though is the fact that these two passages, separated by nearly thirty years of Shakespeare criticism, single out Bradley as the arch enemy; did not Leavis realize that this alone would ensure him a kind of immortality, as his unnamed don exemplified and as the following article makes abundantly clear?

Newton's indictment of the *Scrutiny* writers seems very flimsy, amounting to little more than a dissatisfaction that none of them committed themselves wholeheartedly on paper to the experience of the plays. For instance, he says 'It is oddly as if *Troilus* were for Mr. Traversi something quite tangible, outside himself, not something re-created in his mind and imagination as he has read the play', and 'we don't know what Professor Knights really thinks about any of the plays he writes on'.[78] Newton's own reaction to their criticism is made to do the duty of close critical analysis, and the style in which he presents his findings is indicative of the weight of his article:

All the would-be aces served in *How Many Children?* go into the net. The final result: six-love, six-love, six-love? This is not to say that Professor Knights never plays a good stroke. At this stage in my whole argument it may be enough in the way of general comment to put some personal experience on record. I can still remember vividly

[77] F. R. Leavis, 'A Retrospect', *Scrutiny*, xx (1963), pp. 1–24, at p. 12.

[78] J. M. Newton, '*Scrutiny*'s Failure with Shakespeare', *Cambridge Quarterly* i. 2, Spring 1966, pp. 144–78, pp. 153 and 165 respectively.

> the mental bewilderment and strain I experienced when as a schoolboy and undergraduate I painstakingly tried to take back with me to plays the accounts of them by Professor Knights and Mr. Traversi. . . . The natural effect was that reading the analysis of a play came to make me regularly, want *not* to go back to the play itself.[79]

What he says about Bradley is predictably hardly more substantial, although there is in it enough to make us wish that he had concentrated more attention on Bradley and less on personal reactions to the opposition:

> I should like to end up with a plea for the good old Bradleian approach, which though it does not, and never pretended to, give a complete account, does at least put first things first, and incidentally was neither Bradleian, nor Victorian, nor Romantic, but the natural centre of Shakespeare criticism since Shakespeare criticism has existed. The real problem, of course, is not what Shakespeare's characters are like, but why they affect us as they do. Still the answer to this does inevitably pass through the other, and Bradley gives a substantial part of the answer. The greater part probably lies in the poetry, but not in the poetry *qua* poetry, still less as an esoteric system of semi-philosophical hints and references, but as a means of dramatic expression.[80]

This seems very like a recommendation of *Scrutiny*'s own methods, which is perhaps not really surprising, because it appears that Newton's chief complaint against these critics is that they had 'the effect of discouraging many people from ever reading' Bradley's criticism. Singling out Bradley and Wilson Knight as the only two 'twentieth-century writers known mainly for their "Shakespeare criticism" [who have] proved themselves at the same time talented literary critics'[81] he feels that only the deterrent effect of *Scrutiny* prevents this being universally recognized. As is so often the case with debates of this kind, one is left with a desire to combine the best of both schools: to be able to respect, say, Leavis *and* Bradley, and not only one *or* the other.

This can only be an open-ended survey; and therefore there

[79] J. M. Newton, op. cit., p. 177.
[80] Ibid., p. 178.
[81] Ibid., pp. 150 and 145 respectively.

can be no conclusions. The last word in Bradley criticism has not been said. On the other hand, this survey should have reinforced the impression given by the discussion of his place in Shakespearian criticism. That is that after a period of critical adulation, followed inevitably by ardent reaction (the fashionable nature of which has perpetuated it in some quarters beyond its natural term), Bradley is now after half a century being recognized as one of the accepted Shakespeare critics. This means, among other things, that he is now being read for his own sake, and not merely to satisfy the need of critics to find a whetstone to sharpen their own judgements and a landmark against which they can measure their progress.

9

CONCLUSION

As A. B. Harbage said, 'the terrible thing' about Bradley's criticism, 'is its tremendous success'.[1] Indeed to its immediate success in literary fields and its continued success in teaching could be attributed most of the animosity which his very name has aroused. If in the world of business nothing succeeds like success, in the arts nothing is more doomed to imminent disgrace. To be the darling of one generation is to be the *bête noire* of the next. Bradley's case is a commonplace. Each generation seeks at least to innovate, if not to progress, and this is barely possible in the shadow of success. This was probably exaggerated in Bradley's case by the fact that his book was published at the beginning of the century and that within a decade of its publication a war broke out which made the next generation even more conscious that it must move on. Bradley also offered himself more readily than most as a static symbol of the past because after that war he published nothing reminiscent of his earlier self except perhaps the first essay in *A Miscellany*. He seems to have sunk readily into the role of played-out Victorian; occasional lectures given before respected bodies like the British Academy must have helped to propagate the idea that he had faded from the contemporary critical scene. This was not wholly Bradley's fault. He was fifty-three when *Shakespearean Tragedy* was published, sixty-seven when the war was ended. He felt himself to be an old man.

Harbage, though, was not talking so much of popular success or even fame in the narrow world of Shakespeare criticism; he was talking of the success of Bradley's work as accurate and helpful commentary on the original, Shakespeare. In this sense, too, Bradley's success did harm to his reputation. Bradley chose Shakespeare's four weightiest plays, the plays on which a

[1] A. B. Harbage, *As They Liked It* (New York, 1947), p. 29.

consensus of critical opinion would place the highest value. He discussed the experience of those plays in a way the value of which none who were prepared to acknowledge their greatness could totally deny, because whatever the faults of his criticism, it does make plain Shakespeare's greatness. He discussed the substance and the structure and the individual features of the four plays; those aspects on which he dwelt, the feeling of reconciliation at the end of the tragedy, the characters of those involved in the conflict he discussed exhaustively. What he did has never been done better, and seldom as well.

Shakespeare criticism could not, however, leave empty the ground[2] which Bradley had covered, or at least it could not so totally as to avoid all discussion of the four tragedies. It concentrated on those aspects, therefore, which barely figure in Bradley; firstly historical parallels, Shakespeare seen in perspective against the theatre of his time, Shakespeare's sources, the works from which he took his stories, his audience, the limitations of his stage, a reconstruction as far as possible of Shakespeare as he could have been seen by an almost ideally diligent contemporary; later, concentrated study of the words themselves, the symbols, the reiterated metaphors, the themes, and the poetry; a Shakespeare totally removed in many ways from the reality of his time and theatre, but equally removed from the Shakespeare of Bradley who was concerned to reconstruct an illusion of reality, an illusion occasionally totally convincing but always profoundly meaningful in relation to reality.

Shakespeare became after Bradley a different figure. Not different according to Bradley, however, but as far as possible, different from Bradley. Criticism was not prepared to say: as regards Shakespeare's tragedy seen in terms of human conflict, Bradley has said all that can be said; we must now say something different. It preferred to say categorically: Bradley has mistaken Shakespeare; he was not writing tragedy in terms of human

[2] The desire to do so is best seen in the recent concentration on the late plays and the problem comedies which Bradley, in print, left quite alone. But so strong is the influence of Bradley that Nicholas Brooke, writing about the earlier tragedies, feels he has to justify his deviation from the Bradleian norm. N. Brooke, *Shakespeare's Early Tragedies* (1968), pp. 1 ff.

conflict, he was writing sensational drama suitable for his time, or he was writing exquisite poetry. Shakespeare's interest in human beings was wholly and emphatically denied; Bradley was criticized, at first anyway, for concentrating on an aspect of Shakespeare which did not exist.

Criticism, however, did not ignore Bradley; his judgements were doubted, his methods questioned, in some cases his whole outlook was derided, but attention of some sort or another was constantly being drawn to him. It seems as if in many ways Bradley fulfilled a function for the Shakespeare criticism of the 1930s (for at that time the 'modern' criticism was at its strongest, and Bradley's fortunes were at their lowest). Criticism perhaps needed a testing ground which it found in Bradley and it found its ideal testing ground, which varied as the criticism varied, only by means of distorting Bradley. Bradley had to become simply the antithesis of everything that was modern; he became, therefore, a Victorian, even a 'Romantic', he became exclusively a character critic or exclusively a philosophizing theorist. His criticism was either Aristotle ridden, or suited only to a nineteenth-century novel; in either event it was everything that Shakespeare criticism must not be. It was, of course, because of his success that he made such an admirable touchstone. Not even Dowden (although he is much more like this 'modern' Bradley than Bradley) had the necessary stature. If the moderns were to pit themselves against their predecessors it is a necessary compliment to themselves that they should choose the most eminent. On a practical level also they had to choose a name which would be a cipher for the works of the man: 'The book is too well-known to require much descriptive comment',[3] said L. C. Knights; this too was a necessary feature of the opposition which modern criticism needed. '[H]e is still a very potent and mischievous influence',[4] wrote F. R. Leavis; had he not been, the article in which that was said could hardly have been written at all.

[3] L. C. Knights, *How many Children had Lady Macbeth?* (Cambridge, 1933), p. 5.

[4] F. R. Leavis, 'Diabolic Intellect and the Noble Hero' *Scrutiny*, vi (Dec. 1937), pp. 259–83, at p. 260.

In fact, there is no better testimony, and certainly no earlier testimony in print to Bradley's position as a critic than the works of the 1930s. There is little evidence in literary criticism before this of the fame against which these critics were railing—it must, it seems, have been mostly an affair of hearsay and spoken recommendation. The impression received is that of countless university dons and even more schoolteachers buying copies of *Shakespearean Tragedy* for libraries, passing on (often, no doubt, in garbled form) his judgements and imperceptibly perpetuating his name. Bradley's influence on schoolchildren has long been a source of annoyance to critics; Bertram Joseph's article 'The Problem of Bradley'[5] is evidence of this. In fact, of course, Bradley only has the influence he has on schoolchildren and undergraduates because of the influence he has had on teachers and dons. If a Bradleian approach to Shakespearian tragedy is perpetuated in the notes to school editions of the plays,[6] this is surely because the notes are designed, however naïvely, to help children to give the right answers to the questions they will be asked. While the questions asked are still of the type: 'Coleridge speaks of Iago's "motiveless malignity". Is this the impression you have received from *Othello*?' or more simply: 'Write an account of the characters of Calpurnia and Portia in *Julius Caesar*',[7] then a critic who asked and attempted to answer questions like 'Why did Hamlet delay?' is more help to the student than a critic who has culled obscure parallels of characters from medical treatises or listed the recurrent images which explain a character's function in the drama.

Exactly why Bradley has had such an influence on teachers is difficult to estimate; probably it is the sort of influence which perpetuates itself, though it has been perpetuating itself now for a

[5] B. Joseph, 'The Problem of Bradley', *U.E.*, v (1953–4), pp. 87–91.

[6] An example of this type of edition is *The Warwick Shakespeare* used currently in schools. Cf. Chap. 2, p. 32, for Bradley's views on school editions in his day.

[7] These are respectively university and school essay questions from my own memory. The London University B.A. Honours Shakespeare paper for 1962 produces a further example: 'Those who think Hamlet should have killed Claudius at once regard him as a weakling: those who think he should not have considered such an act at all regard him as a brute. How do you regard him?'

long time. Undeniably the ease with which Bradley can be read and understood must help; however good William Empson's writings on Shakespeare, for example, they will be of little use to the average schoolchild or even undergraduate if they are not understood. Moreover, fame is made by the thousands if not the millions; the only thousands in literary criticism are the schoolchildren and undergraduates who work and read under some sort of compulsion. If Bradley is accepted by these then his fame is assured; ironically the fame accorded to L. C. Knights and F. R. Leavis probably comes from the same source.

Bradley's influence has been widespread and long lasting. There must be other reasons for his influence than his election to the position of adversary to the modern critics. In the face of so much that is merely the dictate of fashion it may seem oddly naïve to think that Bradley's influence has been as great as it is because of any intrinsic characteristic of his; but the inquiry seems worth making.

As a critic Bradley was, as even his opponents have admitted, thorough and honest. Herford in his review of *Shakespearean Tragedy* remarked upon Bradley's 'cautious scrutiny';[8] F. R. Leavis paid respect to his 'scrupulosity';[9] J. F. Danby spoke of his common sense;[10] A. J. A. Waldock of 'the sanity, the care' of Bradley and of his 'masterly thoroughness'.[11] Thoroughness and even honesty, however, are not characteristics likely to have wide influence; although they will serve to perpetuate influence if attention is attracted to them by some other feature. Waldock, who, disagreeing with Bradley on many scores, clearly felt his influence keenly, said:

To read Bradley apart from the play (or, for that matter, with the play) is to be entranced by an exposition built up with deft skill and masterly thoroughness. His *Hamlet* stands four square. . . . It is only

[8] C. H. Herford, review of *Shakespearean Tragedy*, *M.L.R.*, i (1905–6), pp. 128–33, at p. 130.

[9] F. R. Leavis, op. cit., p. 259. He did, however, think it 'misdirected'.

[10] J. F. Danby, *Shakespeare's Doctrine of Nature. A Study of 'King Lear'* (London, 1949), p. 19.

[11] A. J. A. Waldock, *Hamlet: A Study in Critical Method* (Cambridge, 1931), pp. 27 and 49 respectively.

when one inspects a little more closely that one sees that some important members of this construction (a fascinating work of art) have suffered slight alterations from the Shakespearean design. . . . Bradley's *Hamlet* is better than Shakespeare's; it is better in the sense that it has a firmer consistency that it hangs together with a more irresistible logic.[12]

The Times paid its respects to Bradley as 'an effective and winning lecturer',[13] but the University of Glasgow is more precise, and it had in this matter close experience: 'The control of his classes, to those whom he controlled, still offers a startling illustration of the victory of mind over matter. His intellectual influence, owing nothing to external circumstances, was overwhelming and permanent.'[14] It seems unlikely from this that his influence even as a lecturer had much to do with personal magnetism. Bradley seems never to have sought to be and never to have become a 'personality' even in the narrow circle of his university; according to J. W. Mackail he was an 'enigma'[15] to his undergraduates. His influence as a writer similarly does not come from any display of personal charm in the style or content. There are few, if any, jokes; the lightheartedness is only very occasional. If there is a little hyperbole in the conclusion, the book's opening is more indicative of Bradley's manner; scrupulous, businesslike, and quite unembellished:

In these lectures I propose to consider the four principal tragedies of Shakespeare from a single point of view. Nothing will be said of Shakespeare's place in the history either of English literature or of the drama in general. No attempt will be made to compare him with other writers. I shall leave untouched, or merely glanced at, questions regarding his life and character, the development of his genius and art, the genuineness, sources, texts, inter-relations of his various works. Even what may be called in the restricted sense, the 'poetry' of the four tragedies—the beauties of style, diction, versification—I shall pass by

[12] Ibid., p. 49. This view was echoed if not borrowed by J. F. C. Gutteling, cf. Chap. 1, p. 6.

[13] *The Times*, 4 Sept. 1935, p. 14.

[14] From the Minute of a Meeting of the General Council of the University of Glasgow held 30 Oct. 1935—kindly pointed out to me by Mr. Quinn, Librarian of Balliol College, Oxford.

[15] J. W. Mackail, 'Andrew Bradley', *The Oxford Magazine*.

in silence. Our one object will be what, again in a restricted sense, may be called dramatic appreciation.[16]

If this was intended to disarm criticism it failed quite spectacularly; the omissions Bradley boldly admits to were those which caused the modern critics of the thirties to despise him; on the other hand, to the plain reader it has one overwhelming recommendation. It makes quite clear what we can expect from the work; it promises a straightforward manner and style easily understood, a workmanlike attitude to the subject which pays the reader the fine compliment of expecting him to be workmanlike also. Bradley eschews all through his work the unexpected dramatic revelation, the unprepared reversal of the argument, the wilder flamboyances of style. Whether or not the fact that *Shakespearean Tragedy* was delivered first as lectures affected the style or not, it is reminiscent of the best conversational style, coherent and graceful. Sentences chosen at random will illustrate this:

> The Duke of Cornwall, we presume in the absence of information, is likely to live in Cornwall; but we suddenly find, from the introduction of a place name which all readers take at first for a surname, that he lives at Gloster (I. v. 1). This seems likely to be also the home of the Earl of Gloster, to whom Cornwall is patron. But no: it is a night's journey from Cornwall's 'house' to Gloster's, and Gloster's is in the middle of an uninhabited heath[17]

or from the notes where a drier, less accessible style might be expected:

> The likeness between Timon's curses and some of the speeches of Lear in his madness is, in one respect, curious. It is natural that Timon, speaking to Alcibiades and two courtezans, should inveigh in particular against sexual vices and corruption, as he does in the terrific passage IV. iii 82–166; but why should Lear refer at length, and with the same loathing to this particular subject (IV. vi. 112–32)? It almost looks as if Shakespeare were expressing feelings which oppressed him at this period of his life.[18]

A plain straightforward style may seem like an odd feature to create such a widespread influence as Bradley's; but its plainness

[16] *S.T.*, p. 1. [17] Ibid., p. 259. [18] Ibid., p. 443.

is capable of a certain beauty and charm of its own. The almost regularly hyperbolic conclusions of the lectures are examples of the variations in the same conversational style. He ends the first lecture on *Hamlet*:

> It was not that *Hamlet* is Shakespeare's greatest tragedy or most perfect work of art; it was that *Hamlet* most brings home to us at once the sense of the soul's infinity, and the sense of the doom which not only circumscribes that infinity but appears to be its offspring.[19]

The description of Gertrude is masterly in a different way:

> The Queen was not a bad-hearted woman, not at all the woman to think little of murder. But she had a soft animal nature, and was very dull and very shallow. She loved to be happy, like a sheep in the sun; and to do her justice, it pleased her to see others happy, like more sheep in the sun.[20]

The influence of this description is such that it was partly to counteract it that Carolyn Heilbrun wrote her defence of Gertrude in the *Shakespeare Quarterly*.[21]

Not only the manner but the matter of *Shakespearean Tragedy* is seductive; Bradley concentrates his attention on character, because he considers that Shakespearian tragedy is about 'action issuing from character or . . . character issuing in action'. This concentration on character appeals to the reader not only on account of its critical validity, but because it emphasizes that human beings matter. It is the sort of flattery to the human mind that makes character delineation a perpetually fascinating subject. Furthermore, Bradley concentrates on this world, showing it capable of as great heights as depths and this too is reassuring to the reader. The average reader of Shakespeare will conclude for himself that it is the characters who matter; Bradley provides a convincing argument to support this conclusion. When Kirschbaum (in theory not so naïve in his reaction) wrote 'Beatrice and Benedick are as real as you and I',[22] what prompted him to this remark so contrary to all his critical canons seems likely to be the

[19] Ibid., p. 128. [20] Ibid., p. 167.

[21] C. Heilbrun, 'The Character of Hamlet's Mother', *S.Q.*, viii (1957), pp. 201–6.

[22] L. Kirschbaum, *Character and Characterisation in Shakespeare* (Detroit/Toronto, 1962), p. 129.

lurking conviction that he is capable of the wit, the humour, and the charm of the pair. Identification with heroes and heroines is a commonplace reaction; what Shakespeare, as interpreted by Bradley, offers is a more comprehensive identification, with characters capable of glorious if dangerous extremes, with a world magnified and yet obviously related to the world of the audience. It is little wonder that a writer who offers the readers as fellow members of the human race Bradley's Othello, Bradley's Hamlet, or even Bradley's Lady Macbeth should have a widespread influence.

On a lower level but of no less importance Bradley's concentration on the characters of the dramas appeals to the average reader's love of gossip. Leaving aside the question of their relevance to the drama, such issues as 'Where was Hamlet at the time of his Father's death?' have a perpetual appeal to the curiosity of Shakespeare readers. Similarly the mixture of praise and disapprobation which colours many of Bradley's criticisms of the minor characters, appeals to the susceptible and the superior in every reader. The following description is a good example:

> Cassio is a handsome, light-hearted, good natured young fellow, who takes life gaily, and is evidently very attractive and popular. . . . He has warm generous feelings, an enthusiastic admiration for the General, and a chivalrous adoration for his peerless wife. But he is too easy going. He finds it hard to say No; and accordingly, although he is aware that he has a very weak head, and that the occasion is one on which he is bound to run no risk, he gets drunk, not disgustingly so, but ludicrously so.[23]

Such influence may seem at first glance far removed from the legitimate ends of criticism; but this is not wholly true. The above description of Cassio, for example, is unquestionably true to the impression left by the play. Moreover, Bradley inserts proof of the accuracy of the impression: 'Othello, who calls him by his Christian name, is fond of him; Desdemona likes him much; Emilia at once interests herself on his behalf.'[23]

Nor does Bradley let accuracy in portrayal of characters seem

[23] *S.T.*, p. 238.

an end in itself; 'it is just because he is truthful in those smaller things that in greater things we trust him absolutely never to pervert the truth for some doctrine or purpose of his own',[24] which is as good a brief account of the value of verisimilitude in art as any. If characters are not necessarily the most nearly perfect means to understanding tragedy they are, it seems likely, the most accessible. Someone seeing *Othello* for the first time, for example, will rely instinctively on the characters to guide him through the play; however informative a knowledge of Iago's theatrical forebears (or even a sense that he is descended from the medieval Vice) or the observation of repeated sea images may be in the study, it is of little immediate help in the theatre, or in any imaginative reading of the play.

To say that Bradley's is one of the most easily understood and most generally helpful studies of Shakespeare is to make a low claim indeed for one whose influence has been so widespread. On the other hand, if a true understanding of Shakespeare is the end of Shakespearian criticism these two factors must be of paramount importance. Moreover, in the case of a critic harmed as Bradley has been by exaggerated statements about his achievement, the more modest claims may now appear to be the most useful.

Whatever else is debated about Bradley's criticism, however, there can be no denial that he has been one of the most influential Shakespeare critics to write in English. On the whole, and seen now in the perspective of the half-century since *Shakespearean Tragedy* was published, the influence has generally been for good. This is only partly on account of Bradley's intrinsic merits as critic; it is also because while thousands of readers and a proportionate number of critics immediately adopted Bradleian attitudes to Shakespeare, after a certain interval the same people in the next generation deliberately eschewed both Bradleian methods and Bradleian conclusions and explored a diverse and rewarding variety of other methods. This process meant at one time a considerable loss of prestige for Bradley's work, but this is hardly important especially since now the balance is being restored and

[24] Ibid., pp. 238–9.

the excesses of the anti-Bradley movement scorned as the first excesses of his followers.

While it is difficult to put dates to these trends, two periods of more marked transition stand out: the thirties, when Bradley reaction first of all became a real vogue, and the sixties, which have seen the rehabilitation of Bradley the critic. Why these two periods should so stand out is enigmatic. In the first case it is due to the publication within five years of major works by L. B. Campbell, Granville-Barker, G. Wilson Knight, L. C. Knights, Caroline Spurgeon, Dover Wilson, and E. E. Stoll. Between them these seven critics account for most of the essentially modern criticism which this century has produced, and most, if not all, did it by methods which were widely different from Bradley's and some (if not so many as general opinion would think) made explicit the reason for their seeking such an alternative. The word 'modern', however, of its essence cannot for long be true; these critics persisted as the modern critics for a long while because they still had much to say about Shakespeare; this is true of Wilson Knight, L. C. Knights, Dover Wilson, and E. E. Stoll at least. Also they persisted in being modern because other critics, F. R. Leavis, D. A. Traversi, S. L. Bethell, and J. F. Danby, perpetuated their aims and methods. By the middle 1950s, however, the quarter-century which has passed since their works were first published had taken the edge off their newness. While Fluchère still supported the Cambridge approach and Wilson Knight was still publishing his works, the publication in the late forties of H. B. Charlton's *Shakespearian Tragedy* and P. N. Siegel's article on Bradley had been followed by Muir's sympathetic account of Bradley in his summary of Shakespeare criticism, Sewell's independently very Bradleian work *Character and Society in Shakespeare*, and other individually barely significant works which show that the 'modern' criticism had become jaded. 1960 saw the publication of several works which replaced the 'modern' criticism with a new 'modern' criticism which perhaps inevitably turned (as the 'modern' criticism had largely turned to Coleridge) to Bradley for its authority. J. Bayley's *The Characters of Love*, Barbara Everett's article on 'The New King Lear',

Ribner's *Patterns in Shakespearean Tragedy*, and John Lawlor's *Tragic Sense in Shakespeare*, were all published in 1960, and if with the exception of the article they did so with less flamboyance they no less decidedly left the modern critics behind than they, in their turn, had previously left Bradley. Lawlor's work, for example, makes no reference to Leavis, Wilson Knight, or Granville-Barker, it refers only in footnotes to Knights and Spurgeon; instead there are several references to Bradley.

Thirty years, it seems, is the expected life-span of a critical vogue; the real test of any critic, however, is his position after he has ceased to be in vogue. Bradley emerges from thirty years of reaction as a critic of lasting value; it is seen now, as it was not perhaps before, that his interpretation of Shakespeare is as worthy serious consideration as any published in England. It is doubtful now whether a critic could produce a work on a subject which Bradley had handled without paying some attention to Bradley's conclusions on that subject. An article in a recent issue of *Shakespeare Quarterly* is a case in point; the article seeks to prove that *King Lear* is about the 'meaning of chaos'. The argument is conducted with no reference to Bradley and few to any critic. Before concluding, however, the writer feels compelled to add: 'Bradley has subjected *King Lear* to a very different sort of reading from mine, one which has not been enfeebled by its longevity, and I shall have to say a few words about it before summing up.'[25] That Bradley alone of all the holders of 'different' views on *King Lear* should be thus singled out is evidence of the recent pro-Bradley fashion; on the other hand, to have said, over sixty years ago, something about *King Lear* which a modern American critic feels it his duty to pay attention to is an achievement of solid worth.

It is to what Bradley said that attention is now being paid; that what he said so long ago and in conditions widely different from the modern, in a manner far removed from the modern professional style and without the help of research and all the developments which intensive Shakespeare criticism has brought

[25] H. Skulsky, '*King Lear* and the Meaning of Chaos', *S.Q.*, xvii (1966), pp.1–17, at p. 16.

about in the last fifty years, should still be worth consideration is the only tribute of meaning to a critic. For long Bradley was condemned for what later generations assumed he stood for; in fact he stood for nothing except the right reading of Shakespeare. Now Bradley is read on account of what he said and criticism is so much the richer. What he said is not necessarily true or even more true than what many other critics have said, but it was the product of a sensitive, well-educated, honest mind; it is the communication of a reading of Shakespeare, conditioned by 'a vivid and intent imagination' subjected equally and simultaneously to a 'process of comparison and analysis'. The more writings of this kind on Shakespeare that are accessible the better it is for the true understanding of Shakespeare; it is as one among the not very many such readings that Bradley's *Shakespearean Tragedy* makes its best claim to serious consideration.

BIBLIOGRAPHY

NOTE

THE most important reference material for this book has been found in works of Shakespeare criticism, a collection too vast to search comprehensively. Instead, as 'influence' has been the main concern, major works have provided a starting-point, leading to other books by their references, and so on. Such a process does not pretend to exhaust the supply, and as any reader can create his own selection by similar means, I have not thought it necessary to provide a bibliography of this material. The two major Shakespeare periodicals in English, *Shakespeare Quarterly* and *Shakespeare Survey*, provide a useful guide as do the following bibliographies:

W. JAGGARD: *Shakespeare Bibliography*. Stratford-on-Avon, 1911.

C. H. HERFORD: *A Sketch of Recent Shakespeare Investigation, 1893–1923*, London, n.d. [1923]

W. EBISCH and L. L. SCHÜCKING: *Shakespeare Bibliography 1931* (and *Supplement* 1937). Oxford.

A. A. RAVEN: *A Hamlet Bibliography and Reference Guide, 1877–1935*. Chicago, 1936.

G. R. SMITH: *A Classified Shakespeare Bibliography, 1936–58*. Pennsylvania, 1963.

Shakespeare Association Bulletin (becoming *Shakespeare Quarterly* 1950), 1924–66.

The Year's Work in English Studies. London, 1919–63.

A. WORKS BY A. C. BRADLEY IN CHRONOLOGICAL ORDER

'A Sea-Shell', *Macmillan's Magazine*, xviii (July 1868), p. 288.

'Mr. Rossetti's Shelley', *Oxford Undergraduates Journal* (9 Nov. 1870), pp. 846–7.

'Mr. Browning's "Inn Album"', *Macmillan's Magazine*, xxxiii (Feb. 1876), pp. 347–54.

'Aristotle's Conception of the State', *Hellenica*, ed. E. Abbott (Oxford and Cambridge, 1880), pp. 181–243.

'Old Mythology and Modern Poetry', *Macmillan's Magazine* (1881), pp. 28–47.

'Some Points in "Natural Religion"', *Macmillan's Magazine* (Dec. 1882), pp. 144–60.

Ed. T. H. Green: *Prolegomena to Ethics*. Oxford, 1883.

The Study of Poetry: a lecture. Liverpool, 1884 (delivered Winter 1883).

Current Literature: A Review of Julius Caesar, ed. H. C. Beeching', *Liverpool University College Magazine*, ii (1887), pp. 32–4.

'The Nature of Tragedy with Special Reference to Shakespeare.' Address given to the Literary and Philosophical Society, 19 Feb. 1889. Warrington, 1889. (I have not seen this.)

Poetry and Life. An Inaugural Address delivered at the University of Glasgow, 8 Nov. 1889. Published Glasgow, 1889.

The Teaching of English Literature. An Address given to the Teachers' Guild at Liverpool and to the Glasgow Branch of the Association of Teachers in the Secondary Schools of Scotland. Glasgow, 1891.

Ed. (with G. R. Benson) R. L. Nettleship: *Philosophical Lectures and Remains*, vols. i and ii. Vol. i ed. and prefaced with a biographical sketch by A. C. Bradley. London, 1897.

'Shelley and Brunetto Latini', *Atheneum*, No. 3729 (15 Apr. 1899), p. 469.

A Commentary on Tennyson's 'In Memoriam'. London, 1901.

'John Keats', *Chambers Cyclopedia of English Literature*. Edinburgh and London, 1903, pp. 99–106.

'Eighteenth Century Estimates of Shakespeare. A Review of D. Nichol Smith: *Eighteenth Century Essays on Shakespeare*', *Scottish Historical Review* (1904), pp. 291–5.

Shakespearean Tragedy. London, 1904.

'Notes on Passages in Shelley', *Modern Language Review*, i (1905–6), pp. 24–42.

Oxford Lectures on Poetry. London, 1909.

'The Locality of *King Lear* Act I scene ii', *Modern Language Review*, iv (Jan. 1909), pp. 238–40.

The Uses of Poetry. Presidential Address at the Annual General Meeting of the English Association. London, 1912. (Delivered 12 Jan. 1912.)

Coriolanus. Second British Academy Shakespeare Lecture. London, 1912. (Delivered 1 July 1912.)

Short Bibliographies of Wordsworth, Coleridge, Byron, Shelley, and Keats. *E. A. Pamphlet*, 23 (1912).

Preface to J. A. Cramb: *Germany and England*. London, 1914.

'Notes on Shelley's "Triumph of Life"', *Modern Language Review*, ix (Oct. 1914), pp. 441–56.

'International Morality: The United States of Europe', *The International Crisis in its Ethical and Psychological Aspects*. Lectures delivered in February and March 1915 by various speakers at Bedford College for Women. London, 1915.

Ed. and Introduction of *New and Old: Literary Remains of Edith Sichel*. London, 1917.

'Bernard Bosanquet 1848–1923', *Proceedings of the British Academy*, xi (London, 1924).

A Miscellany. London, 1929.

The Ideals of Religion. Gifford Lectures given in the University of Glasgow, 1907. Published posthumously in a text prepared by Mrs. Ernest von Glehn. London, 1940.

Bradley also published in 1885 a translation of Hermann Lotze: *Metaphysic*, Book III (Oxford), and he was responsible for vols. i and vi of *Essays and Studies*, 1910 and 1916.

B. SOURCES FOR LIFE OF A. C. BRADLEY

1. *Himself*

Who was Who, 1929–1940. London, 1941.

M. RIDLEY: 'Andrew Cecil Bradley', *Dictionary of National Biography, 1949*.

Obituary: 'A. C. Bradley', *The Times* (4 Oct. 1935).

J. W. MACKAIL: 'Andrew Cecil Bradley, 1851–1935', *Proceedings of the British Academy*, xxi (London, 1935), pp. 385–92.

—— 'Obituary: Andrew Cecil Bradley', *Oxford Magazine* (17 Oct. 1935), pp. 16–17.

Excerpt from the Minute of a Meeting of the General Council of the University of Glasgow held 30 October 1935. Copy at Balliol College, Oxford.

Correspondence to Gilbert and Lady Mary Murray, 1892–1929. (Manuscript in Bodleian Library.)

G. G. A. MURRAY: *An Unfinished Autobiography*, ed. Jean Smith and A. Toynbee. London, 1966.

2. *Family Background*

GEORGE GRANVILLE BRADLEY: 'Reverend Charles Bradley', *Dictionary of National Biography*, ii (London, 1921) (reprint).

J. S.: 'George Granville Bradley', *Dictionary of National Biography*. Supplement vol. i. London, 1912.

A. E. TAYLOR: 'Francis Herbert Bradley', *Dictionary of National Biography. 1922–30*. London, 1937.

—— 'F. H. Bradley', *Mind*, xxxiv (1925), pp. 1–12.

R. WOLLHEIM: *F. H. Bradley*. Harmondsworth, 1959.

G. R. G. MURE: 'Men and Ideas: F. H. Bradley, Towards a Portrait', *Encounter*, xvi (Jan. 1961), pp. 28–37.

See also for insight into an evangelical Clapham sect family, E. M. FORSTER, *Marianne Thornton*. London, 1956.

3. *Oxford*

J. H. MUIRHEAD: *Bernard Bosanquet and his Friends. Illustrating the Sources in the Development of his Philosophical Opinions*. London, 1935.

W. G. HISCOCK: *Balliol Rhymes, edited from Rare Original Broadsheet with the notes of J. W. Mackail, Lord Sumner, and F. A. Madan together with a MS. from Christchurch Library*. Oxford, 1939.

M. RICHTER: *The Politics of Conscience: T. H. Green and his Age*. London, 1964.

W. R. WARD: *Victorian Oxford*. London, 1965.

N. PEARSON: 'Balliol as I Remember it', *Blackwoods*, clxxxvii (May 1910), pp. 633–42.

4. *English Studies*

D. J. PALMER: *The Rise of English Studies. An Account of the Study of English Language and Literature from its Origins to the Making of the Oxford English School*. London, 1965.

C. BRADLEY CRITICISM

1. *Reviews, etc.*

C. H. HERFORD: review of *Shakespearean Tragedy*, *Modern Language Review*, i (1905–6), pp. 128–33.

J. BUCHAN: 'The Dramatist Shakespeare', *The Spectator*, 28 Jan. 1905. (This article is unsigned: the writer's name was kindly given to me by the Librarian of *The Spectator*.)

J. C. COLLINS: review of *Shakespearean Tragedy*, *Westminster Gazette*, 28 Jan. 1905.

G. G. A. MURRAY: Letter to *Westminster Gazette*, 30 Jan. 1905.

Times Literary Supplement: review of *Shakespearean Tragedy*, 10 Feb. 1905 and 7 Apr. 1905. This latter is reprinted in A. B. WALKLEY: *Drama and Life* (New York, 1907), pp. 148–55.

R. Y. TYRRELL: 'Tragedy', *Academy*, lxviii (11 Mar. 1905), pp. 229–31, and a further review in the same (18 Mar. 1905), pp. 266–7.

T. DE WYZEWA: review of *Shakespearean Tragedy*, and J. W. GRAY: *Shakespeare's Marriage*, *Revue des deux mondes*, xxvi (April–May 1905).

Times Literary Supplement, review of *Oxford Lectures on Poetry*, 10 June 1909.

R. W. CHAMBERS: review of *Shakespearean Tragedy*, *The Hibbert Journal*, iv (1906), pp. 213–17.

2. *Obituary notices*

See above, Section B 1.

Times Literary Supplement. 'A. C. Bradley: The Surrender to Poetry', 25 May 1936.

3. *Critical articles*

This includes surveys and general works with extended passages on Bradley. It does not include works of Shakespeare criticism with treatment of Bradley's criticism, however extended this may be.

C. H. HERFORD: *A Sketch of Recent Shakespearean Investigation, 1893–1923.* London, n.d. [? 1923].

A. RALLI: *A History of Shakespeare Criticism*, vol. ii. London, 1932.

P. N. SIEGEL: 'In Defense of Bradley', *College English*, ix (Feb. 1948), pp. 250–6.

E. J. WEST: 'Bradleyan Reprise: on the Fool in Twelfth Night', *Shakespeare Association Bulletin*, xxiv (1949), pp. 264–74.

K. MUIR: 'Fifty Years of Shakespearian Criticism, 1900–1950', *Shakespeare Survey*, iv (1951), pp. 1–25.

Times Literary Supplement, 'A. C. Bradley', 30 Mar. 1951.

B. JOSEPH: 'The Problem of Bradley', *The Use of English*, v (1953–4), pp. 87–91.

M. EMSLIE: 'Shakespeare: Another Approach', *The Use of English*, v (1954), pp. 174–6.

H. WEISINGER: 'The Study of Shakespearian Tragedy since Bradley', *Shakespeare Quarterly*, vi (1955), pp. 387–96.

P. ALEXANDER: 'Critics who have Influenced Taste', xv: 'A. C. Bradley'. *The Times*, 11 July 1963.

D. J. PALMER: 'A Short Guide to Shakespeare Studies', *Critical Survey*, i (1962), pp. 34–8.

—— 'A. C. Bradley', *Critical Survey*, ii (1964), pp. 18–25.

M. R. RIDLEY: Introduction to Papermac Edition of *Oxford Lectures on Poetry*. London, 1965.

M. WEITZ: *Hamlet and the Philosophy of Criticism*. London, 1965. (First published in America, 1964.)

J. M. NEWTON: '*Scrutiny*'s Failure with Shakespeare', *Cambridge Quarterly*, i. 2 (Spring 1966), pp. 144–78.

MOTHER MARY BLISH: 'Principles and Method in the non-Shakespearean Literary Criticism of Andrew Cecil Bradley'. Unpublished dissertation, St. Louis, 1967 (with a useful Bibliography).

DETAILS OF CONTENTS OF 'OXFORD LECTURES ON POETRY'

'Poetry for Poetry's Sake.' Published Oxford, 1901.

'The Sublime.' Published 1903.

'Hegel's Theory of Tragedy.' Published *The Hibbert Journal*, ii (Oct. 1903 to July 1904), pp. 662–8.

'Wordsworth.' n.d.

'Shelley's View of Poetry.' *English Association Pamphlet*, No. 4. London, 1908.

'The Long Poem in the Age of Wordsworth.' n.d. [? 1903–5].

'The Letters of Keats.' 1905.

'The Rejection of Falstaff.' Delivered 5 Mar. 1902. Published *Fortnightly Review*, lxxi (Jan.–June 1902), pp. 849–66.

'Shakespeare's *Antony and Cleopatra*.' Published *Quarterly Review*, cdvii (Apr. 1906), pp. 329–57.

'Shakespeare the Man.' 1904.

'Shakespeare's Theatre and Audience.' 1902.

DETAILS OF CONTENTS OF 'A MISCELLANY'

'The Reaction against Tennyson.' *English Association Pamphlet*, No. 39. London, 1917. (Lecture delivered to English Association, 1914.)

'Jane Austen.' *Essays and Studies*, vol. ii, pp. 7–36. London, 1911. (Lecture delivered at Newnham College, Cambridge. n.d.)

Coriolanus. Second Annual Shakespeare Lecture. British Academy, 1 July 1912. Published London, 1912.

'English Poetry and German Philosophy in the Age of Wordsworth.' Adamson Lecture. Manchester 1909.

'Shelley and Arnold's Critique of his Poetry.' (Enlarged Leslie Stephens Lecture delivered at Newnham College, Cambridge, 1919.)

'Odours and Flowers in the Poetry of Shelley.' n.d.

'Coleridge Echoes in Shelley's Poems.' n.d.

'Coleridge's Use of Light and Colour', in *A Miscellany Presented to J. M. MacKay*. Liverpool, 1914.

'Keats and "Philosophy"', in *The John Keats Memorial Volume*, ed. G. C. Williamson, issued by the Keats House Committee, Hampstead. London/New York, 1921.

'Feste the Jester', in *A Book of Homage to Shakespeare*, ed. Israel Gollancz. London, 1916.

'Scene Endings in Shakespeare and in *The Two Noble Kinsmen*.' n.d.

'Inspiration.' Read in a Glasgow Church, n.d. (Remark in letters, Sept. 1898, about 'a sermon for Hunter', possibly refers to this.) Published 1889.

'Monosyllabic Lines and Words in English Verse and Prose.' n.d.

INDEX